AF899814

[redacted]

TWO CASES FROM JUNG'S CLINICAL PRACTICE

Vicente L. de Moura takes us on a ground-breaking journey into the previously unknown stories of two of Jung's patients and their impact on the development of key concepts in his work. Examining the original correspondence between the patients, sisters Misha Epper and Maggy Reichstein, and Jung, de Moura investigates what these cases tell us about the evolution of Jung's clinical practice and his shaping of material for publication.

Two Cases from Jung's Clinical Practice places these key cases into the context of Jung's work in the 1920s and provides a complete assessment of their place within his writings. Presented in three parts, it first examines Jung's disappointment with contemporary treatments and theories and his break from Freud and the development of his own ideas, and then summarises the history of his more famous patients. In Part 2, de Moura examines Epper's case, which is recognised as an essential part of the development of the concept of active imagination, as well as how it is connected to the work of Jung's collaborator Maria Moltzer. Finally, Part 3 assesses the case of Reichstein, which emerges as a key contribution to Jung's writings on Eastern and Western psychology, transference and countertransference, mandalas and, in particular, synchronicity. *Two Cases from Jung's Clinical Practice* provides a comprehensive and personable picture of Jung and his interactions with these two patients, giving us valuable data about a time when his practice was still evolving.

A unique and insightful study, this book will be an essential work for academics and students of Jungian and post-Jungian theory, analytical psychology, the history of psychoanalysis and psychology, and the history of ideas. These cases will also be of great interest to analytical psychologists and Jungian analysts in practice and in training.

Vicente L. de Moura is supervisor, docent and training analyst at the C.G. Jung Institute Zürich, Küsnacht Switzerland. Former president of the Susan Bach Foundation, he was curator of the pictures archive of the C.G. Jung Institute Zürich between 1998 and 2015. He works as an analyst and psychotherapist in Zürich. His website can be found at www.de-moura.ch.

"In this publication, in a very careful study, it is described for the first time how C. G. Jung, in contact with patients, was scientifically inspired by their topics and how this influenced his theories as a result. One sees Jung, his colleagues, and patients in a psychotherapeutic field as well as in spiritual exchanges in a time period around 1920. It is to the author's merit that he has managed to collect little known but very interesting material and place it within a stimulating context."

–Prof. Dr. Verena Kast, President of the Curatorium of the C.G. Jung Institute Zürich, Küsnacht, Switzerland

"In this book historical scholarship has struck a seam of gold. Based on previously unexamined archival sources and original interviews, the book gives the reader privileged insight into two female patients of Jung's who played key roles in shaping his understanding of such crucial topics as active imagination, transference and countertransference, synchronicity, and the significance of Eastern thought (especially Kundalini yoga and mandalas). De Moura's historical and comparative scholarship is meticulous, his journey of discovery is deeply engaging, and his findings significantly illuminate several important texts of Jung's."

–Professor Roderick Main, Department of Psychosocial and Psychoanalytic Studies, University of Essex, UK

TWO CASES FROM JUNG'S CLINICAL PRACTICE

The Story of Two Sisters and the Evolution of Jungian Analysis

Vicente L. de Moura

Routledge
Taylor & Francis Group
LONDON AND NEW YORK

First published 2019
by Routledge
2 Park Square, Milton Park, Abingdon, Oxon OX14 4RN

and by Routledge
52 Vanderbilt Avenue, New York, NY 10017

Routledge is an imprint of the Taylor & Francis Group, an informa business

© 2019 Vicente L. de Moura

The right of Vicente L. de Moura to be identified as author of this work has been asserted by him in accordance with sections 77 and 78 of the Copyright, Designs and Patents Act 1988.

All rights reserved. No part of this book may be reprinted or reproduced or utilised in any form or by any electronic, mechanical, or other means, now known or hereafter invented, including photocopying and recording, or in any information storage or retrieval system, without permission in writing from the publishers.

Trademark notice: Product or corporate names may be trademarks or registered trademarks, and are used only for identification and explanation without intent to infringe.

British Library Cataloguing-in-Publication Data
A catalogue record for this book is available from the British Library

Library of Congress Cataloging-in-Publication Data
A catalog record for this book has been requested

ISBN: 978-0-367-14332-9 (hbk)
ISBN: 978-0-367-14333-6 (pbk)
ISBN: 978-0-429-03130-4 (ebk)

Typeset in Bembo
by Apex CoVantage, LLC

CONTENTS

PHOTOGRAPHS AND DRAWINGS

FOREWORD

In the beginning of 2011, a gentle old lady visited the pictures archive at the C.G. Jung Institute in Zürich, where I was the curator. Mrs Lunin was almost 81 years old. She said that she came to donate to the institute the correspondence between C.G. Jung and her mother, Maggy Reichstein, who was one of Jung's patients in the 1920s. Mrs Lunin told me that during and after the treatment they exchanged letters and met on several occasions, and added that she did not understand properly many of the issues discussed in the letters. She wanted to ensure that these documents were not forgotten in a cabinet and wished for a proper conservation thereof.

After a closer look at the material, I realised that the case of Maggy Reichstein was relevant in many aspects. Furthermore, besides the material on Reichstein's case, I also found documents about her sisters in the archives. In particular, the case of her younger sister, Mischa Epper, was relevant for the understanding of their stories and added important historical data about the development of the technique Jung referred to as active imagination. Epper was also the main reason why the sisters left Holland and came to Zürich in the second decade of the last century to be treated by Jung. I checked the material and realised that, although Jung mentioned the events related to the Reichstein's case on different occasions, there was almost no information in Jungian literature about her story, and, furthermore, part of the available information was flawed.

During a second meeting with Mrs Lunin, I asked her for permission to research the documents in depth and for consent for a later publication. She kindly granted my request. I promised her that I would check the material carefully and would ensure its proper preservation.

Many questions appeared during my research: what does this material tell us about Jung and his evolving practice? And, as we shall see, what happened in

Reichstein's case that led Jung to mention her in relation to different subjects? What follows are the results of this quest. The outcome reveals the story of two cases of C.G. Jung, which were unknown until now. The aim of this book is to locate the encounter of C.G. Jung and the two sisters in Jung's methodological development. As we shall see, the cases, and particularly Reichstein's case, were very important to him.

The story of these two patients is discussed in relation to Jung's concepts, and the material presented can be compared to Jung's treatment of other cases in the literature, such as those of Christiana Morgan,[1] Frank Miller[2] or Tina Keller-Jenny,[3] which occurred contemporaneously, and uncovers additional information on how Jung shaped case material.

The most important documents in the research about the stories of Mischa Epper and Maggy Reichstein are three texts, two of them written by Epper herself. The first document is a text from the archives in the Museum Epper, in Ascona, Switzerland. The text is named 'Story of my childhood'[4] and in it Epper described not only her childhood but also the main events of her life. The date when she wrote the text is not clearly known, but she described in a letter dated 21st July 1957 and addressed to Marie-Louise von Franz,[5] a collaborator of C.G. Jung, with whom Epper also went into analysis, how in that year she began to write the story of her own neuroses. She mentioned that Jung himself had told her that it was a good idea, but he wrote to her that, if she felt an uneasy feeling once confronted with the material, either written or in paintings, she should leave it and let it rest for a while. The document ended abruptly, as if it were incomplete.

The second important document is Epper's diary between 1918 and 1919.[6] During these years she was in treatment with Jung's collaborator Maria Moltzer. Epper described her fantasies, how she dealt with them and how the treatment affected her. In her diaries, there are also some notes which Epper added much later, in the 1950s. In these later comments, as we shall see, Epper reviewed her opinions and criticised the treatment she had had with Moltzer. Similarly to the first text, this document is also to be found in the archives of the Museum Epper.

The third important document, which serves as basis for this section, was not signed, but the author was most probably Henriette Louise Quarles van Ufford-Reichstein, the third sister of the Quarles van Ufford family. She was married to Tadeus Reichstein, the winner of the Nobel Prize in Physiology or Medicine in 1950, who was the brother of Maggy Reichstein's husband, Adam Reichstein. Henriette Reichstein wrote a text she called 'Attempt to describe the several neuroses'[7] and started with 'the case story' referring to Mischa Epper as 'the patient'. The reason why she wrote the text is unknown, but in it she gave further information about her upbringing, as well as her opinion on many episodes in her life, in the life of her family and of her sisters. The text is archived in Basel, Switzerland (Staatsarchiv des Kantons Basel-Stadt). Henriette Reichstein was also in treatment with Jung. However, differently than the cases of her sisters, no relevant historical data concerning Jung was found in the available documents. Therefore, her case was not investigated in this book. Besides, a detailed exposure of her personal background would require the written consent of her family, which was not available.

Concerning Reichstein, the relevant documents are the letters exchanged with Jung. In the archive of the C.G. Jung Institute in Zürich there are thirteen letters from Reichstein dated between 1930 and 1949, and nineteen letters from Jung dated between 1924 and 1959. Besides these letters, there are notes and booklets which are the material donated by Mrs Lunin. Also in the archives of the Jung Institute are Reichstein's drawings, which she did while in treatment with Jung. Other important letters from Jung and Reichstein mentioned in this research are from the historical collection of the Eidgenössische Technische Hochschule – ETH – Zürich – Switzerland.

Concerning the interviews: they were conducted by the author between 2011 and 2013. The three interviews with Mrs Lunin, Reichstein's daughter, were conducted at the Jung Institute in Küsnacht, a small town near Zürich, and in her house in Zürich. The first interview, conducted in February 2011, was not structured, whereas the second and third interviews, in June 2011 and March 2013, were half-structured, with questions about her mother's connection with Jung. She added valuable information about her mother's life. Furthermore, she provided the photographs of her family used in this book.

The interview with Helene Hoerni-Jung, Jung's daughter, was conducted in March 2012 and took place in her house in Küsnacht. It was a half-structured interview, and her son, Jost Hoerni, was present, giving further information about Jung's life and practice.

The interview with Emmanuel Kennedy, who disclosed valuable information about people in Jung's inner circle, such as Marie-Louise von Franz and Barbara Hannah, provided further data about Reichstein's case. It was an informal talk and took place in his house in Gommiswald, Switzerland, in March 2012.

The interview with Diana Mirolo, the director of Museum Epper, was conducted in November 2012, in Ascona, Ticino, in the Italian region of Switzerland, where the couple Mischa and Ignaz Epper lived after 1932. She gave me access to the crucial documents mentioned previously and added relevant data about Epper's story.

The interview with Margrit Orsoni in April 2013 was also conducted in Ascona. Mrs Orsoni lived with Mischa Epper for three years after her husband died in 1969, and she added further information about her life.

Finally, an informal talk with Tjeu van der Berk in December 2013 provided more details about the 'Dutch patient' mentioned in the section on Mischa Epper. He visited the pictures archive of the Jung Institute in Zürich during the research for his book *In de ban van Jung*, published in 2014.

The material mentioned previously, i.e., documents and letters, the interviews and the available data in literature revealed the story of Mischa Epper and Maggy Reichstein presented in this book.

Note

1 Douglas, 1993.
2 Shamdasani, 1990.
3 Swan, ed., 2011.
4 ME – Original in German: *Kindheistgeschichte Mischa Epper*.
5 SB – Document PA 979a B 5–1 5 – Letter from Mischa Epper to M.L. von Franz from 21.6.1957, p. 1.
6 ME – Mischa Epper notes of her analysis.
7 SB – Original in German: *Versuch einer Darstellung der verschiedenen Neurosen* – Document PA 979a B 5–3.

References

Douglas, C. (1993) *Translate This Darkness: The Life of Christiana Morgan* (New York: Simon & Schuster).

Shamdasani, S. (1990) "A woman called Frank" in *Spring: Journal of Archetype and Culture* 50:25–56.

Swan, W., ed. (2011) *The Memoir of Tina Keller-Jenny: A Lifelong Confrontation with the Psychology of C.G. Jung* (New Orleans: Spring Journals Books).

PREFACE: INSIDE JUNG'S STUDY

From 1913 onwards, Jung commenced a process of self-experimentation which he termed his 'confrontation with the unconscious', which led to the birth of analytical psychology as a would-be science and therapeutic discipline. At the heart of this project was Jung's attempt to get to know his own 'myth' as a solution to the mythless predicament of secular modernity. This took the form of provoking an extended series of waking fantasies in himself. He later called this method 'active imagination'. He elaborated, illustrated and commented on these fantasies in a work which he called *Liber Novus*, or *The Red Book*, which was at the centre of his later work.[1] This depicted the process through which he regained his soul and overcame the contemporary malaise of spiritual alienation, which was achieved through enabling the rebirth of a new image of God in his soul and developing a new world view in the form of a psychological and theological cosmology. *Liber Novus* presented the prototype of Jung's conception of the individuation process, which he held to be the universal form of individual psychological development.

During this period, he began to reformulate the practice of psychotherapy from being oriented towards the removal of pathology to one having precisely this as its goal: in other words, the higher spiritual development of the individual. This reformulation was to have far-reaching consequences on the subsequent development of psychotherapy, as well as on the plethora of humanistic, new age and alternative therapies that rose up. From his own self-experimentation, Jung attempted to develop an iterable practice of psychotherapy. He encouraged his patients to undertake similar self-explorations through active imagination, which he supervised. He sought to discern whether the conceptions he derived in *Liber Novus* were of value to others, and whether procedures he himself had followed could lead to replicable results.

He eventually decided not to publish *Liber Novus* in his life time, and was reticent to reveal much in public concerning his clinical material. Until recently, not much has been known of what went on in Jung's practice at this time (nor subsequently, for that matter), nor its relation with his own self-experimentation, nor how these both formed the experiential basis of his later works, and his particular form of empiricism. His most extended treatment of the practical aspects of psychotherapy was in *The Psychology of the Transference. Illustrated through an Alchemical Series of Images. For Doctors and Practical Psychologists*, to give its full original baroque title – a work not easy of access to one not already well versed in his work, nor for that matter, with medieval alchemy. Indeed, at the outset of the book, Jung explicitly stated that he took it for granted that the reader would be already familiar with his *Psychology and Alchemy*.[2] Since Michael Fordham's 1974 essay, 'Jung's conception of the transference', there has also been little extended study of Jung's writings on psychotherapy, of the clinical Jung.[3]

Scattered through Jung's works, we find a number of nodal statements regarding his practice, of which the following are a few. Reflecting back on his career in the late 1950s, Jung recalled to Aniela Jaffé that as a medical student, he had never wanted to be a gynaecologist. Ironically, he continued, 'I have had mainly women patients, who often entered into the work with extraordinary conscientiousness, understanding and intelligence. It was essentially because of them that I was able to strike out on new paths in therapy'.[4] Here, Jung stressed what he learnt from his patients, and what they had enabled him to do. A few decades earlier, in his 1925 seminar, he stressed the role of his own self-investigation in his therapeutic work: 'I drew all my empirical material from my patients, but the solution of the problem I drew from the inside, from my observations of the unconscious processes'.[5] In *The Psychology of the Transference*, he spoke of the far-reaching mutual transformation of doctor and patient in psychotherapy, noting that the therapeutic relation between them 'is often of such intensity that we could almost speak of a *bond*. When two chemical bodies combine, both are altered'.[6]

How do these statements interrelate? What hidden histories lie behind them? On the basis of copious previously unknown documentation, Vicente L. de Moura's landmark study provides entrance to such questions. It is a comparative study of the remarkable cases of two sisters – possibly the closest to a 'twin study' in the psychotherapeutics of individuation. One of these, that of Maggy Reichstein, featured anonymously in Jung's writings as a paradigmatic case in more than one significant instance. The other, that of Mischa Epper, opens up a comparison between Jung's practice and that of his assistant and close associate during the period of his confrontation with the unconscious, Maria Moltzer, as well as the question of the relation between active imagination and expressionist artistic practice. Thus this book invites us to enter Jung's study and glimpse some of what transpired there, thus opening a critical window into the co-constitution of Jungian analysis.

Sonu Shamdasani

Notes

1 C.G. Jung, *The Red Book: Liber Novus*, ed. Sonu Shamdasani, trs. Mark Kyburz, John Peck and Sonu Shamdasani, Philemon Series (New York: W.W. Norton, 2009).
2 Jung, *CW* 16, p. 168.
3 *Journal of Analytical Psychology*, 19, 1, 1974, pp. 1–21.
4 Protocols of *Memories, Dreams, Reflections*, Jung collection, Manuscript Division, Library of Congress, p. 316; C.G. Jung and A. Jaffé, *Memories, Dreams, Reflections*, trs. Richard Winston and Clara Winston (New York: Random House, 1963), p. 145.
5 *Introduction to Jungian Psychology: Notes of the Seminar on Analytical Psychology Given in 1925*, ed. William McGuire, revised ed., Sonu Shamdasani, Philemon Series (Princeton: Princeton University Press, 2012), p. 35.
6 *Psychology of the Transference*, *CW* 16, § 358, tr. mod.

ABBREVIATIONS

CW	*The Collected Works of C.G. Jung*, edited by Sir Herbert Read, Michael Fordham, Gerhard Adler and William McGuire, Exec. Editor, Trans. R.F.C. Hull, 20 vols. (London and Henley: Routledge and Kegan Paul, 1981–1994)
ETH	Wissenschaftshistorische Sammlungen, Eidgenössische Technische Hochschule, Zürich, Switzerland
ME	Museum Epper, Ascona, Switzerland
NH	Noord-Hollands Archief, Haarlem, Holland
PA	Pictures Archive of the C.G. Jung Institute, Zürich, Switzerland
Protocols	The protocols of the interviews of A. Jaffé with C.G. Jung from the Library of the Congress, Washington, D.C.
SB	Staatsarchiv des Kantons Basel-Stadt

ACKNOWLEDGEMENTS

I am in debt and grateful to many people, without whom this book would not be possible. I would like to thank Sonu Shamdasani, who guided research during my Ph.D. Studies at the University College London, and told me at the beginning of my research that I would need to approach Jung from a historical perspective, which is totally different from the perspective of an analyst. My answer was that it would be easier to cut my head off. Well, let's say that he decapitated me gently and, in the end, he helped me enrich my analytical work. I would like to thank Martin Liebscher, who can combine gentleness and orientation with the accuracy of a scholar; to Ernst Falzeder, for his feedback and his keen evaluation, which helped me improve my research skills immensely; to Mrs Verena Lunin, for her generosity in allowing me to research and to make public the story of her mother and her aunt; to Helene Hoerni-Jung who, despite old age, gave me the opportunity to interview her on her father's story, and Jost Hoerni and Ulrich Hoerni, for the precious conversations about their grandfather; to Andreas Jung, who granted me access to Jung's library, for the talks, and for his kind and dear support; to Thomas Fischer, from the C.G. Jung Foundation, for allowing me the publication of Jung's letters; to Diana Mirolo, director of the Museum Epper, for her interview and for granting me access to documents without which the research would be much deprived; to Margrit Orsoni, for her precious information on Epper's life; to the curatorium and the board of training of the C.G. Jung Institute – Zürich, in particular to Daniel Baumann, Robert Hinshaw and Ruth Ammann, for granting me the permission to use the material of the pictures archive in this research and in the book; to Emmanuel Kennedy, for his valuable inputs on the case of Reichstein; to Tjeu van den Berk, for the information concerning the case of the Dutch patient of Jung in the book of van Helsdingen; to Wendy Swan, for the material she sent me on Tina Keller-Jenny; to Andreas Schweizer and Georgina Seel, from the Psychological Club in Zürich, for the access to the relevant documents of the club's library; to Verena Kast and Roderick Main, for checking my manuscript; to Arthur Eaton for his essential work in the translations from Dutch; for the kindness of Peter Kenney for helping me with the English corrections. Many others supported me in the development of this work. The list would be too long, if I would thank here all the people who helped me, but for all the ones not mentioned here, my sincere thanks.

Finally, I would like to add here my gratitude to my wife Sonia, and my children Juliana and Leonardo – for their love.

Material from the pictures archive C.G. Jung Institute (images) is made available by the pictures archive of the C.G. Jung Institute Zurich – Küsnacht.
Images of Museum Epper: Copyright Museum Epper – Ascona – Switzerland
Original letters from C.G. Jung: © 2007 Foundation of the Works of C.G. Jung, Zürich.

PART 1

C.G. Jung

1
INTRODUCTION

Historical research on Carl Gustav Jung (1875–1961) has constituted the focus of much scientific research in recent years. Different authors unveiled the story of some of his patients, such as, for instance, the case of Sabina Spielrein published in Carotenuto's book from 1982, which describes the connection between Jung, Spielrein and Freud.[1] Later books and articles on other patients followed, such as the works of Shamdasani (1990) on Frank Miller,[2] of Ellenberger (1991) on Helene Preiswerk,[3] of Douglas (1993) on Christiana Morgan,[4] of Reid (2001) on Catharine R. Cabot,[5] or of Swan (2011) on Tina Keller-Jenny.[6] However, besides the story of his patients, the development of his method has also been in focus since the publication of *The Red Book* in 2009.[7] In this publication, one can follow the process Jung went through exploring his own fantasies. Contemporaneous with the break with Freud, he began a personal process, a phase of self-experimentation, which had a major impact on both his concepts and on his way of working. This development was mirrored in the way he treated his patients.

According to Ellenberger, the impact of the theorist's personal experiences and of some patients on the formulation of hypotheses can be observed throughout the history of psychiatry.[8] In the 1960s, Ellenberger stressed that many of the most important psychiatric discoveries were frequently the result of irrational speculations, personal intuitions and emotional preoccupations of all sorts. He described two additional typical situations in this respect: first, a psychiatrist who had a personal crisis, which he succeeds in overcoming and, second, a patient who becomes a special object of investigation.

In the first case, that out of a crisis a new method or theory may appear, Ellenberger gave examples in the works of Robert Burton (1577–1640) and his description of *melancholy*; George Cheyne (1671–1733) and *hypochondria*; George Beard (1839–1883) and *neurasthenia*. In the 19th century, he mentioned Pierre Janet (1859–1947), the crisis in his youth and his later writings on *psychasthenia* and Sigmund Freud (1856–1939), who observed neurasthenic symptoms in himself and through a process of introspection discovered the hate for his father, which later led him to formulate general concepts based on it.

With reference to the second case, Ellenberger mentioned how concepts and ideas in psychiatry emerged out of the encounter of the doctor with patients, usually women suffering from hysteria. As examples, he mentioned in the history of Anton Mesmer (1734–1815) the importance of the case of Francisca Oesterlin in 1774 for his discovery of animal magnetism, and the case of Maria-Theresa Paradis in 1777 for the development of his career. Further, he cited Justinus Kerner (1786–1862), an important figure in the history of dynamic psychiatry, and the case of Friedericke Hauffe, about whom Kerner wrote in 1829 the book *The Seeress of Prevost*. Kerner studied her clairvoyant gifts and published one of the first monographs dedicated to the study of one single patient. Next, Ellenberger mentioned Jean-Martin Charcot (1825–1893), the French neurologist, who studied the case of Blanche Wittmann, who became the prototype of the phenomenon of the three stages of hypnotism he described. Ellenberger also mentioned the importance of the case of Leonie Boulanger in the beginning of the career of Pierre Janet and his studies on hypnotism and somnambulism and, finally, the case of Bertha Pappenheim for Freud and his studies on hysteria with Josef Breuer (1842–1925).[9]

There are many factors which may exert an impact on a theorist while he or she is developing a concept or method, such as the personal events in his life, the academic background, the *Zeitgeist*, contemporaneous theories, events in society and politics, and so on.

However, among the most important factors for the development of the theorist are the personal events in his life and the encounter with paradigmatic patients, as presented previously in Ellenberger's essay about how some of the most important theories in psychology originated out of this complex interaction. This book follows Ellenberger's historiographical approach in focusing on Jung's self-experimentation related to the development of his method and its impact on the treatment of two of his patients in this crucial phase of the development of his theory.

The first part of the book is concerned with the development of Jung's psychotherapeutics. I initially focus on the early days of Jung as a psychiatrist, his work at the Burghölzli hospital in Zürich and his disappointment with the manner in which he believed psychiatry approached the patients. Subsequently, I present his studies on the word association experiment and the encounter with Freud's psychoanalysis, following their collaboration until their break in 1913. Thereafter, I present a section on the psychotherapeutics contemporaneous with Jung's self-experiment, giving an overview of the available treatments and theories in those days. This section shows the scientific surroundings in which Jung developed his ideas after his break with Freud.

Special attention is then given to his self-experimentation which occurred from 1913 onwards. It was a key personal event, for it had great impact on the development of his method and, particularly, on the development of the technique of active imagination. Concerning Jung's method, in an interview with Helene Hoerni-Jung from 2012, the daughter of C.G. Jung, I asked her about the method her father used with his patients. She stated with reference to her father that *Er habe keine Methode!* – to English: *He would have no method!* This interesting statement triggered a question, which will be later addressed. Next, I summarised the history of Jung's patients, who attracted historical attention to the present day, in order to situate these two unknown cases that are unveiled in my research in a comparative framework. In Part 1, therefore, I present the development of Jung's ideas and practice with his patients based predominantly on published sources.

In the second and third parts of the book, I present the story of and Jung's interaction with two patients, two sisters, about whom little was known until now: Mischa Epper and Maggy Reichstein. Epper's and Reichstein's stories, Epper's analysis with Jung's collaborator, Maria Moltzer, the development of her analysis, the interpretations and active imaginations and further elements of the story of the two sisters form the essence of this part of the book. To this subject, I will add information about the case of the Dutch patient described in Rene van Helsdingen's book *Images from the Unconscious – A Case of Jung's*.[10] Jung wrote in the preface for this book that van Helsdingen's patient was Reichstein's sister, but Jung's comment was flawed. I present the available material about the case in van Helsdingen's book, which shows the parallels and similarities between the story of Reichstein, Epper and this third case, and the possible reasons for Jung's flawed comment.

After the presentation of Epper's and Reichstein's stories, the book focuses on Jung's use of Reichstein's case in his writings. It was Reichstein's wish to help her sister, who had suffered a psychic disturbance, which led Reichstein to come to Zürich and enter treatment with Jung after her sister. I will discuss the important topics of her analysis, focusing on those which Jung used as example for his postulations. The next section will describe and contextualise the development of Jung's ideas related to the themes present in Reichstein's story. As we shall see, Reichstein's case was particularly important, and deepened Jung's interest in Eastern symbolism; he also used her drawings in his publications as examples of European mandalas. Besides, Reichstein's case challenged Jung's therapeutic relationship and his understanding of the concepts of transference and countertransference. Furthermore, Jung wrote that her case was unique concerning the concept of synchronicity. Finally, I will present the correspondence between them after 1940 on religion and psychology, which indicates that Jung extensively discussed his concepts with Reichstein.

Jung did not include detailed information about his patients in his publications. My intention in this book is to add information about the lives of the patients and to discuss them in relation to Jung's concepts mentioned previously. I use unpublished sources and interviews with relatives and persons close to these patients, offering a comprehensive picture of the interaction between them and Jung. Their treatments give us further information about Jung's development of his psychotherapeutic practice and ideas. As we shall see, the encounter with these sisters gives us valuable data about a time when Jung's practice was still evolving and offers us an example of how Jung shaped case material in his publications.

My goal is to offer additional information on a critical phase of Jung's development, namely, when he began to use the insights of his self-experimentation with patients and to teach them to his collaborators. Additionally, the research unveiled important cases of Jung, cases which have not been studied to date and that he used as examples for his concepts.

Notes

1 Carotenuto, 1982.
2 Shamdasani, 1990.
3 Ellenberger, 1991.
4 Douglas, 1993.
5 Reid, 2001.
6 Swan, ed., 2011.
7 Shamdasani, ed., 2009.
8 Micale, ed., 1993.
9 Ibid., pp. 239–249.
10 van Helsdingen, 1957. Original in Dutch: *Beelden uit het Onbewuste – een geval van Jung.*

References

Carotenuto, A. (1982) *A Secret Symmetry: Sabina Spielrein between Freud and Jung* (New York: Pantheon).
Douglas, C. (1993) *Translate This Darkness: The Life of Christiana Morgan* (New York: Simon & Schuster).
Ellenberger, H. (1991) "The story of Helene Preiswerk: A critical study with new documents" in *History of Psychiatry* 2:41.
Micale, M., ed. (1993) *Beyond the Unconscious: Essays of Henri F. Ellenberger in the History of Psychiatry* (Princeton: Princeton University Press).
Reid, J.C. (2001) *Jung, My Mother and I: The Analytic Diaries of Catharine Rush Cabot* (Einsiedeln: Daimon Verlag).
Shamdasani, S. (1990) "A woman called Frank" in *Spring: Journal of Archetype and Culture* 50:25–56.
———, ed. (2009) *The Red Book: Liber Novus/C.G. Jung* (New York: Norton & Company).
Swan, W., ed. (2011) *The Memoir of Tina Keller-Jenny: A Lifelong Confrontation with the Psychology of C.G. Jung* (New Orleans: Spring Journals Books).
Van Helsdingen, R.J. (1957) *Beelden uit het Onbewuste* (Arnhem: Van Loghum Slaterus).

2

THE DEVELOPMENT OF JUNG'S CAREER

Psychology and psychotherapy underwent considerable changes in the beginning of the 20th century. There was a great deal of experimentation on visions, dreams and fantasies, and the boundaries between psychology and other sciences and arts were not clearly defined. As individuals were searching for new expressions of inner experiences, there was a quest for spiritual and cultural renewal.[1]

In 1900, C.G. Jung started his work as a practitioner doctor at the Burghölzli mental hospital in Zürich. Jung's initial interest was in studies related to anatomical brain research,[2] a passage not included by A. Jaffé in *Memories, Dreams, Reflections*.[3] One of his studies was on the brain of the dementia praecox patient. But during conversations with his friend and director of the laboratory at the Burghölzli, Alexander von Muralt, Jung came to the conclusion that there was no real reason for conducting this research, because he could detect no difference between the anatomy of the brain of a patient with dementia praecox and that of a healthy person.[4] The lack of results derived from those research studies led Jung to write in a paper from 1908 that the future of psychiatry could only be in the area of psychology. He then turned to the psychological investigation of mental illnesses.[5]

He started to apply and develop the word association experiment in order to study normal and abnormal psychology. In 1900, Eugen Bleuler (1857–1939), the director of the Burghölzli mental hospital at that time, sent one of the doctors under his supervision, Franz Riklin (1878–1938), to learn the association method with Emil Kraepelin (1856–1926) in Heidelberg, Germany. After his return, Riklin taught Bleuler and Jung how to apply it. The method was the most important research study of the Burghölzli hospital at the time.[6]

Jung's initial aim with the word association experiment was to provide a tool to differentiate mental disorders, and later he focused on the disturbances in the responses. Jung dedicated his studies to understanding the meaning of mistakes, such as a longer time of reaction, enhancement of physiological changes or strange associations of words. He focused on what were considered failures or lack of attention by the patient.[7]

It was his research with the word association experiment that built his reputation in the international psychiatry scene and provided the basis to describe what he called the emotionally charged complex. He postulated that every person was affected by feelings and ideas, which were not present in the consciousness, i.e. the complexes. According to Jung, complexes have enough psychic energy to disturb conscious behaviour. He showed that these disturbed reactions were not meaningless and that there was a link between the disturbed reaction and the complexes. In 1905, Jung presented his conclusions as follows:

> Such a recollection, which is composed of a large number of component ideas, is called a complex of ideas. The cement that holds the complex together is the feeling-tone common to all the individual ideas, [. . .]. We are therefore speaking of an emotionally charged complex of ideas, or simply of a complex. In our case the complex has the effect that the subject does not react by arbitrary or random connections of words, but derives most of his reactions from the complex. The influence of the complex on thinking and behaviour is called a constellation.[8]
>
> *(Translation modified)*

The aim of Jung's work was to explore how consciousness reacts under the influence of the complex. The research on the reactions during this experiment allowed him to show manifestations of unconscious psychological processes in a statistically meaningful way.

Besides his research studies, he treated patients using techniques which were commonly employed in the Burghölzli hospital. One of the techniques was hypnosis. The importance of hypnosis at the turn of the 19th to the 20th century was manifold: it was one of the main tools of psychological research and therapy and was used to treat and explore phenomena such as multiple personality, hysteria and spiritualism. All these phenomena were considered variants of somnambulism, a term which referred to any complex act performed while asleep or in a trance-like condition.[9]

The method was introduced at the Burghölzli by Auguste Forel after learning it from Hippolyte Bernheim in France in 1886. Jung used hypnosis mainly in the earlier stages of his career,[10] between 1900 and 1906, and he mentioned its use in different passages, for instance, in his text from 1902.[11] Nevertheless, Jung considered that what was missing in the psychiatry of the time was an adequate knowledge about the psychological processes that occurred in the psyche of the patient. One may conclude that Jung missed a psychology which allowed him to understand what was going on in the psyche of the patients, in particular, and that could explain the expressions of the psyche, in general. Remembering his impressions of the time at Burghölzli he commented:

> The years at Burgholzli were my years of apprenticeship. Dominating my interests and research was the burning question: 'What actually takes place inside the mentally ill?' That was something which I did not understand then, nor had any of my colleagues concerned themselves with such problems. Psychiatry teachers were not interested in what the patient had to say, but rather in how to make a diagnosis or how to describe symptoms and to compile statistics. From the clinical point of view which then prevailed, the human personality of the patient, his individuality, did not matter at all. Rather, the doctor was confronted with Patient X, with a long list of cut-and-dried diagnoses and a detailing of symptoms. Patients were labeled, rubber-stamped with a diagnosis, and, for the most part, that settled the matter. The psychology of the mental patient played no role whatsoever. At this point Freud became vitally important to me, especially because of his fundamental researches into the psychology of hysteria and of dreams. For me his ideas pointed the way to a closer investigation and understanding of individual cases. Freud introduced psychology into psychiatry, although he himself was a neurologist.[12]

Around 1904, Jung started to apply Freud's psychoanalytical method, but he considered that there were uncertainties about it and that his studies with the association experiment were a contribution to its development.[13] It is important to note that Jung initially applied the method based on his readings of Freud's publications. Freud himself, however, criticised in 1905, those who applied psychoanalysis only by readings, i.e., without direct contact with him. He wrote:

> It seems to me that there is a widespread and erroneous impression among my colleagues that this technique of searching for the origins of an illness and removing its manifestations by that means is an easy one which can be practised off-hand, as it were. I conclude this from the fact that not one of all the people who have shown an interest in my therapy and passed definite judgements upon it has ever asked me how I actually go about it. There can be only one reason for this: that they think there is nothing to enquire about, that the thing is perfectly self-evident. Again, I am now and then astonished to hear that in this or that department of a hospital a young assistant has received an order from his chief to undertake a 'psychoanalysis' of a hysterical patient. I am sure he would not be allowed to examine an extirpated tumour unless he had convinced his chiefs that he was conversant with the histological technique.[14]

In her book on the development of psychoanalysis, Leitner postulates, however, that up to this date, Freud's descriptions of the method in his publications were too general and therefore not sufficient to be applied properly. Accordingly, his followers were necessarily developing their own techniques, based on what they interpreted of Freud's texts.[15]

The encounter with Freud led Jung to give up the use of hypnosis and turn to psychoanalysis as an instrument of research and treatment.[16] We can follow the change in Jung's practice in his correspondence with Freud, which started in 1906. For instance, in a letter to Freud in May 1907, Jung commented on the good results of the experiments of two of his colleagues conducted with hypnosis.[17] In his answer, Freud wrote that the positive results, should they last, were probably due to the transference process to the doctor.[18] Just a few months later, in June 1907, Jung reported his encounter with Pierre Janet, noting that Janet understood nothing of Freud's theory, and that the 'Paris complex' was no more. Freud answered:

> I should be very sorry if your Vienna complex had been obliged to share the available cathexis with a Paris complex. Luckily, as you tell me, nothing of the sort happened, you gained the impression that the days of the great Charcot are past and that the new life of psychiatry is with us, between Zürich and Vienna. So we have emerged safe and sound from the first danger.[19]

From the preceding notes it is clear that the encounter with Freud's ideas caused a shift in Jung's practice with his patients; namely, his method of treatment began to change. He began to apply less suggestive therapy and became closer to Freud's psychoanalysis.[20]

However, Jung shared the opinion of Bleuler, who succeeded Forel as director of the Zürich mental hospital in 1898, considering psychoanalysis both a complementary method as well as one of the possibilities for treatment at the hospital. Jung believed that hypnosis could lead to better results with uneducated patients.[21] Jung knew that hypnosis and suggestive methods were effective, but he did not know how and why hypnosis worked. In a correspondence with Dr Löy in 1913 about his ideas on hypnosis at that time, Jung wrote:

> What alienated me once and for all from this comparatively effective, indirect method of suggestion, based as it is on an equally effective false theory, was the simultaneous recognition that behind the bewildering and deceptive maze of neurotic fantasies there is a *conflict* which may best be described as a moral one. With this there began for me a new era of understanding. Research and therapy now joined hands in the effort to discover the causes and the *rational* solution of the conflict.[22]

As mentioned, Jung's studies of psychoanalysis and his contact with Freud were significant for his understanding of the unconscious processes. Nevertheless, according to Shamdasani, the Freud–Jung encounter was mythologised, and the assumption that Freud was the main source of Jung's work misplaced Jung in the history of psychiatry.[23] Jung would protest against such an assumption such as, for instance, in the following passage of an unpublished article from the 1930s:

> I in no way exclusively stem from Freud. I had my scientific attitude and the theory of complexes before I met Freud. The teachers that influenced me above all are Bleuler, Pierre Janet, and Theodore Flournoy.[24]

Besides, Jung was critical towards Freud's postulations at various points. In a passage from 1925, in which Jung retrospectively considered Freud's theories and his association experiments, he wrote:

> The fact that convinced me of the truth of Freud's theory was the evidence of repressions, which I could find in my association experiments. Patients could not respond to certain tests where pain entered in, and when I asked why they could not respond to the stimulus word, they always said they did not know why, but when they said this it was in a peculiar, artificial manner. I said to myself that this must be the thing that Freud described as repressions. Practically all the mechanisms of repression became clear in my experiments. As to the content of repression, I could not agree with Freud. In those days, he was speaking only of sexual trauma and shocks to explain the repression. I had then considerable experience with cases of neurosis in which sexual things were of quite secondary importance compared with the role played by social adaptation.[25]

Leitner points further in her book on the development of psychoanalysis that around 1908, Freud's followers were uncertain concerning the use of the technique of dream interpretation and the handling of the transference. Besides, she notes that there was a controversy related to Freud's technique of free association and the use of Jung's method based on the word association experiment by some of Freud's pupils.[26]

In the protocols of the Vienna Psychoanalytical Society it is noted how in 1908 Freud was ambivalent towards the word association experiment, and his ambivalence can be understood by considering, on the one hand, that it was important for him because it brought Jung and Burghölzli close to psychoanalysis and Jung's engagement attracted the attention of a wider group; on the other hand, Freud believed that once the word association had played its role as a learning method, it would no longer be important.[27] One could further add that Jung's research brought a missing element to psychoanalysis, namely, the scientific observation of the concepts and its quantification in a psychological experiment.

Between August and September 1909, Freud and Jung went to the US to present a series of lectures at Clark University. It was an important event, because it was considered to be a landmark for the introduction of psychoanalysis in America.[28] 1909 was the year when Jung resigned from his position at Burghölzli and focused his activities on his practice. He described this period in his life in an unpublished letter from the 4th of November 1909, possibly to Ferenczi, who also participated in the journey to the US. Jung wrote about his practice and research at that time and the happenings he was involved with as follows:

> Dear Colleague,
>
> It is very good that you convinced yourself to write the letter. You are completely right: one should not let a companionship like ours break apart. On the other hand, the complexes are active enough to keep such memories always fresh anyway. Transference could be most highly transformed into hatred and we are too reasonable for that. I feel towards you exactly as during our trip, even if I did not write. I very often had the impulse to communicate to you how I feel. Since (the trip) I had experienced quite a lot. The very, very first thing I did after my return was to lay down to my wife all the aspects of my complexes, with the resolute consequence and with all psychoanalytic openness. It worked out extremely well, and I realised that I was such a fool, not having told her much before. The improvement in my peace and calmness is enormous.
>
> At the moment I just have three patients who do pay well. I would have enough patients if I would accept them paying me very little, but I don't like to offer psychoanalysis for tip money. I can and even must use my time better, namely, for my students, who I have still 3 to 5. They required too much time. I ask for a three weeks course (3 to 4 times weekly, 2 hours each time) 100 Swiss francs.[29] Otherwise people would just devour me. Regarding my clients I have great satisfaction with them because of their precious psychology. I also analysed a budding catatonic with success. [. . .] Experimental scientific work, which I have to do at the moment, is tedious and long-lasting. The way of experimentation is almost too exhausting to be followed permanently.
>
> With best regards
> Yours faithfully
>
> Jung[30]

The letter presented here gives us valuable information about Jung's situation at the end of the year 1909: firstly, in the letter, Jung described his impressions of the trip to America, when the complexes were active and transference could be transformed into hatred, if one was not reasonable enough. This remark is particularly interesting, because Jung mentioned later, in 1925, that it was on this trip that something important changed in his relationship to Freud. Jung mentioned that he and Freud analysed each other's dreams and when he analysed the symptoms and a dream that Freud had had, Jung asked for more details of Freud's private life. Freud denied his request, saying that he could not risk his authority. Jung mentioned that at that moment Freud lost it. Jung mentioned that it was a fatal impression of Freud's limitations, because he put authority above truth.[31]

Besides, Jung also told Freud his dream about the medieval house, with many stairways and rooms. He went downstairs and found a cellar with gothic structures and the further down he went, the more ancient the structure looked, until he reached a prehistoric place with bones and skulls. Freud analysed it, saying that there were people around him that he (Jung) wanted dead. In the seminars of 1925, Jung noted that he disagreed with Freud's interpretation and that the dream was the origin of his book *Transformation and Symbols of the Libido* from 1912, in which he analysed the fantasies of Ms Miller.[32]

Secondly, in one passage of the letter, Jung commented that he is not prepared to offer psychoanalysis without adequate payment. This passage adds an interesting comment about Jung's view on the payment of his work as a psychoanalyst. This was an important issue in Jung's treatment of Sabina Spielrein, which will be presented later in this book, and in which the issue about the payment was one of the queries. Concerning Spielrein, it is interesting to note Jung's comment about his students, because when he wrote this letter, Spielrein was possibly among them. She was writing her dissertation in those days and asked him to read it in September 1909.[33]

Thirdly, the letter indicates once more the importance of Emma Jung in Jung's development and in his psychological balance in his private life. Jung spoke to her openly and it helped him to feel calmness and peace. Furthermore, it also revealed how Jung stood in his work after he left the Burghölzli hospital at the end of 1909. At that time, Jung was occupied in his private practice mostly by his students, not by too many patients.

Finally, the scientific work based on the experiment Jung referred to was probably his word association experiment. One of his lectures at Clark University had the title 'the Association Method' and was about his work on the topic. Jung's research had given him a scientific reputation in America. However, his comment in the letter shows that the experiment was becoming increasingly dull for him. Besides, there was possibly another reason for Jung's declining interest in his work with the association experiment, namely, that he concluded that the experimenter himself could affect the results. It would mean that there was a personal equation in the experiment which could disturb the results and introduce an incalculable factor of variation, a factor impossible to exclude.[34] It is not clear when Jung stopped using the method, but his last paper on his experiments 'The Psychological Methods of Investigation Used in the Psychiatric Clinic of the University of Zürich' appeared in 1910.

In the following year, 1911, the controversies between Jung and Freud grew. Jung wrote a letter to Freud on the 11th of December 1911, describing the 'libido problem', expressing his doubts about applying Freud's ideas in his studies on dementia praecox and that he considered that what he observed could not be reduced to a repressed sexuality.[35] Freud considered the loss of reality in the dementia praecox as being caused by a recession of the libidinal interest, but Jung contested this explanation, pointing out that in his experience, it was not only the sexual interest that disappeared but all interest, and one cannot consider that all the interest in reality (Janet's *fonction du réel*) was due to sexuality.[36]

As the divergences grew, Freud proposed the abandonment of their personal relations in a letter to Jung dated 3rd of January 1913. On the 20th of April 1914, Jung also resigned from his position in the International Psychoanalytic Association, writing that his views contrasted with the views of most of its members, and he could no longer hold the position of president.[37]

By 1914, Jung had developed a busy therapeutic practice. He worked five days a week, with an average of five to seven hours a day.[38] But although he was experiencing success in his professional life, an important change occurred in his approach to psychology: Jung began a process of investigation of his own fantasies. It led him to develop his theories and ideas to a further extent, and it had a strong impact on his way of working with his patients. But for a proper understanding of Jung's ideas and his experiment, it is important to review the contemporaneous scientific context in which he was involved.

Notes

1 Shamdasani, ed., 2009, p. 194.
2 Protocols, p. 77.
3 Shamdasani, 2003, p. 45.
4 Ibid., pp. 45–46.
5 Jung, 1908a, par. 332, CW 3.
6 Schröter, 2012, p. 14.
7 McGuire, 1990, p. 8.
8 Jung, 1905, par. 733, CW 2.
9 Haule, 1999, p. 245.
10 Shamdasani, 2001.
11 Jung, 1902b, pars. 262ff, CW 1.
12 Jaffé A., ed., 1989, p. 114.
13 Jung, 1906, pars. 660–664, CW 2.
14 Freud, 1905, p. 261. It is not known if Freud meant Jung as 'a young assistant', but at that time Burghölzli was the only hospital to use the psychoanalytical method.
15 Leitner, 2001, p. 87.
16 Shamdasani, 2001, p. 10.
17 McGuire, ed., 1974, p. 49.
18 Ibid., p. 53.
19 Ibid.
20 Nevertheless, as we shall see later, some elements of hypnosis will be relevant in the method of treatment he developed after his self-experiment. He will call it active imagination.
21 Shamdasani, 2001, p. 8.
22 Jung, 1914, par. 583, CW 4.
23 Shamdasani, ed., 2009, p. 196.
24 Ibid.
25 McGuire, ed., 1990, p. 14.
26 Leitner, 2001, pp. 95–111.
27 Nunberg and Federn, eds., 1976, p. 315.

28 For the context and importance of this event, see Shamdasani, 2012a.
29 100 Swiss Francs in 1909 would be approx. 1'100 Swiss Francs or £850 nowadays.
30 PA – Letter from Jung to Ferenczi (?) from the 4th of November 1909 (unlabelled document).
31 In an interview with John Billinsky in May 1953, Jung mentioned that, from his visit to Freud in Vienna in 1907 and from the dreams he analysed in the trip to America in 1909, he supposed that Freud had an affair with his sister-in-law, the younger sister of his wife. Jung thought that it could be the reason for Freud's symptoms, but Freud refused to talk about it. Jung mentioned that his knowledge about Freud's triangle became one of the main aspects that led to the break with Freud. Billinsky, 1969.
32 McGuire, ed., 1990, pp. 22–23. See also Jung's interview with Eissler in 1953 in the Library of the Congress – Sigmund Freud Papers: Interviews and Recollections 1914–1998; Set A, Jung, 1953.
33 Carotenuto, 1982, p. 8.
34 Shamdasani, 2003, pp. 47–50.
35 McGuire, ed., 1974, p. 471.
36 Jung, 1912a, pp. 122–123.
37 McGuire, ed., 1974, p. 551.
38 Shamdasani, ed., 2009, p. 201.

References

Billinsky, J.M. (1969) "Freud and Jung (the end of a romance)" in *Andover Newton Quarterly* November;10(2).

Carotenuto, A. (1982) *A Secret Symmetry: Sabina Spielrein between Freud and Jung* (New York: Pantheon).

Freud, S. (1904/1905) "On Psychotherapy" *The Standard Edition of the Complete Psychological Works of Sigmund Freud, Volume VII Psychoanalytic Electronic Publishing – PEP online Version.*

Haule, J.R. (1999) *Jung in Contexts: A Reader* (London and New York: Routledge).

Jaffé, A., ed. (1989) *Memories, Dreams, Reflections, by C.G. Jung* (New York: Vintage Books).

Jung, C.G. (1902b) "A case of hysterical stupor in a prisoner in detention" in *The Collected Works of C.G. Jung* (London: Routledge), 1993, vol. 1.

——— (1905) "The psychological diagnosis of evidence" in *The Collected Works of C.G. Jung* (London: Routledge), 1992, vol. 2.

——— (1906) "Psychoanalysis and association experiment" in *The Collected Works of C.G. Jung* (London: Routledge), 1992, vol. 2.

——— (1908a) "The content of the psychosis" in *The Collected Works of C.G. Jung* (London: Routledge & Kegan Paul), 1981, vol. 3.

——— (1912a) *Wandlungen und Symbole der Libido – Beiträge zur Entwicklungsgeschichte des Denkens* (Leipzig und Wien: Franz Deuticke).

——— (1914) "Crucial points in Psychoanalysis" in *The Collected Works of C.G. Jung* (London: Routledge), 1993, vol. 4.

Leitner, M. (2001) *Ein gut gehütetes Geheimnis: die Geschichte der psychoanalytischen Behandlungstechnik von den Anfängen in Wien bis zur Gründung der Berliner Poliklinik im Jahr 1920* (Giessen: Psychosozial, Verlag).

McGuire, W., ed. (1974) *The Freud-Jung Letters* (NJ: Princeton University Press).

——— (1990) *C.G. Jung: Analytical Psychology Notes of the Seminar Given in 1925* (London: Routledge).

Nunberg, H. and Federn, eds. (1906–1908/1976) *Protokolle der Wiener Psychoanalytischen Vereinigung* (Frankfurt a. M: Fischer), vol. 1.
Schröter, M., ed. (2012) *Sigmund Freud-Eugen Bleuler "Ich bin zuversichtlich, wir erobern bald die Psychiatrie" Briefwechsel 1904–1937* (Basel: Schwabe Verlag).
Shamdasani, S. (2001) "The magical method that works in the dark: C.G. Jung, hypnosis, and suggestion" in *The Journal of Jungian Theory and Practice* 3(1).
——— (2003) *Jung and the Making of Modern Psychology: The Dream of a Science* (Cambridge: Cambridge University Press).
———, ed. (2009) *The Red Book: Liber Novus/C.G. Jung* (New York: Norton & Company).
——— (2012a) "Psychotherapy, 1909: Notes on a Vintage" in *After Freud Left: A Century of Psychoanalysis in America*, J. Burnham (ed.) (Chicago: Chicago University of Chicago Press).

3

CONTEMPORANEOUS PSYCHOTHERAPEUTICS

Jung began his self-experiment at a time when different methods were used for the treatment and investigation of the psyche. He referred to these works, commented on and evaluated them, and, as we shall see, some of these procedures have parallels to Jung's later development of his method. Among the psychiatric authors of the time, there was often a lively debate about theories, in which they questioned their validity or supported their assumptions. What follows is a description of the contemporary psychotherapeutic landscape in the first decades of the 20th century.

What is called today treatment by hypnotism and suggestion was one of the most used methods in the turn of the 19th to the 20th century. The term hypnosis was coined by James Braid in his book *Neurypnology – the Science of Nervous Sleep*, in 1843, as part of a terminological revision.[1] But at the end of the 19th century, the method was not accepted in the medical community. A revival came with the studies of two schools in France: Salpêtrière, with Jean Martin Charcot (1825–1893) and Nancy, with Hippolyte Bernheim (1840–1919). Charcot was a famous neurologist of international reputation. His personal engagement and his prestige gave a great impulse to the legitimation and to the respectability of hypnotism and his studies led to hypnotism being accepted by the Academy of Science in France.[2] But Charcot's main focus was on the clinical features of the phenomenon, while Bernheim's focus was the practical use of suggestion for therapeutic purposes. Bernheim was a French internist, who was initially known for his research on typhoid fever and on heart and pulmonary diseases. He began to apply hypnosis in 1882, using a method he learned from Ambroise A. Liébeault (1823–1904). Bernheim, in opposition to Charcot's postulations, affirmed that hypnotic states were not exclusive to hysterical patients, but a condition which could be observed in nearly all persons. Based on his studies, he asserted that hypnotic sleep was not pathological, that the phenomena observed under hypnosis were due to suggestion and that the suggestibility also exists in the waking condition. The only difference was that in a waking state, suggestibility was diminished or neutralised by the faculties of reason, attention and judgment. However, he added:

> In spontaneous or in induced sleep these faculties are dull and weakened; imagination rules supreme; impressions are accepted without verification, and the brain transforms them into actions, sensations, movements and images. The psychical state is thus modified and the new state of consciousness induced. [. . .] It is this susceptibility increased by suggestion which we employ in the most efficacious way for a therapeutic end.[3]

Regarding the therapeutic applications of hypnotism, Bernheim mentioned that imagination and confidence caused effects upon the patient, and those were the reasons why the artifacts, the 'magnetically charged' tools and objects used by the magnetisers, worked. For Bernheim, it was suggestion which caused the therapeutic result.[4] In 1887, he considered therapeutic suggestions as follows:

> It is a psychological law, that sleep puts the brain into such a psychical condition that the imagination accepts and recognises as real the impressions transmitted to it. To provoke this special psychical condition by means of hypnotism, and to cultivate the suggestibility thus artificially increased with the aim of cure and relief, this is the role of psychotherapeutics.[5]

Hypnotism underwent a rapid decay with Charcot's death in 1893. The decline began in France and neighbouring countries, such as Belgium and Switzerland, the three countries where hypnotism had arisen. Among the exceptions was the Burghölzli hospital in Zürich under the supervision of Forel.[6] Concerning Jung, his critique of hypnotism was not aimed at its efficacy but rather arose from the fact that he did not understand the psychological mechanism behind it,[7] and as late as 1913, he was still using the method occasionally, as noted in his correspondence with Dr Loy.[8]

Another important contemporary treatment method for neurasthenia and hysteria was the treatment of Silas Weir Mitchell (1829–1914), described in his book *Fat and Blood*.[9] Weir Mitchell's method is important to note because it was integrated, applied and modified by different authors. In the third edition,[10] from 1884, Weir Mitchell described his treatment as mainly based on seclusion (basically in removing the patient from his negative surroundings and bad habits); rest (physical activities were reduced or under the supervision of a physician); massage (to avoid muscle atrophy), electricity (for exercising the muscle of the patient and, he believed, causing a rise of the temperature, which influenced the nutritive changes in the body positively); and dietetics and therapeutics (largely based on milk, following diets adapted to the needs of the patient). He noted that the individual conditions of each patient should be considered and the method must be adapted accordingly. Further, he mentioned that he did not refer to a mere addition of blood and flesh in the patient, but that their gradual increase would lead to a visible result of manifold changes in the digestive, assimilative and secretive powers of the body of the patient.[11] He added:

> If I succeed in first altering the moral atmosphere, which has been to patient like the very breathing of evil, and if I can add largely to the weight and fill the vessels with red blood, I am usually sure of giving general relief to a host of aches, pains, and varied disabilities.[12]

Jung knew Weir Mitchell's writings, and so, for instance, he mentioned him in 'A case of hysterical stupor in a prisoner in detention' from 1902, commenting on one of his cases in relation to the loss of intellectual faculties and alternating states of consciousness in hysteria. Jung, however, did not comment on Weir Mitchell's method.[13]

One of the most important figures in the psychotherapeutics of the time was Pierre Janet, who in his book *Psychological Healing* from 1919, gave a contemporaneous 'thorough and systematic treatise on psychology comprising more than 1,100 pages'.[14] Janet described and discussed a great number of case reports and treatments, and classified them in groups. Besides, he provided a historical background of the methods and his criticism about what he considered to be their mistakes. Janet's main method was hypnotism and suggestion, but he also used other treatments similar to Weir Mitchell's method, such as, for instance, inducing a deep sleep by hypnosis and suggestion, leaving the patient in a state of artificial sleep for days or weeks.[15]

A possible link between Jung and Janet, which may indicate the impact of Janet's ideas on Jung's theorising, was Janet's criticism of Freud's exaggeration of sexuality as the only pathogenic factor in mental illness. Janet considered the symbolical construction around the sexual aetiology as flawed, because, for him, this was not found in every case. Janet referred to his earlier publications, in which he pointed to the connection between traumatic events and what he referred to as neuropathic disorders. For Janet, the studies of Freud and Breuer were basically the same as his earlier studies, albeit using a new nomenclature for the observed processes, and he took them as confirmations of his own findings.[16] He also considered the method of free association to be inadequate, but in this book from 1919 he appreciated Jung's word association test, considering that the procedure could be utilised to disclose memories of incidents and their influence on the subject's emotions, perhaps revealing traumatic memories.[17]

There is another point in Janet's concepts which has parallels to Jung's method, namely in dealing with transference. Janet mentioned treatments by *moral guidance*,[18] in which the personal influence of the doctor was the main tool in psychotherapy. He termed 'period of influence'[19] the phase when the patient is being treated, when he usually has a confident belief in the benevolent action of the doctor. One effect of this phenomenon, he noted, was that after the session, some patients carried on with their conversations with the doctor in their imagination with a sense of guidance or protection. This last point is interesting to note, because Jung used this procedure as part of his technique to deal with transferential issues in some of his cases, which possibly shows how Janet's ideas had an effect on Jung's practice. For the time after the treatment, Jung, similarly to Janet's preceding description, suggested to some of his patients that they develop a dialogue with their inner representation of him.[20]

Another central figure in the psychotherapeutic landscape at the time was August Forel (1848–1931), who was the director of the Burghölzli hospital in Zürich until 1898. He was distinguished by his studies in brain anatomy, which led him to take up the post of professor of psychiatry at the University of Zürich. Initially a convinced organicist, he became interested in the psychological aspects of the mental illnesses with his work on alcoholism.[21] After reading Bernheim's book on suggestion, Forel went to Nancy in 1886 and learned the therapeutic use of hypnosis with Bernheim, which he then introduced at the Burghölzli.[22]

In the fifth revised edition of his book *Hypnotism or Suggestion and Psychotherapy* from 1907 (the first edition was published in 1889), Forel gave an account of the main factors in, and the contemporary up-to-date theories on, the method. He presented his view of psychotherapy as follows:

> Psychotherapy is suggestive therapy, but is developed in markedly different ways, in accordance with the requirements of the case. The usual verbal suggestion will mostly suffice to remove a simple headache. But if one is dealing with a disposition, one will, as a rule, find out all sort of habits, inherited predispositions, frames of mind, etc., which are connected with the disposition; it then becomes the function of psychotherapy to regulate this.[23]

During his time at the Burghölzli, Jung used some of Forel's suggestive techniques, such as, for instance, transposing a patient into a particular situation in order to facilitate associations.[24] Forel's writings are present in different passages in Jung's work, as in his writing from 1907, *The Psychology of Dementia Praecox*,[25] in which he referred to concepts such as the dissociation from Forel's book mentioned earlier.

As mentioned, the work developed at the Burghölzli clinic in the beginning of the 20th century was pioneering in relation to the methods of treatment of mental diseases. From the preceding notes, it is possible to observe that controversies about methods and their authors were the order of the day. Besides hypnotism and psychoanalysis, an approach of those days, which is important to note and was used in that institution, was the one proposed by Dumeng Bezzola (1868–1936), a Swiss psychiatrist, who was close to Forel and developed a method which had some importance in those days, constituting a variation of Freud and Breuer's cathartic method.[26] He was Forel's pupil and, like him, did not agree with Freud's postulation published in 1905 in the *Three Essays on the Theory of Sexuality*.

In a paper from 1907, entitled 'On the Analysis of Psychotraumatic Symptoms'[27] and published in the *Journal für Psychologie und Neurologie*, Bezzola proposed a modification of Freud and Breuer's cathartic method. The proposed modification was explained by Bezzola as follows:

> My attempt was to modify Freud's method in the sense that the pathogenic event should be activated and made conscious under medical control, not through the analysis and interpretation of secondary associations, but through the synthesis of primary sensations.[28]

Out of these considerations, he proposed a method he referred to as psychosynthesis. The method consisted of a reinforcement of the afterimage of all separated stimulations of the senses, which occurred in the event. This procedure should be conducted without the patient's conscious criticism and the goal was to revitalise all the subconscious associated components. Through this procedure, a retroactive development of the whole event would occur in the patient's consciousness and the psychic trauma would be solved.[29]

Jung and Freud's reaction to Bezzola's paper can be followed in their correspondence. Freud wrote, in a letter dated the 7th of April 1907,[30] that he was not struck by the paper. For him, Bezzola tried to conceal that his psychosynthesis was identical to psychoanalysis and that Bezzola was back to the point where he (Freud) and Breuer were twelve years before. In his answer on the 11th of April 1907, Jung noted that he found Bezzola's paper infuriating, a 'hoarder of details with no clear over-all vision'.[31] Later, in May of the same year, Jung briefly commented in his letter to Freud that he tested Bezzola's method with some good results, but he considered it to be identical to the cathartic method. Further, he noted that the effect of the method was not altogether comprehensible for him.[32] In his answer, Freud mentioned that the results were undoubtedly, the results of the transference.[33]

But one of the most important names in the landscape of psychiatry and psychology in those days, who was related to Forel, Freud and Jung and must be mentioned, was Eugen Bleuler (1857–1939), who assumed the post of director of the Burghölzli hospital in Zürich after Forel left. While Forel's style of running the hospital was based on the personal authority of the director, an attitude also present in his approach to hypnosis and suggestive therapy, Bleuler ran the institution in a more participative style, which was also mirrored in his proposals for treatment.[34]

Among his many contributions to psychiatry, a particularly important one was his definition of schizophrenia. He coined the term in order to specify a group of mental illnesses, which had been until then grouped in the psychiatric literature under the term Dementia Praecox. He described it in his book from 1911, *Dementia Praecox or the Groups of Schizophrenia*,[35] noting that the term Dementia Praecox was unspecific to the illnesses it referred to. This justified his minting the term schizophrenia.[36]

Concerning therapeutics, Bleuler believed that hospital treatment should be considered only if necessary, for instance, when the patient was a danger to himself or to others, or when it was not possible to influence the patient in his behaviour any longer. If possible, the patient should be kept in his ambiance. He affirmed that improvement could be achieved by psychic influence. It could come from the outside, if a change in the life conditions of the patient sets it in motion, or from the inside, if the patient learned to come to terms with his complexes. It could also happen if a dream-like condition ended, or if the affect behind it was consumed. He noted that the fact that healing emerges from psychic processes was not fully comprehended, but postulated that some kind of self-healing process must exist.[37]

Bleuler noted that there was no prophylaxis to the outbreak of the illness, but in the initial stages some measures could be helpful, such as corporeal hygiene with enough sleep and nourishment, the avoidance of any kind of excitement of a psychic or toxic nature, as well as strong affects. Opposition and obligations tended to make it worst, as they enhanced the negativism of the patient.

He commented on many other practical aspects of the treatment, such as the use of medications, physical restriction or isolation, even advising patients with other cases of schizophrenia in their families to avoid having children. One particularly important aspect of the treatment was related to education and retaining contact with reality. In this sense, he recommended work therapy for the patient, i.e., the engagement of the patient in some activities such as gardening, housework and other simple activities. For him, work therapy was the most suitable approach for these purposes, because the patient used the normal functions of the psyche and had opportunities to keep contact with reality. It pushed the patient to think about a normal life and the possibility of adaptation. Particularly important was the personal interaction of the patient with the personnel of the hospital, who through this work were in constant contact with the patient.[38]

Bleuler's importance for Jung's development was manifold. As director of the Burghölzli hospital, it was Bleuler who approved and supported the topic of Jung's dissertation in 1902 'On the Psychology and Pathology of So-Called Occult Phenomena'.[39] He called and directed his work with the association experiments and endorsed Jung's findings on the notion of unconscious affects and their role in symptom formation.[40] Besides, Jung's first therapeutic experience with hypnosis occurred while he was in the Burghölzli clinic under Bleuler's guidance, and this was also a time when Jung gave lectures on hypnosis with demonstrations.[41] A few years later, they were both connected with Freud.

It is interesting to note that in a letter from the 5th of October 1906, Jung wrote to Freud that he called Bleuler's attention to the existence of Freud's ideas and 'converted' him to psychoanalysis.[42] However, Bleuler contested Jung's comment. In a letter to Freud from the 20th of November 1912, Bleuler mentioned his interest in his theory and that it was the other way around – he presented Jung to Freud's ideas.[43] Jung mentioned and commented on Bleuler's works on many occasions, for instance, in his review in 1911 of the concept of negativism in the

Jahrbuch für Psychoanalytische und Psychopathologische Forschung, in which Jung discussed Bleuler's concepts of ambivalence, ambitendency and the schizophrenic split of the personality.

Another author important for Jung's practice was Alfred Adler (1870–1937), one of Freud's closest pupils, who became a dissident due to his critical approach to Freud. He was one of the first collaborators of Freud, a member of the committee in the Psychoanalytical Association and, together with W. Stekel, the editor of the *Zentralblatt für Psychoanalyse*.[44]

Adler's approach considered a parallel between psychic and organic processes, and postulated that abnormal psychic developments are related to a morphological or functional weakness in the body.[45] He concluded that all neuroses and psychoses could be traced to this organ inferiority, and, depending upon the degree and type of the psychic compensations for it, the individual could develop enhanced or pathological psychic conditions.[46] For him, the neurotic builds psychological structures to keep power over others, aiming to end the feelings of insecurity and inferiority. These feelings require a goal to make life tolerable, but the goal is unattainable, for it is based on infantile expectations. Concerning his method to treat the neurotic disposition, Adler noted:

> The mechanism itself he (the neurotic) never understands neither is he able to explain and break down unaided his mode of apperception by means of analogy and the conduct resulting therefrom. This can only succeed by means of an analytic process which permits us to divine and understand his infantile analogy by means of abstraction, reduction and simplification. In this way, one finds regularly apparent that the neurotic always apperceives after the analogy of a contrast, indeed, that usually he only recognises and gives value to relations of contrast. This primitive mode of orientation in life [. . .] originates also in the feeling of uncertainty and illustrates a simple device of logic.[47]

The doctor should firstly understand these models, the life plan of the neurotic, because it compresses in one point the past, the present, the future and the desired goal of the patient, and, secondly, should remove the strong opposing attitude of the patient, the resistance towards the doctor and its exposures, i.e., the patient should take these as an attachment to the neurotic ideal.[48]

In 1917, Jung compared Adler's and Freud's assumptions. He questioned whether all that appears in sexual form needs to be sexuality and concluded that the sexual theory is partially correct, but one-sided. It would be a mistake both to discard it and to regard it as universally valid. He explained therefore what he considered a counterpoint to Freud's perspective on the psychology of the unconscious, namely, Adler's ideas. He cited Nietzsche's Zarathustra and compared it to Nietzsche's life, pointing to the drive to self-preservation and the will to power. Jung considered Freud's and Adler's perspectives from these two equally strong impulses (sexuality and will to power) and presented a case story and analysed it firstly with Freud's perspective and then with Adler's and mentioned the principles of Adler's psychology.[49]

Jung postulated that the controversy between the two hypotheses has its roots in the different typologies of the theorist. Freud would be guided by an extraverted feeling attitude, while an introverted thinking attitude would be characteristic of Adler. Jung noted:

> With that the incompatible contradictions of both theories are solved, for the theories are products of one-sided psychologies.[50]

He went on to mention that both theories could be helpful if properly used, but none could claim to be valid for all cases. They should be used 'locally', for both theories were reductive.[51]

The controversies and dissidences within the psychoanalytical movement in Europe did not stop its expansion to other countries. One important author in America, who referred to psychoanalysis, was Morton Prince (1854–1929). He was the founder and editor of the *Journal of Abnormal Psychology* to which Jung contributed a paper in 1907 named 'On psychophysical relations of the associative experiment'.[52] Prince was invited to deliver a lecture at the first congress of psychoanalysis in 1908 in Salzburg, Austria, but he signed off.[53] Besides his interest in psychoanalysis, Prince experimented with hypnosis, for instance, using crystal gazing and automatic writing, and he studied dream processes, developing his own methods and postulations.[54]

Prince stated that the process that creates both kinds of complexes, functional (normal) and dysfunctional (abnormal), was educational. This process could be intentional or not, and its principle could be used in psychotherapeutics. He wrote:

> A functional disease is a perversion of the normal process brought about by some acute, intense experience or by repetition of an experience, i.e. by education. Theoretically it would follow that what can be done by education can be undone by the same method, and, in practice we find this to be true.[55]

Prince considered dissociation as a normal mechanism of the mind, which was pathological only in marked form and presented the principle of automatism, as one can observe in the habitual and absent-minded acts, which served the mind for the economy of effort. In pathological cases, the complex developed an intense grade of automatism, acting outside the normal inhibitory control of the consciousness, for its action is due to dissociation. The goals in psychotherapy were to reassociate what was split up, to form healthy complexes of ideas and to support the will to slow down undesirable complexes.

He stressed the importance of emotions in the process described, noting that exalting emotions had an intense synthesising effect, while depressing emotions had a disintegrating one. He praised hypnosis as a means to modify the personality, because it can activate fields of ideas and memories which were dissociated by the fatigue, by the tensions with the environment or by other disintegrating factors. He added that psychotherapy made use of the normal mechanism of the mind and body to bring about a restitution of the disordered functions and restore the individual to health. Furthermore, he said that suggestion could only act by stimulating the physiological mechanism and could not create anything anew. Prince summarised his psychotherapeutics as follows:

> The point of view, the attitude of mind, the beliefs, the habits of thoughts, must be modified by the introduction of new points of view, of data previously unknown to the patient and drawn from the wider experience of the physician; by instruction in the meaning of symptoms and in their organisation and causes; by suggestion of expectations that justly may be fulfilled; of ambitions that ought rightfully to be entertained; of duties to be assumed but too long neglected; of confidence and hope; and above all, by the suggestion of the emotion and joy that go with success and a roseate vista of a new life. There is no fact of life that does not have more than one aspect, no conduct that does not have more than one interpretation, no judgment that does not have an alternative, no conduct that does not have more than one relation. Thus the old system of ideas carrying with them apprehensions, anxieties, and depressive emotions are modified by being interwoven with new ones, and new systems of ideas or complexes are artfully created and substituted for the old.[56]

Prince considered this procedure an educational method, which, in both hypnotic and waking states, gives to the patient insights into the meaning of his trouble; lets him see new points of view and introduces new ideas and feelings into his complexes.[57]

Interesting to note is that in 1929, Jung described the four stages of psychological treatment, in which education was one of them. He described the four stages as confession (the patient sharing and becoming conscious of his unconscious secrets), elucidation (to know where the neurosis came from), education (to learn new habits to replace the negative ones caused by neurosis) and transformation (the mutual change caused by the interaction between patient and the doctor).[58] As we shall see later, the case of Reichstein was particularly important for Jung concerning the stage of transformation.

Jung already mentioned Prince's studies in his dissertation published in 1902, comparing Prince's patients with the case of S.W. in his writings,[59] and in 1911 he wrote a review on Prince's paper concerning dream interpretation. He considered Prince an unprejudiced investigator, competent and with a firm reputation in researching psychopathological disorders. Jung pointed out the aspects in which Prince supported Freud's postulations, but countered when Prince criticised the assumption that every dream is a wish fulfilment. Jung noted that

Prince's paper only considered the formal and not the dynamic element of the dream he analysed.[60]

Besides the authors who applied psychoanalytic and hypnotic methods in their treatments, another approach was relevant in the psychotherapeutic landscape of the time. It was mentioned by Jung in some of his writings and this approach had its focus mainly on the use of will and reason. One of the main figures among them was Paul Dubois (1848–1918), a Swiss medical doctor who practiced in the Viktoria hospital in Bern, Switzerland. Dubois, who was the president of the Swiss society for neurology between 1911 and 1916, used a variation of Weir Mitchell's method of rest, basically, to isolate the patient from his family and close friends, keeping him in bed with a healthy and controlled diet.[61] He was against hypnosis and critical about the use of medication for psychic illnesses.

Dubois applied what he called a 'Socratic dialogue' or 'rational psychotherapy', which in the literature was called a persuasion method. His main goal was to convince the patient that the origin of his complaints and symptoms was mostly of a psychic nature (not an organic one) and the improvement in his condition was possible through a modification of his false moral values. To achieve this modification, the patient should give up the flawed conceptions he constructed about the illness and put reason in the first place.

In the introduction of the seventh English edition of his book *The Psychic Treatment of Nervous Disorders – the Psychoneuroses and Their Moral Treatment*[62] published in 1909, with a preface note from Dejerine (an author we shall see later), Dubois pointed to the differences between his approach and the treatments by suggestion. He postulated four characteristics of the psychoneuroses, namely, exaggerated suggestibility, sensitiveness, impressibility and emotional hysteria. He considered that in their origin all these characteristics were caused by fear. He noted that it is not enough to treat the crisis by physical or psychical means, or removing a particular cause. What was necessary was 'to prevent the recurrence of attacks by making the primary mentality less sensitive', and this happens when the doctor teaches the patient useful ideas about how to conduct his life.[63] Using a paralogism to explain the difference between what he understood as persuasion and suggestion Dubois wrote:

> The means that men have always adopted in order to come to a mutual conviction is called simply persuasion. It is arrived by proof, for it is also possible by experience and demonstration to prove things in medicine. Persuasion is practiced by affirmation, pure and simple, which can never come under the head of suggestion if one believes oneself in what one is affirming. Suggestion is nothing more than a form of persuasion, and I refute it for the precise reason that it is artificial, illusive, that it arrives at its conclusion by surreptitious means.[64]

One may conclude that for Dubois, suggestion meant to use what was actually causing the patient illness to get a false improvement, while his method aimed at strengthening the patient's autonomy by enhancing his rationality. Further, he presented the philosophical fundaments of his ideas and the different illnesses, which he ordered under the term psychoneuroses. He summarised his method as follows:

> The nervous patient is on the path to recovery as soon as he has the conviction that he is going to be cured; and he is cured on the day when he believes himself to be cured.[65]

The doctor must be convinced of this idea, for only through his sincerity could he implant it in the patient and help him. Dubois stated that although suggestion and persuasion are identical in their action, suggestion was based on blind faith and kept the patient in a dependent position, while persuasion was based in clear and logical reason, pushing the patient to be autonomous. Furthermore, he added:

> The best precaution against this psychic slavery would be imperturbable confidence in his independence, and a calm reason which detects the secret of this weakening influence.[66]

His method sought to immunise the patient from all suggestive influence, appealing to his *ego* in the highest individual sense, making his mind critical and giving him a conscious sense of independence. The doctor could achieve it by education of the intellect.[67]

Jung knew Dubois' work and had some of his books in his library. Among them the two volumes of *The Psychic Treatment of Nervous Disorders (The Psychoneuroses and Their Moral Treatment)*[68] from 1905 and 1910 and a collection of offprints of Dubois. In one of them, 'Pathogenesis of the neurasthenic condition'[69] from 1909, there is a dedicatory note from Dubois. He commented on Dubois' method in different papers, for instance, in 1908, when he wrote that psychoanalysis could be called an educative method, for the patient learns an independent attitude towards his complexes, and in this respect resembled Dubois' educative method.[70] Furthermore, in his book originally written in 1913, *The Theory of Psychoanalysis*, he stated that he was well acquainted with hypnotic suggestion and Dubois' method of persuasion, but did not use them for they were comparatively ineffective.[71] And also in 1913, in a paper called 'General Aspects of Psychoanalysis', he countered the criticism that psychoanalysis was a suggestive method, in which a systematic teaching was instilled into the patient. He affirmed that the psychoanalytical method was in direct contrast to suggestion therapy and countered that psychoanalysis was comparable to the ratiocinative method of Dubois, which was essentially a rational procedure.[72]

An important psychotherapeutic contemporaneous approach, which was not mentioned by Jung in his writings, was that of Joseph Jules Dejerine (1849–1917), who used a method which had parallels to that of Dubois. He was a French neurologist who became interested in psychology, particularly the study of emotions. He also applied Weir Mitchell's method and considered that the cause of neurasthenia and hysteria were to be found outside organic symptoms, namely, in the mind of the patients. Dejerine was the director of the Salpêtrière hospital in Paris after 1910 and opposed methods based on hypnotism and suggestion.[73] In 1913, he published *The Psychoneuroses and Their Treatment by Psychotherapy* in collaboration with one of his former assistants, Edouard Gauckler.[74]

For Dejerine and Gauckler, psychotherapy was a mental pedagogy and although they used isolation, an element of Weir Mitchell's method, they considered that it was not mandatory in all cases. They postulated that psychotherapy could only be effective if the patient had absolute confidence in the doctor, which was the basis for the patient to confess his entire life to him. For Dejerine and Gauckler, reasoning and its acceptance, i.e., the idea alone, had no effect, unless it was supplemented by an emotional appeal, which leads to conviction. They considered that reason was dependent on the sentiment or feeling present in the therapeutic relationship.[75]

Concerning therapeutic procedures, they did not support the use of drugs for psychoneuroses, because they postulated that the therapeutic effect was caused by suggestion and all suggestions were a medical trick. Therefore, treatments based on them (direct or indirect suggestion) should not be used either. They criticised hypnotism, which they believed suppresses the free will of the patient, making them helpless. They considered it a direct and negative attack on the personality of the patient.[76] For them, the only proper treatment was the treatment by persuasion. They explained the method as follows:

> It consists in explaining to the patient the true reason for his condition, and the different functional manifestations which he presents. It consists, on the other hand, moreover and you must say almost wholly, in establishing the patient's confidence in himself and awakening the different elements of his personality capable of becoming the starting-point of the effort which will enable him to regain his self-control. The exact comprehension of the phenomena which he presents must be grasped by the patient by means of its own reasoning. [. . .] The part that the physician plays is to recall, awaken and direct. He has nothing to do with suggestions. [. . .] When the physician shows a patient in what way he has erred, what are the faults of his character and his moral condition and his reasoning which are the cause of the genesis of his affection, he does not demand that he shall accept what he has told him as an article of faith: he asks only one thing, – that he should force himself to reflect and to understand.[77]

Further, they noted the conditions for the successful use of the method and described that the physician in the first meeting should achieve a reciprocal sympathy with the patient, gaining his confidence during the examination and questioning. The doctor should acquire, as much as possible, the most complete picture about the patient's condition and the mechanism of his symptoms before beginning the debate, weighing his words carefully. After having gained confidence, the doctor should learn the whole story of the patient's life and should show a kind sympathy, proving to the patient that he (the doctor) is ready to give him a little affection and a little of himself. This allows the patient to tell the doctor the emotional cause of the disturbance and his whole story, allowing the doctor to form a complete and coherent picture of his mental and moral condition. Their therapeutic action was basically strengthening emotions, i.e., to support all emotional action, which would lead to the sense of reorientation of the personality. The therapy consisted in addressing these feelings, and rarely pure reason. The therapist should point to the events, which would confirm these emotions with confidence. This emotional stimulation exercised a synthetic action of orientation in the personality of the patient.[78] Depending of the diagnosis, for instance, in cases of hysteria, they proposed an affirmative and authoritative intervention of the doctor, contrary to the experience of helplessness of the patient (e.g., to command the patient to move his paralysed arm). Patients who did not show improvement should be punished in some way (e.g., to receive no letters), but to the ones who showed improvement, they should be rewarded (e.g., to go out for a walk). The method consisted in doing it with absolute firmness, with the patient knowing that the doctor had the patient's interest at heart.[79]

Finally, it is important to consider the methods for investigating the unconscious, which were contemporaneous with, and that can be related to Jung's self-experiment.

The first important method to mention was the one proposed by Herbert Silberer (1882–1923). Silberer was active in Freud's psychoanalytical movement and a part of the Viennese Psychoanalytical Society. In his investigations, he came to the conclusion that certain figures in dreams were symbolic representations of the dreamer, and that images in hypnagogic states were symbolic representations of the condition of the person, who was half-way between waking and dreaming states.[80]

He presented his method to explore these phenomena in 1909 in the *Jahrbuch für Psychoanalytische und Psychopathologische Forschung* in a paper titled 'Report on the method to call and observe symbolic hallucinatory visions'.[81] He described that he came to investigate the phenomena after a spontaneous curious occurrence, in which he was in a drowsy state of mind on his sofa, thinking about the concepts of Kant and Schopenhauer. He wanted to recall some elements of Kant's ideas in his mind, but he could not and, suddenly, like in a dream, with closed eyes, he received a vivid impression of a secretary who denied his services. Shocked by the vivacity of the image, he decided to investigate how to access such experiences willingly.

He mentioned two conditions for the use of his method, namely, a state of somnolence and exertion of thinking. Both elements must be in balance, i.e., neither of them must dominate the state of mind, which would then be in a hypnagogic state. These opposite conditions characterised the conditions for hallucinatory visions, marked by the activation of an appropriate symbol for the specific feeling or idea of the moment. He referred to it as 'auto-symbolic phenomena'. Silberer's goal was to research these elements linked to Freud's postulations on dream formation.

Analysing the visions in hypnagogic states, Silberer identified three classes of such phenomena, classifying the visions by their content (when it expresses some of the elements present in an ideational process); by their functional element (when it expresses the state of the consciousness, how it is functioning in the moment) and by their somatic element (when it expresses the perceived external and internal corporeal sensations). He noted that these classes were frequently mixed up with each other, and finished his paper with examples for the classes mentioned earlier, giving interpretations for the occurred symbol.

Initially, he considered the phenomena using Freud's concept of regression. However, he revised this later, in 1914, in *Problems of Mysticism and Its Symbolism*, using Jung's concept of introversion instead of regression. He added that introspection was an important condition in the practice of both religion and mysticism.[82] He also mentioned the magical experiments of Staudenmaier (an author we shall see next), pointing to the interesting results of the effects of an intense introversion.[83] In several places, Silberer referred to Jung's work with symbols, and his concept of the elementary types has similarities to Jung's idea of the archetypes, as the following passage demonstrates:

> We understand only half of the psychic impulses, as we indeed do all spiritual development, if we look merely at the root. We have to regard not merely whence we come but also whither we go. Then only can the course of the psyche be comprehended, ontogenetically as well as phylogenetically, according to a dynamic scheme as it were. [. . .] The solution of the riddle is found the instant we regard these images as types, for a few fundamental forces of the soul, with which we are all endowed, and whose typical symbols are for that reason of general applicability (I will therefore call these types the human elementary types).[84]

He added that the process of intro-determination and its symbols represent a collection of our spiritual powers, and from it comes the force for our future development.[85]

From the material just presented, one might see that Silberer's definitions, his method for exploring unconscious images and his notion of a spiritual development expressed in symbols have parallels to Jung's self-experiment with images of the unconscious, his concepts of the individuation process and of the archetypes. Jung was interested in Silberer's work and in his experiments with hypnagogic states,[86] and commented on Silberer's experiments with intentional somnambulistic states in 1912 in *Transformations and Symbols of the Libido*, pointing to the fact that in dealing with the fantasies, a certain willingness to listen to them must be present in order to perceive the inner experience. Jung noted the importance of an attentive attitude to the inward-flowing current of libido, which leads to an unknown goal.[87]

Jung commented on Silberer's ideas in other passages, for instance, analysing one of the visions of Ms Miller concerning a 'swarm of people'. Jung noted that he followed Silberer's postulation and considered the vision as functional,[88] and he agreed with Silberer that mythological symbolism is a cognition process at a mythological level.[89] He mentioned Silberer's work related to mythological symbolism in other papers, such as *General Aspects of Psychoanalysis* from 1913.[90] In the same year, he supported Silberer's postulation on the mythological stage of cognition that apprehends symbolically.[91]

Finally, a contemporaneous method to investigate the unconscious that is important to consider in this context is the method of Ludwig Staudenmaier (1865–1933). He was a theologian and professor of chemistry at the Munich University, and mysticism and magic were among his interests. In 1912, he wrote a book entitled *Magic as Experimental Science*,[92] based upon the self-experiments he conducted, which included conscious and unconscious awareness and enhanced hallucinations. He gave instructions for carrying out practical experiments with the conscious and unconscious mind and decided to call it magic, because such phenomena had been known since antiquity by this name.[93] Jung had Staudenmaier's book in his library, but did not mention this work in his writings. According to Shamdasani, Jung's self-experiment resembles Staudenmaier's procedures.[94]

In his book, after giving a brief overview of the history of magic, Staudenmaier described how he decided to go through a self-experiment triggered by the spiritualistic occurrences he had gone through These were, according to him, automatic writing and acoustic, visual and sensory hallucinations, with ghosts around him. He experienced these phenomena over several years aiming to explore and postulate the psychic laws behind them. He commented that he knew that a great part of what he observed came from him, and not from the action of ghosts.[95] Staudenmaier's 'psychic ghosts' were personified in different figures like a child, an emperor, a fool, a divine or demonic being. The opposite demands of these figures led to psychic confusion and he recognised that it was a pathological condition. But he took it as evidence that man represents a psychic unity, i.e., that all these figures were part of himself.[96]

Regarding his method, Staudenmaier wrote that it was based on the concepts of hallucination and of the subconscious. Concerning hallucinations, he suggested exercises to produce them consciously, focusing attentively on an object (initially with simple images such as a circle, then with more complex ones) and enhancing its visualisation through concentration and imagination, until the image becomes more distinctive and clear. The same procedure could be used to develop any sensory impression. Staudenmaier postulated that some people could even produce a real image outside of themselves, which would be visible for other people, and also that telepathy was possible. He described a series of practical exercises to develop this ability for all senses and added that, although simple in itself, this technique could trigger problems such as the fragmentation or exaggeration of the images, caused by an irritation of the nerves.[97]

Staudenmaier cited Prince's studies on the dissociation of personality, noting that Prince used the term personalities for the split off parts of his patients, while he used the term personifications. He wrote that in one of Prince's patients a new character took control of the greater part of the functions of their consciousness, which would justify why Prince called it 'personality'. Staudenmaier contested, however, that in his experiments with personifications he went through the same process as Prince's patients. He explained that it would be difficult for some characters such as the child or the girl to fit into Staudenmaier's real physical appearance and, if so, his conscious *ego* would take control again, unless he suffered under a real psychic illness.

He considered cases of a second personality as a kind of dispute between two enemies to take the upper hand. Differently, he postulated that the personifications had to do with the excessive use of everyday functions, such as eating, drinking and walking. He considered that the psychic illness in Prince's case was not caused by the appearance of the personifications but mainly by the wrong way of living and mental extrapolation. He noted, however, that personifications could increase psychic damage.[98]

Staudenmaier's experiments resemble those of Jung,[99] if one considers the personifications of and interaction with psychic elements. However, there are important differences which must be noted. Staudenmaier trained the conscious intensification of hallucinations, while Jung suggested a trance-like condition for the latter. Besides, Staudenmaier considered that the inner figures were mainly interested in the pleasant elements of everyday life, while Jung considered that the interaction with the inner figures had a teleological aspect to it. Furthermore, Jung's interactions with the inner figures are like an enacted drama of imagination, while Staudenmaier's do not have this character.

As presented previously, in the beginning of the 20th century, there were a variety of approaches to psychological treatments and of ways to explore the manifestations of the unconscious. It was a time when self-experimentation and introspection were current methods of research in medicine and psychology.[100] Jung was familiar with these different approaches and applied psychotherapeutics from different contemporaneous authors such as Freud, Adler, Janet, Bleuler, Bezzola, Prince, Forel, Staudenmaier and Silberer. Jung knew and used the different approaches of those days in treatments and related them to the results of his own research and ideas. In 1935, in 'Principles of practical psychotherapy', Jung wrote:

> The more deeply we penetrate the nature of the psyche, the more the conviction grows upon us that the diversity, the multidimensionality of human nature requires the greatest variety of standpoints and methods in order to satisfy the variety of psychic dispositions.[101]

He also stated that the theory developed by someone, including himself, was a kind of subjective confession and based on the personal assumptions of its author.[102] In a paper called 'The Realities of Practical Psychotherapy', from 1937, Jung considered the importance of a method not only in relation to the doctor who applied it, but also to the patient who interacts with the doctor. The story of the case used as an example in this paper will be presented later in this book.

It was in the turmoil of theoretical and political disputes, personal and methodological issues that Jung began his self-experiment. As we shall see, out of his self-experiment he developed what he later called the technique of active imagination, which was a method for both exploring the unconscious and treating the psyche. His method was embedded in a historical context and had some similarities to the practices mentioned previously. As we shall see, these elements are present in the treatment of the cases of Mischa Epper and Maggy Reichstein.

Notes

1 Gauld, 1992, p. 281. Similar procedures were used before, but under different names.
2 Ibid., p. 306.
3 Bernheim, 1887, p. x.
4 Ibid., pp. 193–196.
5 Ibid., p. 203.
6 Janet, 1976, vol. 1, p. 200.
7 Shamdasani, 2001.
8 Jung, 1914, p. 252, CW 4.
9 Mitchell, 1884.
10 First edition published in 1877.
11 Mitchell, 1884, p. 43.
12 Ibid., pp. 43–44.
13 Jung, 1902b, p. 137, CW 1.
14 Ellenberger, 1970, p. 345.
15 Janet, 1976, vol. 1, p. 457.
16 Ibid., p. 602.
17 Nevertheless, Janet criticised Jung's association method in a congress in London in 1913, noting that Jung's studies collapsed due to failures in experimental methodology. Shamdasani, 2003, p. 48.
18 The word *morale* in French can have different translations such as ethic, conscience or state of humour.
19 Janet, 1976, vol. 2, p. 1134.
20 Swan, ed., 2011, p. 23.
21 Ellenberger, 1970, p. 287.
22 Shamdasani, 2001, p. 6.
23 Forel, 1907, p. 208.
24 Shamdasani, 2001, p. 9.
25 Jung, 1907, CW 3.
26 Wieser, 2001.
27 Original in German: *Zur Analyse Psychotraumatischer Symptome.*
28 Bezzola, 1907, p. 206.
29 Ibid., p. 207.
30 McGuire, ed. 1974, p. 29.
31 Ibid., p. 32.
32 Ibid., p. 50.

33 Ibid., p. 53.
34 Bernet, 2013, p. 198.
35 Original in German: *Dementia Praecox oder Gruppe der Schizophrenien.*
36 Bleuler, 1911, p. 6.
37 Ibid., p. 374.
38 Bleuler, 1911, pp. 380–395.
39 Protocols, p. 75.
40 Falzeder, 2015, pp. 182–184.
41 Protocols, p. 317.
42 McGuire, ed., 1974, p. 5.
43 Schröter, 2012, p. 188.
44 Wehr, 1996.
45 Adler, 1907, pp. 2–4.
46 Ibid., p. 69.
47 Adler, 1916, pp. 24–25.
48 Ibid., p. 446.
49 Jung, 1917, p. 57.
50 Ibid., p. 59.
51 Ibid., p. 62.
52 McGuire, ed., 1974, p. 117.
53 Ibid., p. 142.
54 Taylor, 1928, pp. 21–73.
55 Prince, 1910, p. 21.
56 Ibid., p. 35.
57 Ibid., pp. 43–44.
58 Jung, 1929a, pars. 122–174. CW 16.
59 Jung, 1902a, par. 110, CW 1.
60 Jung, 1911, p. 56, CW 4.
61 Dubois, 1909, p. 235.
62 Ibid.
63 Ibid., p. viii.
64 Ibid., pp. ix–x.
65 Ibid., p. 210.
66 Ibid., p. 220.
67 Ibid., pp. 221–222.
68 Original in German: *Die Psychoneurosen und ihre psychische (seelische) Behandlung.*
69 Original in German: *Pathogenese der neurasthenischen Zustände.*
70 Jung, 1908b, par. 41, CW 4.
71 Jung, 1913b, par. 414, CW 4.
72 Jung, 1913a, p. 229, CW 4.
73 Ellenberger, 1970, p. 343.
74 Dejerine and Gauckler, 1913, p. iv.
75 Ibid., p. viii.
76 Ibid., pp. 274–278.
77 Ibid., p. 283.
78 Ibid., pp. 295–297.
79 Ibid., pp. 371–372.
80 Ellenberger, 1970, pp. 719, 729, 834.
81 Silberer, 1909. Original in German: *Bericht über eine Methode, gewisse symbolische Halluzinations-Erscheinungen hervorzurufen und zu beobachten.*
82 Silberer, 1917, pp. 233 ff.
83 Ibid., p. 272.
84 Ibid., pp. 251–252.
85 Ibid., pp. 254–255.
86 Swan, 2008.

87 Jung, 1912b, par. 253, CW 5.
88 Ibid., par. 302, CW 5.
89 Ibid., par. 659n, CW 5.
90 Jung, 1913a, par. 478, CW 4.
91 Jung, 1913c, par. 1061, CW 18.
92 Original in German: *Die Magie als Experimentelle Naturwissenschaft.*
93 Staudenmaier, 2003, p. 39.
94 Shamdasani, ed., 2009, p. 200.
95 Staudenmaier, 2003, pp. 28–29.
96 Ibid., p. 37.
97 Ibid., pp. 40–61.
98 Ibid., p. 87.
99 Shamdasani, ed., 2009, p. 200.
100 Swan, 2008 and Shamdasani, ed., 2009, p. 199.
101 Jung, 1935b, par. 11, CW 16.
102 Jung, 1935a, par. 275, CW 18.

References

Adler, A. (1907) *Studie über Minderwertigkeit von Organen* (Berlin und Wien: Urban & Schwarzenbach).

——— (1916) *The Neurotic Constitution: Outlines of a Comparative Individualistic Psychology and Psychotherapy* (New York: Moffat, Yard and Company).

Bernet, B. (2013) *Schizophrenie – Entstehung und Entwicklung eines psychiatrischen Krankheitsbild um 1900* (Zürich: Chronos Verlag).

Bernheim, H. (1887) *Suggestive Therapeutics: A Treatise on the Nature and Uses of Hypnotism* (New York: The Knickerbocker Press).

Bezzola, D. (1906/1907) "Zur Analyse psychotraumatischer Symptome" in *Journal für Psychologie und Neurologie* 8(3):204–219.

Bleuler, E. (1911) *Dementia Praecox oder Gruppe der Schizophrenien* (Leipzig und Wien: Franz Deuticke).

Dejerine, J. and Gauckler, E. (1913) *The Psychoneuroses and Their Treatment by Psychotherapy* (Philadelphia and London: J.B. Lippincott Co.).

Dubois, P. (1909) *The Psychic Treatment of Nervous Disorders: The Psychoneuroses and Their Moral Treatment* (New York and London: Funk and Wagnalls Company).

Ellenberger, H. (1970) *The Discovery of the Unconscious* (New York: Basic Books).

Falzeder, E. (2015) *Psychoanalytic Filiations: Mapping the Psychoanalytic Movement* (London: Karnac Books).

Forel, A. (1907) *Hypnotism or Suggestion and Psychotherapie* (New York: Rebman Company).

Gauld, A. (1992) *A History of Hypnotism* (Cambridge: Cambridge University Press).

Janet, P. (1976) *Psychological Healing: A Historical and Clinical Study* (New York: Arno Press), vols. 1 and 2.

Jung, C.G. (1902a) "On the So-Called Occult Phenomena" in *The Collected Works of C.G. Jung* (London: Routledge), 1993, vol. 1.

——— (1902b) "A case of hysterical stupor in a prisoner in detention" in *The Collected Works of C.G. Jung* (London: Routledge), 1993, vol. 1.

——— (1907) "The psychology of Dementia Praecox" in *The Collected Works of C.G. Jung* (London: Routledge & Kegan Paul), 1981, vol. 3.

——— (1908b) "The Freudian theory of hysteria" in *The Collected Works of C.G. Jung* (London: Routledge), 1993, vol. 4.

——— (1911) "Morton Prince, 'The mechanism and interpretation of dreams: A critical review'" in *The Collected Works of C.G. Jung* (London: Routledge), 1993, vol. 4.
——— (1912b/1952) "Symbols of transformation" in *The Collected Works of C.G. Jung* (London: Routledge & Kegan Paul), 1986, vol. 5.
——— (1913a) "General aspects of psychoanalysis" in *The Collected Works of C.G. Jung* (London: Routledge), 1993, vol. 4.
——— (1913b) "The theory of psychoanalysis" in *The Collected Works of C.G. Jung* (London: Routledge), 1993, vol. 4.
——— (1913c) "A comment on Tausk's criticism of Nelken" in *The Collected Works of C.G. Jung* (London: Routledge), 1993, vol. 18.
——— (1914) "Crucial points in psychoanalysis" in *The Collected Works of C.G. Jung* (London: Routledge), 1993, vol. 4.
——— (1917) *Der Psychologie der Unbewussten Prozess* (Zürich: Rascher und Cie.).
——— (1929a) "The problems of modern psychotherapy" in *The Collected Works of C.G. Jung* (London: Routledge), 1993, vol. 16.
——— (1935a) "Analytical psychology: Its theory and practice: The Tavistock Lectures" in *The Collected Works of C.G. Jung* (London: Routledge), 1993, vol. 18.
——— (1935b) "Principles of practical psychotherapy" in *The Collected Works of C.G. Jung* (London: Routledge), 1993, vol. 16.
McGuire, W., ed. (1974) *The Freud-Jung Letters* (Princeton, NJ: Princeton University Press).
Mitchell, S.W. (1884) *Fat and Blood: An Essay on the Treatment of Certain Forms of Neurasthenia and Hysteria* (Philadelphia: J.B. Lippincott & Co).
Prince, M. (1910) "The psychological principles and field of Psychotherapie" in *Psychotherapeutics: A Symposium* (Boston and Toronto: The Gorham Press).
Schröter, M., ed. (2012) *Sigmund Freud-Eugen Bleuler "Ich bin zuversichtlich, wir erobern bald die Psychiatrie" Briefwechsel 1904–1937* (Basel: Schwabe Verlag).
Shamdasani, S. (2001) "The magical method that works in the dark: C.G. Jung, hypnosis, and suggestion" in *The Journal of Jungian Theory and Practice* 3(1).
——— (2003) *Jung and the Making of Modern Psychology: The Dream of a Science* (Cambridge: Cambridge University Press).
———, ed. (2009) *The Red Book: Liber Novus/C.G. Jung* (New York: Norton & Company).
Silberer, H. (1909) "Bericht über eine Methode, gewisse symbolische Halluzinations-Erscheinungen hervorzurufen und zu beobachten" in *Jahrbuch für psychoanalytische und psychopathologische Forschung* 1:513–525.
——— (1917) *Problems of Mysticism and Its Symbolism* (New York: Moffat, Yard and Company).
Staudenmaier, L. (2003) *Die Magie als experimentelle Naturwissenschaft* (Langen: Verlag Wolfgang Roller).
Swan, W. (2008) "C.G. Jung's Psychotherapeutic Technique of Active Imagination in Historical Context" in *Psychoanalysis and History* 10(2).
———, ed. (2011) *The Memoir of Tina Keller-Jenny: A Lifelong Confrontation with the Psychology of C.G. Jung* (New Orleans: Spring Journals Books).
Taylor, W.S. (1928) *Morton Prince and Abnormal Psychology* (New York and London: D. Appleton and Company).
Wehr, G. (1996) *Gründergestallten der Psychoanalyse Profile-Ideen-Schicksale* (Zürich: Artemis und Winkler).
Wieser, A. (2001) *Zur frühen Psychoanalyse in Zürich: 1900–1914*. Dissertation zur Erlangung der Doktorwürde der Medizinischen Fakultät der Universität Zürich, Zürich.

4

THE SELF-EXPERIMENT

In the autumn of 1913, Jung, in retrospect, mentioned that he felt a sense of oppression, as if something was coming in the air. He referred to it not just as if it were coming from a psychic situation, but also from concrete reality. As this feeling grew more intense, Jung described an overpowering vision he had, which involved the whole of Europe. He described:

> It happened in October of the year 1913 as I was leaving alone for a journey, that during the day I was suddenly overcome in broad daylight by a vision: I saw a terrible flood that covered all the northern and low-lying lands between the North Sea and the Alps. It reached from England up to Russia, and from the coast of the North Sea right up to the Alps. I saw yellow waves, swimming rubble, and the death of countless thousands. This vision lasted for two hours, it confused me and made me ill. I was not able to interpret it. Two weeks passed, then the vision returned, still more violent than before, and an inner voice spoke: 'Look at it, it is completely real, and it will come to pass. You cannot doubt this'. I wrestled again for two hours with this vision, but it held me fast. It left me exhausted and confused. And I thought my mind had gone crazy.[1]

Nevertheless, he decided to go through an experiment with his fantasies. From December 1913 onwards he deliberately evoked them in waking state, as a kind of enacting dramas in his imagination.[2] Besides, he mentioned the need to find a criterion to understand the fantasies he had, to find a reference to deal with them. Further, he said:

> I asked myself whether these visions pointed to a revolution, but could not really imagine anything of the sort. And so I drew the conclusion that they

> had to do with me myself, and decided that I was menaced by a psychosis. The idea of war did not occur to me at all.[3]

He tried to find inner images that were behind the emotions and noted that, if he would have not done it, he could fall into a neurosis and would be torn apart by the emotions. Jung then had a sequence of dreams which he did not understand. In the summer of the following year, he described:

> In the year 1914 in the month of June, at the beginning and end of the month, and at the beginning of July I had the same dream three times: I was in a foreign land, and suddenly, overnight and right in the middle of summer, a terrible cold descended from space. All seas and rivers were locked in ice, every green living thing had frozen. The second dream was thoroughly similar to this. But the third dream at the beginning of July went as follows: I was in a remote English land. It was necessary that I return to my homeland with a fast ship as speedily as possible. I reached home quickly. In my homeland I found that in the middle of summer a terrible cold had fallen from space, which had turned every living thing into ice. There stood a leaf-bearing but fruitless tree, whose leaves had turned into sweet grapes full of healing juice through the working of the frost. I picked some grapes and gave them to a great waiting throng.[4]

In the interviews with Jaffé, Jung commented in retrospect that he worked on the material in the way it was given by the unconscious, and stated that this was the correct approach.

However, Jung's preceding comments that he could not imagine a revolution or that the idea of a war was unexpected must be considered critically. If we take into consideration the events of that time, there were many signs indicating that tensions between nations in Europe were rising and that an armed conflict among them was a tangible menace. The different political ambitions and rivalries among the most important European countries led them to invest a considerable amount of their resources in their military and increased the risk of a war in the beginning of the 20th century. Around 1910, the investment of many important European nations in their military force had met an unprecedented increase and military expenditures were consuming over a third of the national budgets of some countries.[5]

Even so, the years before 1914 were also marked by a strong movement for peace. One of the most active peace movements was in Germany, with protests against the hard-line of the government. In September 1911, a march involving 250,000 participants assembled in Berlin to demonstrate against war. In Switzerland, prior to 1914, there were also important movements, which aimed at the prevention of war. The most significant was the Second International from the Socialist Movement held in Basel in November 1912. The participants wrote a 'Manifesto against War' noting that 'the governments should not forget that they could not start a war without risks for themselves'. At the political level, there were meetings in May 1913 between the members of the French and German Parliaments in Bern, Switzerland, in an attempt to reduce armaments and find agreement on arbitration, none of these with any results. All these events were broadly discussed in Swiss newspapers.[6]

Important to mention is that Jung was not alone insofar as he was having visions about the menace of a major conflict in Europe. There were many people who had premonitions about a coming catastrophe. Just before the war, apocalyptic imagery was common throughout Europe in the arts and literature, in the work of artists such as Wassily Kandinsky and Ludwig Meidner. Particularly in the work of authors and people linked to spiritualism, such as Leonora Piper and Arthur Conan Doyle, there was a sense of prophetic warning about a war.[7] To many contemporaries, the outbreak of the war was an inevitable occurrence after a long series of local conflicts, menaces, national disputes, serving as a release of the great tension in Europe.[8]

Jung was in Aberdeen, Scotland, in July 1914. He was there at the invitation of the British Medical Association to deliver a lecture at a congress. He presented the paper 'On the Importance of the Unconscious in Psychopathology'. At this point, Jung was in active engagement with his dreams and visions and, as mentioned before, he initially interpreted them as referring to his own psychic conditions. However, with the outbreak of the war, Jung later commented that nobody was happier than him, because he said that he was finally able to understand his dreams and visions. He concluded that they were prospective, that they anticipated the war and that what his dreams and visions referred to were the actual events to come over Europe.[9] Jung's conclusion that his fantasies were prospective may be considered as one of the events which led him to the elaboration of the concept of synchronicity and, as we shall see later, the case of Reichstein was particularly striking for him with regard to this concept.

Another important occurrence related to this event was mentioned by Jung in the seminar he gave in 1925. There he noted that, as he initially did not know what to do with those fantasies, he decided to write them down in sequence. As he asked himself if what he was doing was science, an inner voice of a woman said that this was art. In the sequence, he described what happened as follows:

> Well, I said very emphatically to this voice that what I was doing was not art, and I felt a great resistance grow up within me. Then I got another shot like the first: 'That is art'. This time I caught her and said, 'No, it is not', and I felt as though an argument would ensue. I thought, well, she has not the speech centers I have, so I told her to use mine, and she did, and came through with a long statement. This is the origin of the technique I developed for dealing directly with the unconscious contents.[10]

As mentioned before, Jung's conversation with an inner figure resembles the techniques of Staudenmaier and Silberer to explore unconscious contents. Jung would later call his technique active imagination, and the case of Mischa Epper that I present in this book will shed light on its development. Also important to note is that the editor of the seminar of 1925 speculated that the woman's voice in Jung's fantasy was that of Sabina Spielrein, whereas Shamdasani has argued that it was the voice of Maria Moltzer,[11] a close collaborator of Jung in those days, who, as we shall see, will play an important role in Epper's treatment.

Up to 1914, Jung had developed and articulated many of the concepts in his psychology. He had a) described his theory of the emotionally charged complex based in his word association experiment; b) differentiated his concept of libido from Freud, postulating it as a non-sexual psychic energy; c) postulated the idea of an unconscious phylogenetically acquired and expressed in mythic images; d) presented his general types with the extroverted and introverted libido; e) described his understanding of dreams as having a prospective and a compensatory function; and f) considered fantasies and dreams with a synthetic and an analytic approach. The processes he went through during his self-experimentation added a new method, which he would later call active imagination, and a new element to his concepts and theories, mainly connected to what Jung would later refer to as the process of individuation. This is the notion that personality develops over time to a higher state, expressed in symbolic changes, which have parallels in mythology and religions.[12]

In 1950, in the foreword to the fourth edition of *Symbols of Transformation*, he reviewed those days of self-experimentation as follows:

> I did not know that I was living a myth, and even if I had known it, I would not have known what sort of myth was ordering my life without my knowledge. So, in the most natural way, I took it upon myself to get to know 'my' myth, and I regarded this as the task of tasks, for – so I told myself – how could I, when treating my patients, make due allowance for the personal factor, for my personal equation, which is yet so necessary for a knowledge of the other person, if I was unconscious of it? [. . .] This resolve led me to devote many years of my life to investigating the subjective contents which are the products of unconscious processes, and to work out methods which could enable us, or at any rate help us, to explore the manifestations of the unconscious.[13]

Notes

1 Shamdasani, ed., 2009, p. 231.
2 Ibid., p. 200.
3 Jaffé, ed., 1989, p. 176. In the protocols he added in this passage that the idea of the war came unexpeted not only for him, but for everyone.
4 Shamdasani, ed., 2009, p. 231.
5 Blom, 2008, p 163.
6 Kreis, 2014, p. 22.
7 Shamdasani, ed., 2009, p. 199.
8 Ellenberger, 1970, p. 822.

9 Shamdasani, ed., 2009, pp. 201–202.
10 McGuire, ed., 1990, p. 42.
11 Shamdasani, ed., 2009, p. 199.
12 Shamdasani, 2012b, pp. 366–367.
13 Jung, 1912b/1952, CW 5, p. xxv.

References

Blom, P. (2008) *The Vertigo Years: Europe, 1900–1914* (New York: Basic Books).

Ellenberger, H. (1970) *The Discovery of the Unconscious* (New York: Basic Books).

Jaffé, A., ed. (1989) *Memories, Dreams, Reflections, by C.G. Jung* (New York: Vintage Books).

Jung, C.G. (1912b/1952) "Symbols of transformation" in *The Collected Works of C.G. Jung* (London: Routledge and Kegan Paul), 1986, vol. 5.

Kreis, G. (2014) *Insel der unsicherer Geborgenheit – Die Schweiz in den Kriegsjahren 1914–1918* (Zürich: Verlag Neue Zürcher Zeitung).

McGuire, W. (1990) *C.G. Jung: Analytical Psychology Notes of the Seminar Given in 1925* (London: Routledge).

Shamdasani, S., ed. (2009) *The Red Book: Liber Novus/C.G. Jung* (New York: Norton & Company).

——— (2012b) "After Liber Novus" in *The Journal of Analytical Psychology* 57:366–367.

5

ON THE SEARCH FOR A SCIENTIFIC LANGUAGE

As indicated earlier, Ellenberger postulates three possible ways of how experiential aspects in the lives of scientists may impinge upon their theorising. The first possibility is direct self-observation – one turns to one's self as an intimate source of information; the second is a kind of objectification, by the intellectualisation of a painful psychological experience that he lived; and the third is a full-scale 'creative malady', in which he enters a period of distress, with neurotic and even psychotic symptoms, from which he emerges with a new insight or theory.[1] One may find these aspects in Jung's theoretical and practical work, which occurred during and after his period of self-experimentation.

Shamdasani, however, noted the problems in considering Jung's self-experiments only as a 'malady'. He pointed to the many (mis)interpretations by authors, who speculated about Jung supposedly having psychotic episodes apparently due to his 'traumatic' break with Freud. He added authors who did not reduce it to the psychopathological criteria alone and pointed to parallels in the history of Christian esotericism, such as the 'night sea journey', i.e., it could also be considered as a religious experience.[2]

In the *Liber Novus*, Jung referred to the influence of the spirit of the time and the spirit of the depths, and described how he was forced to consider the irrational. Meaning would come from the 'melting' of both: rational and irrational. He wrote:

> I have learned that in addition to the spirit of this time there is still another spirit at work, namely that which rules the depths of everything contemporary. The spirit of this time would like to hear of use and value. I also thought this way, and my humanity still thinks this way. But that other spirit forces me nevertheless to speak, beyond justification, use, and meaning. [. . .] The spirit of the depths took my understanding and all my

> knowledge and placed them at the service of the inexplicable and the paradoxical. He robbed me of speech and writing for everything that was not in his service, namely the melting together of sense and nonsense, which produces the supreme meaning. But the supreme meaning is the path, the way and the bridge to what is to come.[3]

In the preceding passage, Jung reports having received the impression that he was 'robbed' of his belief in science and his joy of explaining and ordering things, i.e., the rational world. He felt he was forced to consider the irrational due to the spirit of the depths, and a sense that rationality alone was not enough to grasp the plenitude of life. As mentioned before, he added commentaries to the fantasies in an attempt to interpret the material of his self-experiment,[4] but it is clear that the commentaries and interpretations he put in there were not enough. Jung needed to find a proper way to express his insights in a scientific language.

A hypothesis for Jung's reasons to search for a scientific language to describe his findings from his self-experimentation can be drawn from some of his later writings and presentations. In a seminar given in 1925, Jung presented the process he went through in order to develop his main concepts. He said that a man wants to present to the public a finished product of his thinking, to present it as if it was produced by his mind free of weakness, without weaving of mistakes or impure thinking.[5] Jung added:

> Just so with a man about his books. He does not want to tell of the secret alliances, the *faux pas* of his mind. This it is that makes lies of most autobiographies. [. . .] And just as a woman erects her stronghold of power in her sexuality, and will not give away any of the secrets of its weak side, so a man centres his power in his thinking and proposes to hold it as a solid front against the public, particularly against other men. He thinks if he tells the truth in this field it is equivalent to turning over the keys of his citadel to the enemy.[6]

Although in the preceding passage Jung was describing his opinion concerning his book on typology and the differences between the opinions of Freud, Adler and his own, in general, his argumentation can also be applied to the presentation of the insights he received out of his self-experimentation.

Another possible reason for Jung's search for a scientific language to describe his findings was the link between his fantasies and the fantasies of Ms Miller, whom he analysed in the book he published in 1912.[7] He mentioned in 1925 that he later realised whilst analysing her fantasies, which he considered semi-morbid, that he was also analysing his own fantasy function. Jung assumed that Ms Miller would in that context serve as a description of his own impure thinking. He added that he elaborated Miller's morbidity into myths in a way satisfactory to him, and by this assimilated the Miller side of himself.[8]

It is important to note that Jung did not consider his personal fantasies as the only basis for his theory and concepts. As mentioned before, he was interested in historical parallels between his inner experiences and symbolic materials, as presented in myths, religion and primitive psychology. In this respect, his studies on alchemy were vital. In retrospect he said:

> As my life entered its second half, I was already embarked on the confrontation with the contents of the unconscious. My work on this was an extremely long-drawn-out affair, and it was only after some twenty years of it that I reached some degree of understanding of my fantasies. First I had to find evidence for the historical prefiguration of my inner experiences. That is to say, I had to ask myself, "Where have my particular premises already occurred in history?" If I had not succeeded in finding such evidence, I would never have been able to substantiate my ideas. Therefore, my encounter with alchemy was decisive for me, as it provided me with the historical basis which I had hitherto lacked. Analytical psychology is fundamentally a natural science, but it is subject far more than any other science to the personal bias of the observer. The psychologist must depend therefore in the highest degree upon historical and literary parallels if he wishes to exclude at least the crudest errors in judgment.[9]

Besides, he noted the parallels between his ideas and the research studies and experiments of other scientists in psychology and areas related to the topics. It is nevertheless clear that his self-experimentation gave him the direction for the development of his theories. His self-experimentation also changed the treatment he offered to his patients, because he applied to them the procedures that he had experienced within himself, which had, in turn, led him to the development of the technique of active imagination. It is also important to note that Jung's way to work on the material went through some changes as he developed his method.

In Jung's notes in *The Red Book*, Shamdasani identified two different layers in the text. The first layer is indicated with [1] and in these notes Jung wrote down what happened to him without questioning or interpreting the material he was experiencing, mostly waking visions and fantasies. This first part of his experiment was conducted during the years 1913 and 1914. In retrospect, Jung remembered his attitude to the self-experiment as if it were a scientific research. He described it as follows:

> From the beginning I had conceived my voluntary confrontation with the unconscious as a scientific experiment which I myself was conducting and in whose outcome I was vitally interested. [. . .] I was voluntarily submitting myself to emotions of which I could not really approve, and I was writing down fantasies which often struck me as nonsense, and toward which I

> had strong resistances. For as long as we do not understand their meaning, such fantasies are a diabolical mixture of the sublime and the ridiculous. [. . .] A cogent motive for my making the attempt was the conviction that I could not expect of my patients something I did not dare to do myself. The excuse that a helper stood at their side would not pass muster, for I was well aware that the so-called helper – that is, myself – could not help them unless he knew their fantasy material from his own direct experience, and that at present all he possessed were a few theoretical prejudices of dubious value. This idea – that I was committing myself to a dangerous enterprise not for myself alone, but also for the sake of my patients – helped me over several critical phases.[10]

Therefore, at the beginning of his experiment, Jung did not interpret his fantasies. He took notes of the images, and felt as if he were passive in front of them. In his retrospective remarks, it is clear that he did not understand the images, but wanted to check if they had a meaning or not. Another goal was to gain a better understanding for the sake of his patients.

After July 1914, Jung began a draft of what would become the *Liber Novus*, transcribing the fantasies from the black books and explaining each episode, adding a lyrical elaboration.[11] The second layer of texts added to the fantasies were identified with a [2] by Shamdasani, who considered them the first major attempt to develop a new constructive method and an interpretation Jung himself gave to the material.[12]

Up to this point, Jung's approach was firstly to observe and to record the fantasies and, secondly, to elaborate the material with amplifications and interpretations. Therefore, one could say that Jung had a prototype of a method, based on his own self-experimentation, which he could apply to his practice.

A further development in the procedure followed in 1915, as Jung began to paint the images to accompany his text. These images could be considered as active imaginations in their own right.[13] Jung transcribed the fantasies to *The Red Book*, altered titles and edited the material, but only in the second layer; the original fantasies were kept almost unchanged.[14]

Summarising the development of Jung's method, we can see that Jung firstly experienced the fantasies towards the end of 1913. Up to this point, he had visions and conversations with the inner figures. Then he began to elaborate these experiences explaining the significance of each episode and to combine it with lyrical elaborations and interpretations. After 1915, he began to express the contents in a visual form through his paintings.

In 1916, Jung wrote 'The transcendent function' in which he tried to conceptualise his procedure and turn it in a replicable psychotherapeutic method. However, he did not present it to the public, because he was not satisfied with the text. Much later, in 1958, in the prefatory notes to the revised and edited text, Jung wrote about its limitations and that 'the essay may therefore stand, with all its imperfections, as a historical document'.[15] He pointed to the question: how does one come to terms in practice with the unconscious?[16] His description of the method in this text runs as follows:

> He (the patient) must make himself as conscious as possible of the mood he is in, sinking himself in it without reserve and noting down on paper all the fantasies and associations that come up. Fantasy must be allowed the freest possible play, yet not in such manner that it leaves the orbit of its object, namely, the affect, by setting off a kind of 'chain-reaction' association process. The whole procedure is a kind of enrichment and clarification of the affect, whereby the affect and its contents are brought nearer to consciousness, becoming at the same time more impressive and more understandable.[17]

Jung's preceding comment regarding the procedure indicates the difference between his method and Freud's method of free association, namely, that the associations must stay related to the initial affect and not leave it. Jung went further, pointing to the fact that it required a specific training, namely, the elimination of critical attention, producing a kind of vacuum in consciousness.[18]

He further added that, because the method activates the fantasies which were right under the surface, it was not without dangers, for the intensified content could irrupt spontaneously into the conscious mind.[19] As we shall see later, this approach was the one applied to the case of Mischa Epper. However, Jung went on developing the technique, specifying some features as we can see in his seminar from the year 1930, in his presentation of the case of Christiana Morgan, which will be presented briefly in the next sections of this book.

Notes

1 Micale, ed., 1993, pp. 71–72.
2 Shamdasani, 2005, pp. 69–86.
3 Shamdasani, 2009, p. 229.
4 Shamdasani notes Jung's commentaries in *The Red Book* as layer [2].
5 McGuire, ed., 1990, p. 32.
6 Ibid., pp. 32–33.
7 Jung, 1912b, CW 5.
8 McGuire, ed. (1990) p. 31.
9 Jaffé, ed., 1989, p. 200.
10 Ibid., pp. 178, 179.
11 Shamdasani, ed., 2009, p. 202.
12 Ibid., p. 203.
13 Ibid.
14 Ibid.
15 Jung, 1916/1957, p. 67, CW 8.
16 Ibid.
17 Ibid., par. 167, CW 8.
18 Ibid., par. 155, CW 8.
19 Ibid., p. 68, CW 8.

References

Jaffé, A., ed. (1989) *Memories, Dreams, Reflections, by C.G. Jung* (New York: Vintage Books).

Jung, C.G. (1912b/1952) "Symbols of transformation" in *The Collected Works of C.G. Jung* (London: Routledge & Kegan Paul), 1986, vol. 5.

——— (1916/1957) "The transcended function" in *The Collected Works of C.G. Jung* (London: Routledge), 1991, vol. 8.

McGuire, W., ed. (1990) *C.G. Jung: Analytical Psychology Notes of the Seminar Given in 1925* (London: Routledge).

Micale, M., ed. (1993) *Beyond the Unconscious: Essays of Henri F. Ellenberger in the History of Psychiatry* (Princeton, NJ: Princeton University Press).

Shamdasani, S. (2005) *Jung Stripped Bare by His Biographers, Even* (London: Karnac Books).

———, ed. (2009) *The Red Book: Liber Novus/C.G. Jung* (New York: Norton & Company).

6

JUNG'S CRITICISM OF METHODS

As mentioned before, Helene Hoerni-Jung stated that her father usually said that 'he would have no method'. This intriguing statement, however, must be elucidated.

In 1937, Jung asserted that analysis must consider the patient's individuality and for patients to whom analysis was indicated, rigid methods could cause harm. He said:

> Psychogenic disturbances, quite unlike organic diseases, are atypical and individual. With growing experience, one even finds oneself at a loss in making a diagnosis. The neuroses, for example, vary so much from individual to individual that it hardly means anything when we diagnose 'hysteria'. [. . .] What we have said about diagnosis is also true of therapy in so far as this takes the form of an individual analysis. It is just as impossible to describe a typical course of treatment as it is to make a specific diagnosis. This radical, not to say nihilistic statement, naturally does not apply to cases where a *method* is employed as a matter of principle.[1]

He pointed out that an approach which only considered general aspects could cause considerable damage to the personality of the patient. Therefore, Jung criticised a blind application of methods.

A method could work as long as the personal psychic conditions of the patient coincided with those of the method proposed. In these cases, methods could be applied. But not all cases would fit into this category described earlier. For Jung, it was imperative that patients should not be reduced to the limits of a method, and that the uniqueness of the personality of the patient was considered. He recognised, however, the importance of different methods, such as that of the Adlerian and Freudian methods, pointing out the importance of different approaches for individual patients. About his personal way of working with patients he said in the lecture of 1937:

> Speaking for myself, I must confess that experience has taught me to keep away from therapeutic 'methods' as much as from diagnoses. The enormous variation among individuals and their neuroses has set before me the ideal of approaching each case with a minimum of prior assumptions. The ideal would naturally be to have no assumptions at all. But this is impossible even if one exercises the most rigorous self-criticism, for one is oneself the biggest of all one's assumptions, and the one with the gravest consequences. Try as we may to have no assumptions and to use no ready-made methods, the assumption that I myself am will determine my method: as I am so will I proceed.[2]

Further, in a letter to Dr Karl Srnertz from the 19th of December 1942, he stated that every postulation about the psyche must be considered, and that every psychological theory is a subjective statement. However, when someone presents a new standpoint, it gives the wrong impression that it turned obsolete what was before. For him, this conclusion was erroneous. In some cases, the most primitive method could achieve better results than the most sophisticated ones. Besides, he wrote that some scientific achievements have no psychotherapeutic value if these were only empty words without life in them.[3]

Jung's approach was also singular in another particular way: he considered that the treatment with some patients might develop into a dialectical process. For him, the psychological similarities between the analyst and the patient established the foundations of mutual understanding, but the differences would require a new approach, and no general method based on general premises could be of any help here. Jung referred to analysis as a dialectical process inside one's psyche. He wrote as follows:

> There is in the analytical process, that is to say in the dialectical discussion between the conscious mind and the unconscious, a development or an advance towards some goal or end, the perplexing nature of which has engaged my attention for many years.[4]

Jung's view was that the inner dialectical process led to the development of the individuation process. Besides, he noted that another dialectical process also occurred during the analysis, namely, the dialectical process between the analyst and the patient. He postulated that the encounter between the qualitative differences of the patient, i.e., his individuality and the individuality of the analyst required a specific approach. A general method would be inappropriate in this context. He commented:

> If one wants to give a name to the process of coming to terms with them, one could call it a dialectical procedure – which means no more than an encounter between my premises and the patient's.[5]

In a text from year 1953, he assumed that the patient in analysis could continue this process alone, in the form of an inner dialogue, and that the dialectical dialogue with the unconscious still continues and follows much the same course as it does with those who have not given up their work with the doctor.[6]

We can observe that Jung developed this approach out of his self-experiment and that he used it with the patients in analysis. Jung had had in his experience the interaction and the inner dialogue with the figures of his fantasies. Furthermore, he expressed them in his writings, paintings and sculptures, and used his critical understanding to assimilate the content.

Therefore, concerning Jung's approach, one may conclude that after 1914, he developed it mainly out of the procedures he had used in his personal experiences, which evidently impacted on his theories and way of working. It can be postulated, then, that the comment Jung made to his daughter – that he would have no method – was an expression of his criticism towards the use of methods without consideration of the patient's individuality.

Notes

1 Jung, 1937, pars. 540–541, CW 16.
2 Ibid., par. 543.
3 Jaffé, ed., 1973, Band 1, p. 401.
4 Jung, 1953, par. 3, CW 12.
5 Ibid., par. 544.
6 Ibid., par. 4.

References

Jaffé, A., ed. (1973) *C.G. Jung: Briefe* (Olten und Freiburg im Breisgau: Walter-Verlag), Band 1 und 2.

Jung, C.G. (1937) "The realities of practical psychotherapy" in *The Collected Works of C.G. Jung* (London: Routledge), 1993, vol. 16.

——— (1953) "Psychology and alchemy" in *The Collected Works of C.G. Jung* (London: Routledge), 1992, vol. 12.

7

IMPORTANT PATIENTS IN THE LITERATURE

In his books and presentations, Jung often referred to case material as illustrations for his theories and assumptions. It can also be postulated that some cases affected Jung's theorising. Although Jung did not reveal the identity of his patients in his writings, some of them were identified later.[1] The published case stories certainly increased the understanding of Jung's way of working for practitioners and researchers of Jungian psychology. It is important to note, however, that the additional information in some aspects supported and in others questioned Jung's presentation and understanding of the case. What follows are some of the materials available in the literature. The presented cases were chosen for their importance in Jung's career or for their connection to the concepts related to this research.

The 'paradigmatic' patient

In his 1902 dissertation 'On the psychology and pathology of so-called occult phenomena', Jung discussed what one could name today as altered states of consciousness and related them to the so-called occult phenomena. To illustrate his thesis he discussed mainly the case of a young medium girl. Jung gave a relatively extended report of her somnambulism and spiritualistic manifestations and he noted that her family had exhibited symptoms of eccentricity and personality disorders. The girl was reserved and susceptible to mood changes. However, differently than the medium herself, the spirits who spoke through her were highly eloquent and mature, cited biblical passages and elaborate theories.

As time went by, the somnambulistic attacks became less frequent and intense and Jung stopped the recordings of the sessions when he caught the medium lying and pretending the manifestations of the spirits. Jung postulated that in the beginning of the sessions the spirits that spoke through her in the spiritualistic sessions were split parts of the medium's personality.

The medium that Jung named 'S.W.' was in fact his cousin Helene Preiswerk. In 1975, biographical data were published on her case by her niece, Stefanie Zumstein-Preiswerk,[2] who consulted documents and interviewed Emmy Zinsstag, a close friend of Preiswerk. Years later, Ellenberger[3] wrote an article adding information to the story of Preiswerk, mentioning the rivalry between Jung's family (C.G. Jung's father) and the Preiswerk family (C.G. Jung's mother) and the sociocultural constellation in the city of Basel where they lived. He also briefly described the influence of the Protestant and Jewish religion in Basel and the general interest in Spiritism at that time. Ellenberger, who based his writings on the text of Zumstein-Preiswerk, pointed out several differences compared to what Jung presented in his dissertation, for instance, in the chronology of events and the concluding phase of the experiments. Ellenberger noted:

> Today, in retrospect, we are drawn to consider another facet of Carl Gustav's relationship to Helene Preiswerk. At first it seems that he was not much interested in her personality; she was the subject of an intellectual inquiry. Gradually, he became bored with her, the more so when he perceived that she was in love with him. The picture he gave of her in his dissertation is one governed by contempt. Later, when he saw her in Paris, he realised that she was a sensible and charming personality. He was attracted to her, but she was reserved. This is quite plainly stated by Emmy Zinsstag: 'the roles were reversed'.[4]

Ellenberger added that Jung wrote about the early death of Helene Preiswerk due to tuberculosis in 1911, and that she was in a condition of mental disintegration, while her niece described her as entirely clear minded. Jung therefore, changed elements in his presentation of the case in a way to support his assumptions. As we shall see, similar criticism can be formulated with reference to the parallels Jung traced in the case of Maggy Reichstein, relating her symptoms to the yoga Kundalini, which will be later discussed in this book.

The story of patients related to concept of transference and countertransference

In 1904, at the Burghözli mental hospital, Jung had a patient, a young Russian woman, whom he treated using the word association experiment and psychoanalytically oriented interpretations until 1905 or possibly even until 1906.[5] He mentioned her treatment in the article 'The Freudian theory of hysteria' (1908b),[6] which was a report of a paper he presented in the First International Congress of Psychiatry and Neurology in Amsterdam in September 1907.

In his paper, Jung mentioned that her diagnosis was a psychotic hysteria and that the earliest symptoms were at the early age of three or four, when the patient developed problems to defecate, holding the faeces until pain forced her to evacuate. At the age of seven the symptoms were related to masturbation, and the patient felt sexually excited when her father smacked her on her buttocks. At puberty, the symptoms became obsessive and the patient was not able to eat without thinking of defecating and could not avoid feeling excited while looking at the hands of her father. The natural impulse in this age to have a relationship was jeopardised by her problems. At the age of eighteen she got depressed, crying and screaming with attacks of laughing. Jung presented the case as a concrete example for Freud's ideas on infantile sexuality and discussed the case with Freud in their letters.[7]

The patient was identified as Sabina Spielrein. In 1977, Aldo Carotenuto, an Italian Jungian analyst, received Spielrein's letters and diaries from the Geneva Institute of Psychology and later published his findings.[8] Spielrein was the psychoanalytic test case for Jung, in which he applied the treatment as proposed by Freud, however, Jung's knowledge of psychoanalysis up to this point in his career came only from his readings.[9] The affair between Freud, Jung and Spielrein was a matter for much speculation and controversy. Based on the documents found after the publication of Carotenuto's books, some authors affirmed that they had an erotic affair; while others pointed out that the nature of the relationship was romantic, but not necessarily sexual.[10] Many studies were published analysing their relationship. This repercussion makes the case probably the most 'popular' and romanticised case in psychoanalytical literature.[11]

The affair led to a debate about the boundaries in psychoanalytic treatment, and was important for the future development of psychoanalysis. It triggered the discussion about the effect a patient may have on the doctor and led Freud to coin the term countertransference.[12] As we shall see, the case of Reichstein presented later in this research also had an impact on Jung's understanding of countertransference, but it is related to aspects other than the ethical boundaries in the analytical relationship.

Besides the case of Spielrein, another relevant case related to the concept of countertransference involving Freud and Jung happened around 1908. Jung treated briefly a patient who was previously in analysis with Freud and who returned to Freud after seeing Jung. This case was relevant because, like Spielrein, it affected the relationship between Freud and Jung and also the development of the concept of countertransference. The case partially overlapped Spielrein's treatment with Jung. She was identified as Elfriede Hirschfeld.

Falzeder, in his article about her case, shows the importance of this patient for Freud,[13] and noted that he (Freud) mentioned her case in at least six of his papers with different names. Although it was an important case, it remained unnoticed in the psychoanalytic literature for a long time. Hirschfeld was treated by important psychiatrists, psychotherapists and psychoanalysts of the time like Pierre Janet, O. Pfister, L. Binswanger and E. Bleuler.[14] Her longest treatment, however, was with Freud, between 1908 and 1914 (nearly seven years, but with interruptions). All the treatments she went through failed in the end. According to Freud the reason for her psychic disturbance was the problem in her marriage, which was childless. After eight years, her husband confessed to her that he was infertile. Hirschfeld's illness began after she was informed. She suffered initially under 'anxiety hysteria' and later this anxiety neurosis changed into a severe obsessional neurosis. During and after the treatment of Hirschfeld's case, between 1911 and 1915, Freud wrote the papers defining more clearly the psychoanalytical method.

It seems that Freud had an ambivalent attitude towards the case of Hirschfeld. On one hand caring and close to her (he sometimes called her by her first name – a quite personal way to refer to a patient in those days) and sometimes referred to her in his letter as his Grand Patient. On the other hand, the difficulties of the case and the lack of development led Freud to call her also his Chief Tormentor. The treatment was discussed mainly in the letters between Freud, Jung and Pfister and, as Falzeder pointed out, it was an important case, because it showed their differences in the posture in front of the patient, namely, in the process of countertransference.

On the 31st December 1911, in his answer to a missing letter from Jung in which Jung supposedly criticised the handling of the case by Freud and in which Hirschfeld was referred to as Frau C, Freud replied that both Jung and Pfister did not have enough experience with the technique and the analyst should remain unaprochable. Freud also warned Jung of Hirschfeld's influence and about using her case to express any resentment towards him.[15]

In his answer on the 2nd January 1912, Jung noted that all that Hirschfeld wanted was a little bit of sympathy, which, she noted, Freud withheld. Jung, however, couldn't withhold and was glad to offer this kind of sympathy.[16] Freud's answer in his letter 10th January 1912, suggested Jung to modify a little his technique and be more reserved towards the patient.[17]

But Falzeder points that Freud, although suggesting that he (Jung) had to work on his technique, did not admit that he (Freud) was involved, and that he had feelings towards Hirschfeld. Jung noted that the patient apparently sensed this, but did not comment further, because he did not know what had happened. But Freud just pointed to the lack of experience of Jung and Pfister. Falzeder writes:

> Given Freud's affection for Frau Hirschfeld, it becomes apparent that he was warning not only Jung, but also himself against the dangers inherent in too much emotional involvement. In theory, this was to remain Freud's position; in practice, however, we see him vacillating between sensitive and sympathetic empathy on the one hand and a distant and sometimes harsh and crude behaviour on the other.[18]

The question presented was mainly: how much feeling towards the patient is the doctor allowed to have and to show? Freud, in his later papers, advises the practitioners of psychoanalysis basically to remain opaque to the patient, surely considering the problems that Jung had had with Spielrein. However, in Falzeder's paper it is clear that Freud in his practice did not have a clear position at the time of Hirschfeld's treatment. In her case, it is possible to observe further the difficulties between Jung and Freud, namely, the question of how to deal with countertransference and the risks related to it, as well as the personal queries between them.

The cases just presented had consequences for the training of future psychoanalysts. Around 1911, Jung treated a Dutch hypnotist named Van Renterghem for about two months. As reason for his treatment Van Renterghem mentioned his interest in experiencing psychoanalysis. Later, in 1913, Van Renterghem wrote an article presenting two cases Jung told him during his analysis as examples of the psychoanalytical method of treatment. It is not precisely known when Jung treated the two patients mentioned in Van Renterghem's text, but the inferences in the text suggest a time around 1910.[19] The cases were named 'Analysis and cure of a case of nervous prostrations' and 'Analysis of a case of sleeplessness' and they give a brief insight into Jung's use of the psychoanalytical technique at that time, namely, dreams as self-representations in the psyche as well as Jung's interpretations of transference. Van Renterghem's case is important to note, because it was one of the first known cases of training analysis.[20] Training analyses later became one of the pillars in the procedures to become a psychoanalyst as an attempt to reduce the emergence of problems in the relationship between patient and the doctor, i.e., in the process of transference and countertransference, as observed in the cases of Spierein and Hirschfeld.

The story of a patient related to the concept of primordial ideas

In 1912, Jung published the second part of *Transformations and Symbols of the Libido*, in which he interpreted essays written by a woman, Ms Frank Miller. He considered them signs of a coming schizophrenia, and related them to the concept of primordial images, a term that he would later refer to as archetypal symbolism. Although her essays were not the result of a psychological treatment, Jung interpreted them in the same way he would work with clinical material during analysis.[21]

Jung considered that she was not consciously aware of the erotic impact of her encounter with an Italian officer and, mentioning the available comments of Miller about the episode, used mythological parallels to interpret her poem. He noted that it was a product of a religiously and poetically introverted libido, related to the father-imago, and that it appeared as a substitute of her erotic problem.[22] Furthermore, he interpreted the fantasies of Miller as indicating that she was not able to deal with her feelings and instincts, and that her conscious mind was not ready yet to take its own decisions.[23] Jung concluded that Miller did not have the conscious understanding to deal with, and to assimilate, the primordial images that the unconscious produced, which were compensatory to the attitude of her conscious mind.[24]

According to Shamdasani, every time Jung reviewed this book, he adapted its reading in a way that confirmed the teleological aspects he had seen in Ms Miller's writings. Shamdasani concludes that in so doing, Jung's intention was to endorse his interpretation of the case, confirming the view that Miller's poem was an indication of a coming schizophrenia.[25] Furthermore, he points out that in Jung's model of 1912 the presence of archaic or mythological material was enough to indicate this condition, but this view changed in his later writings, when Jung considered that it was the attitude of consciousness which was decisive.[26] As we shall see, the problems in the relation to the father-imago and the relation to reality, i.e., the attitude of consciousness, was also a main element in Jung's understanding of the Mischa Epper case.

A patient from when Jung began to use his new method

In 1915, during the main phase of his self-experimentation, Jung treated a Swiss woman who exhibited symptoms of anxiety. Her name was Tina Keller-Jenny. The work with Jung lasted until 1924 and she was also in analysis with Jung's collaborator Toni Wolff. In 2011, Swan[27] published Keller-Jenny's memoir presenting her lifelong confrontation with Jung's psychology. Her notes provide us with an interesting insight into her treatment with Jung in a period when he had begun to apply the insights of his self-experimentation with his patients. It is, therefore, contemporaneous with the treatments of Mischa Epper and Maggy Reichstein. As will be later presented in this book, both women, similarly to Keller-Jenny, developed a lifelong connection with Jung and his ideas.

Besides her impressions of the time and her experiences as a daughter, wife and mother, Keller-Jenny described in her memoir a series of techniques, which Jung applied during her analysis. Jung required from her a particular attitude towards the material she got from her unconscious. She wrote:

> I remember Dr. Jung telling me: 'Follow that which is alive in you'. He felt this would lead to God, even if at first it seemed to lead in another direction. He believed that whatever was a vital interest or need was legitimate and must be pursued, or at least examined carefully.[28]

The preceding note is particularly interesting, because it indicates that around 1915 Jung directly suggested that she should observe carefully what her psyche produced, but also told her what to expect. Furthermore, Jung advised her to develop 'mental hygiene by giving in to inner needs such as extra sleep and relaxation',[29] and, as we shall see, this was also suggested in the treatment of Mischa Epper. Another parallel in Jung's approach between Keller-Jenny and Epper was Jung's suggestion about 'painting a picture or writing in a spontaneous way'.[30] Jung requested her to be prepared for the sessions by writing down her dreams and the associations to each of the elements included,[31] so that she would learn to work with the material by herself.

Keller-Jenny pointed out, however, that the most important technique she learned with Jung was 'writing from the unconscious' and said that in an early stage of her analysis Jung told her the following:

> You must at once begin to prepare for the time when you will no more be coming to me. Each time, as you are leaving, even as you go downstairs, you have more questions. Write these as if they were letters to me. You do not need to send these letters. When you ask a question, in the measure that you really want an answer, and you are not afraid of that answer, there is an answer deep inside you. Let it come up.[32]

Keller-Jenny described that after initial difficulties she gradually learned to access this inner answer, and she mentioned that the technique was a great help for her. She developed inner dialogues and 'let it become an interweaving of rational and irrational elements as a continuum'.[33] As we shall see later, we find similar elements in the therapy of Epper, in which her analyst M. Moltzer, most probably under Jung's guidance, supported Epper to have dialogues with inner figures.

Jung's preceding comment also indicates one aspect of how Jung dealt in his practice with the transferential process in 1915. Suggesting that Keller-Jenny wrote letters to him, Jung prepared the patient for the time after the analysis was completed. This indicates that Jung taught his patients to focus on an element in the psyche that would give answers to them and help them once they were not in treatment any longer.

A patient related to active imagination

In 1926, Jung treated an American woman who had a great number of visual fantasies using the process of active imagination. Later, between 1931 and 1934, Jung gave seminars about her visions. He commented extensively on her fantasies during these seminars, which are known in Jungian literature as the Visions Seminars.[34] Her name was Christiana Morgan. Jung thought that she was naturally gifted in experiencing images using active imagination. He pointed out that her rationality separated her from people and that she got stuck in life, lacking connectedness with others.

Interesting to note is that, as in the case of Morgan, Jung also believed that in Reichstein's case, her difficulties were partially due to the exaggeration of rationality. And regarding Jung's handling of visual arts from imagination, the case of Epper will add valuable information for the development of his practice.

In the technique of active imagination, the patient was trained to let the images follow their own path. For Jung, the conscious mind should observe and interact but not define what happens in the sequence of the fantasy. This required from the patient to give up the control of the images, i.e., the images should flow of their own accord and not according to the patient's conscious intention.

But there is an important difference which suggests that Jung changed his use of the technique between Epper's case in around 1918 and Morgan's case, in 1926. In Morgan's notes of analytical hour with Jung on 2nd July 1926, there is an unpublished passage when Jung told her about the use of the will. He told her to give up the will instead of trying to impose it to the world. If she imposes her will on the world she would take from other people. She would hurt them and hurt herself. Jung's suggestion was that she should turn her will into herself, to know what is inside. He added he had before the wish to cure his patients, but would not have this wish any longer, because in doing so he would take from them and nothing would grow. His wish to cure could kill life in himself and in the patients.[35]

Morgan's notes may indicate a shift in the use of the technique. As we shall see, the way Jung's collaborator Maria Moltzer applied the technique in the treatment of Epper in 1918 was different from Jung's use thereof in 1926 with Morgan. In 1918, the focus was on *guiding the patient to follow* the images according to the interpretation given by the analyst, while in 1926 the focus was to allow the patient *to have his own experience* of the material produced by the unconscious. It is not clear, however, if the shift was mainly due to Jung's development of the technique or due to Moltzer's use thereof.

Patients related to the concept of individuation

In 1928, Jung analysed the case of a woman, whose dreams and fantasies he related to alchemical processes and his concept of individuation. Jung presented her case in a lecture he delivered at the Eranos Conference in 1933. Jung described that in 1920s he met a woman in the USA, whom he called Miss X.

Jung analysed her case, tracing parallels between the symbol in his drawings and alchemy. She painted mandalas throughout her analysis and continued to make drawings until her death in 1945. Jung revised and published this case in1950 in his paper 'A Study in the Process of Individuation'.[36] He related the development of the mandalas of the patient to his understanding of the individuation process.

In his book *The Occult Establishment*,[37] James Webb presented the history of so-called occultism. He noted that Jung was interested in this subject since his dissertation published in 1902 and identified Jung's patient as Kristine Mann.[38] Webb pointed out that Jung was interested in alchemy prior to his encounter with Richard Wilhelm in 1928, and Jung's comment that the patient was the daughter of a remarkable father led him to mention the possible influence of Charles H. Mann, Kristine Mann's father, regarding her interest in alchemy. Charles Mann was Swedenborgian and deeply involved with alchemical literature. Webb pointed out that Jung's statement that Mann's drawings were spontaneous expressions of archetypal material unknown to her must be disputed, because they would rather be expressions of her conscious knowledge about the topic.

In 2015, in her article about Mann, Darlington mentioned that, through her father, Swedenborgian ideas influenced Mann since her early years and that the similarity between these ideas and Jung's postulations 'probably strengthened the affinity that drew her to Jung's work later in her life'.[39] Darlington wrote further that it was the alchemical symbolism in Mann's material that called Jung's attention and that 1928, the year of Mann's treatment, was the same year that he received the German translation of the Taoist text *The Secret of the Golden Flower* from Richard Wilhelm. However, Darlington agrees with Webb in that, as opposed to Jung's claim that Mann did not know about alchemy, she probably had knowledge of alchemy through her father.[40] Furthermore she wrote:

> Significantly, at the conclusion of the 1939 revision of his Eranos lecture on Mann's case material, Jung baldly states that when she came to him he had no knowledge of alchemy and that 'this very case . . . led (him) to the study of alchemy'. He omitted this statement in the 1959 publication, and James Webb points out that Jung had in fact encountered alchemical concepts much earlier in reading the work of Silberer.[41]

Mann's case gives us an example of how Jung used case material to support his postulations. We will also observe Jung's shaping of case material in the history of Reichstein.

Besides Kristine Mann, there is a second case which is relevant concerning alchemical symbolism. It is the case of a young man whose dream symbolism Jung linked with alchemical processes. The patient was identified as Wolfgang Pauli, who won the Nobel Prize for physics in 1945. In the case, Jung analysed that the irrational archetypal images, which appeared in his dreams, were opposed to Pauli's rational mind and the analytical work. The symbolism of the mandala appeared as an attempt to balance the rational-irrational opposition and heightened spiritual awareness.[42] As we shall see, the mandala is one of the elements in Reichstein's case which will be discussed.

Another important aspect of the encounter between Jung and Pauli was their collaboration with the postulation of a scientific link between quantum physics and psychology in their discussion of the concept of synchronicity, an aspect that is relevant in the case of Reichstein and which will be presented later in this thesis in greater detail.

A patient related to Jung's stages of the development of the personality

In 1929, Jung treated a young American woman who took notes of her sessions with him during 25 years. Her name was Catharine Rush Cabot. Throughout her life, she participated in the inner circle of the Zürich group around Jung. Problems with her inferiority complex, anxieties and depression brought her to treatment. In a note from 1932, she wrote about Jung's comment that she missed a *Weltanschauung*, because 'I haven't a fundamental philosophy of my own which I hold to sincerely amid the storms & stress of life'.[43] The themes in analysis were related to Cabot's relationships, and the personalities around Jung in the Zürich group. Jung's advice and interpretations indicate that she needed to settle down from her frivolous way of living. In 1935, describing a depressive reaction after someone told her that 'there was nothing in her', Jung pointed to the need of confronting her shadow side.[44] Later that year, she described the confrontation with her Animus, and Jung's interpretation that she was then divorced from her Animus helped her.[45] Right after this interpretation, Cabot wrote about Jung's comments on the very difficult mission 'to go into yourself' and mentioned that Jung amplified her dreams with mythological analogies.

Besides her naturally extraverted attitude, Cabot developed an introverted side during her analysis, which she called a sea captain. Reid summarises the result of Jung's analysis with her mother as follows:

> Jung did much for her over the three decades she worked with him. She was eventually rid of most of the panics and claustrophobia, and her desire to shine in society lessened. But the father complex in the lump, a factor in her failure to grow up, continued to prove elusive, leaving her in the dark about the neurosis which stopped her development at eighteen. Despite Jung's help, she remained a teenager, pleased all her life with a youthfulness that kept her psychically and mentally less stiff than her contemporaries.[46]

The sequence of the themes reported in Cabot's analysis is interesting, because it gives us an approximation of Jung's scheme of development in the individual analysis: personal complexes, aspects of the transference, confrontation with the shadow, confrontation with the animus/anima, and the difficulties in the realisation of the self. As we shall see later, Reichstein was close to Jung in the Zürich circle too, but mainly related to academic discussions.

Jung's cases presented earlier could be summarised as follows: Helene Preiswerk, although not a patient of Jung's, was considered by Ellenberger his 'paradigmatic patient',[47] and her case gives us an idea of Jung's shaping of case material; Sabina Spielrein was Jung's psychoanalytical test case and opened the discussion about the concept of transference-countertransference; a discussion which was also observed in the case of Hirschfeld. Both cases had impact and possibly changed the requirements for future psychoanalyst, as see in the training analysis of Van Renterghem. Frank Miller's case, who like Preiswerk was not Jung's patient, was used by Jung to present his concept of the primordial ideas, discussing his postulation about a mythological layer of unconscious; with Tina Keller-Jenny, we have a treatment which happened during Jung's self-experiment, with whom he had begun to use his insights; Christiana Morgan was an example of his later use of the technique of active imagination; Kristine Mann's case is related to Jung's ideas about alchemy expressed in her mandala paintings and to the concept of individuation; the case of Wolfgang Pauli was also related to alchemy, but also to Jung's later development of the concept of synchronicity; and, finally, Catherine Rush Cabot participated in Jung's inner circle.

The material presented in this chapter and the cases presented here give us an overview of Jung's evolving psychotherapeutic practice; his methods, concepts and ideas; his considerations about different approaches of treatments and well as his shaping of case material. As we shall see, all these elements give us a framework to understand the treatments of Mischa Epper and Maggy Reichstein, which follow next.

Notes

1 Strictly speaking, as we shall see next, Preiswerk and Miller were not patients of Jung, but they were case studies presented in his writings.
2 Zumstein-Preiswerk, 1975.
3 Ellenberger, 1991.
4 Ibid., p. 52.
5 Carotenuto, 1982, p. 140.
6 Jung, 1908b, par. 52 ff.
7 McGuire, ed., p. 228.
8 Carotenuto, 1982, p. xv.
9 Lothane, 1999.
10 Ibid., pp. 1197 and 1201.
11 After Carotenuto's book from 1982, other authors wrote about the subject, such as Kerr in 1993; articles by Skea in 2006, Hofer in 2001, Fusar-Poli in 2012, Heuer in 2012; as well as theatre plays and films such as *Ich hiess Sabina Spielrein* (2002) and *A Dangerous Method* (2011).
12 McGuire, ed., 1974, p. 231.
13 Falzeder, 1994.
14 Ibid., p. 302.
15 McGuire, 1974, pp. 475–476.
16 Ibid., pp. 476–477.
17 Ibid., p. 479.
18 Falzeder, 1994, p. 311.
19 Shamdasani, 1992, p. 39.
20 Ibid., pp. 38–43.
21 Shamdasani, 1990, p. 44.
22 Jung, 1912b, pars. 64–90, CW 5.
23 Ibid., pars. 462–463.
24 Ibid., par. 468.
25 Shamdasani, 1990, p. 41.
26 Ibid., p. 51.
27 Swan, ed., 2011.
28 Ibid., p. 22.
29 Ibid.
30 Ibid.
31 Ibid., p. 23.
32 Ibid.
33 Ibid., p. 24.
34 Douglas, ed., 1997.
35 Notes from Cristiana Morgan's diary in the Francis A. Countway library of Medicine, Boston, USA. There is a handmade copy of this passage done by Morgan herself in the

pictures archive in the Jung Institute in Zürich, with small differences from the notes mentioned here.

36 Jung, 1950, CW 9i.

37 Webb, 1976.

38 Ibid., p. 388.

39 Darlington, 2015, p. 374.

40 Ibid., p. 385.

41 Ibid., pp. 384–385.

42 Lindorff, 2004, pp. 27–28.

43 Reid, 2001, p. 61.

44 Ibid., p. 91.

45 Ibid., p. 102.

46 Ibid., p. 182.

47 Ellenberger, 1991.

References

Carotenuto, A. (1982) *A Secret Symmetry: Sabina Spielrein between Freud and Jung* (New York: Pantheon).

Darlington, B. (2015) "Kristine Mann: Jung's Miss X and a Pionier in psychoanalysis" in *Spring: A Journal of Archetype and Culture* (New Orleans, Lousiana: Spring Journal), vol. 92.

Douglas, C., ed. (1997) *Jung, C.G. Visions: Notes of a Seminar Given in 1930–34* (Princeton, NJ: Princeton University Press), vol. 1 and 2.

Ellenberger, H. (1991) "The story of Helene Preiswerk: A critical study with new documents" in *History of Psychiatry* 2:41.

Falzeder, E. (1994) "My grand-patient, my chief tormentor: A hitherto unnoticed case of Freud's and the consequences" in *Psychoanalytic Quarterly* 63:297–331.

Fusar-Poli, P. (2012) "Sabina Spielrein" in *The American Journal of Psychiatry* 169(1): p. 21.

Heuer, G. (2012) "A most dangerous: And revolutionary: Method: Sabina Spielrein, Carl Gustav Jung, Sigmund Freud, Otto Gross, and the birth of intersubjectivity" in *Psychotherapy and Politics International* Oct;10(3):261–278.

Hofer, A. (2001) "Jung's analysis of Sabina Spielrein and his use of Freud's free association method" in *The Journal of Analytical Psychology* Jan;46(1):117–128.

Jung, C.G. (1908b) "The Freudian theory of hysteria" in *The Collected Works of C.G. Jung* (London: Routledge), 1993, vol. 4.

——— (1912b/1952) "Symbols of transformation" in *The Collected Works of C.G. Jung* (London: Routledge & Kegan Paul), 1986, vol. 5.

——— (1950) "A study in the process of individuation" in *The Collected Works of C.G. Jung* (London: Routledge), 1991, vol. 9i.

Lindorff, D. (2004) *Pauli and Jung: The Meeting of Two Great Minds* (Wheaton, IL: Quest books).

Lothane, Z. (1999) "Tender love and transference: Unpublished letters of C.G. Jung and Sabina Spielrein" in *International Journal of Psycho-Analysis* 80:1189–1204.

McGuire, W., ed. (1974) *The Freud-Jung Letters* (Princeton, NJ: Princeton University Press).

Reid, J.C. (2001) *Jung, My Mother and I: The Analytic Diaries of Catharine Rush Cabot* (Einsiedeln: Daimon Verlag).

Shamdasani, S. (1990) "A woman called Frank" in *Spring: Journal of Archetype and Culture* 50:25–56.

——— (1992) "Two unknown early cases of Jung" in *Harvest: Journal for Jungian Studies* 38:38–43.

Skea, B. (2006) "Sabina Spielrein: Out from the shadow of Jung and Freud" in *Journal of Analytical Psychology* Sep;51(4):527–552.
Swan, W., ed. (2011) *The Memoir of Tina Keller-Jenny: A Lifelong Confrontation with the Psychology of C.G. Jung* (New Orleans: Spring Journals Books).
Webb, J. (1976) *The Occult Establishment* (La Salle, IL: Open Court Publishing Company).
Zumstein-Preiswerk, S. (1975) *C.G. Jungs Medium: Die Geschichte von Helly Preiswerk* (München: Kindler).

PART 2
Mischa Epper

8

THE STORY OF MISCHA EPPER AND MAGGY REICHSTEIN

In February 1929, Jung wrote a letter to Maggy Reichstein mentioning the progress in the analysis of her second sister, Henriette Louise Quarles van Ufford-Reichstein, who was in treatment with him. He mentioned that her condition was improving and wrote:

> It is unbelievable what familial severity lays on the Quarles children. But I learned a lot from you, which will help other people. Therefore, I always think of you with gratitude.
>
> Yours Faithfully,
>
> C.G. Jung[1]

Jung's sentence indicates that the familial story of the Quarles children impressed him. More remarkable, however, was his comment that he learned a lot from her (Reichstein). It indicates the importance of her case. But for the proper presentation of the material it is important to know the story of Mischa Epper and Maggy Reichstein. Mischa Epper had a psychic disturbance and this was the reason why the sisters came to Zürich. As we shall see, the lives and treatments of Reichstein and Epper are closely intertwined.

As mentioned before, Jung did not write detailed information about the personal story of his patients in his books. In general, it can be said that he usually reduced the information related to personal aspects to a minimum and carefully focused his analysis on the images and fantasies of the patient. One possible reason for his attitude can be found in a comment he made in the 1930s. He wrote:

> I omit personal details intentionally, because they matter so little to me. We are all spellbound by external circumstances, and they make our minds

> deviate from the real thing, which is that we ourselves are split inside. Appearance blinds us and we cannot see the real problem.[2]

Jung's main interest in his case presentations was focused on the complexes that he considered relevant and on the archetypal background he observed in them. He amplified the images of dreams and active imaginations, for instance, with comparative mythology and religious motifs. Detailed information about the personal story of his patients became available in a few cases in the complementary literature in Jungian psychology, as in the books and articles presented before. But with the additional information on his cases it becomes evident that the patient's story allows us a better understanding of Jung's work as well as aspects of how Jung framed them, including some bias and omissions.

Madeleine Reichstein-Quarles van Ufford, often referred to by her nickname, Maggy,[3] was born in Batavia (Indonesia) on the 15th of May 1894 into a well-situated family. Although she was born in Asia, her whole family was European. According to Epper's notes the roots of the family on her father's side can be traced to the Middle Ages. The family lived in the British Isles until the 17th century, particularly in England and Scotland. Some members of the family were part of the royal court and one of her forefathers was the viceroy of Ireland.

Her cousin was the president of the *Federation Équestre Internationale* (FEI) between 1927 and 1929 and therefore, in this position, predecessor of Prince Bernhard of the Netherlands and Prince Phillip of the UK. Her grandfather, Hendrik Quarles van Ufford, owned an indigo plantation in India and was very wealthy, but he died at the early age of thirty-two, due to tuberculosis. But this last note in the archives in Basel contrasts with a different source about the age of the death of Reichstein's grandfather. In the official register of the family he was born in 1822 and his death is noted in 1868, which would mean that he died at age forty-six.

Her grandmother, Anne Madelaine Quarles van Ufford (born Scheltema), lived in India until she was seventeen, and married the grandfather at that age. After his death, the family had financial problems and she took care of four children alone. At the age twenty-five, in 1868, Anne Madelaine decided to come back to Holland with her four children. Shortly after, she went to Switzerland for health reasons. The kind of treatment she searched for in Switzerland was not mentioned but, considering the death of the father by tuberculosis, it is possible that she had a similar health problem. Switzerland had many sanatoria in the turn of the 19th to the 20th century and, in those days, doctors believed that the pure air of the mountains was one of the best treatments for tuberculosis. She managed to offer her children a good education and was cautious to keep the education of her children in connection with the Dutch school system, although the family in those days lived in humble conditions. The preceding description indicates that Reichstein's family had connections to Switzerland even before Reichstein was born.

One of Anne Madeleine's four children was Reichstein's father, Charles Gerard Quarles van Ufford, born in 1865 in Klaten, in the Surakarta region in Indonesia. He began his professional life modestly and became a self-made man. He was known as an excellent administrator and did well at the stock market. He was a high-ranking officer in the Netherlands Marine Corps and was the founder and director of a port in Sabang, in the north of Sumatra. He made a fortune and became very wealthy with his business. He found himself faced with financial problems only after the Second World War, when the Dutch economy was in a difficult situation and he lost a large amount of money then. Nevertheless, he helped his three daughters financially during their lives.

Reichstein's mother, Hermine Marie Elisabeth Didok van Heel (Figure 8.1), born in 1868, was known as a warm-hearted woman. She married Charles Quarles von Ufford in 1891. Reichstein was the firstborn child of the couple Charles and Hermine.

Around 1897, Reichstein fell ill with malaria and the family decided to return to Holland. They lived in Bloemendaal, a small town close to Amsterdam. In 1898, during the birth of her second child, Henriette Louise, Hermine Marie became very ill, for she had severe complications during childbirth. She had a prolapse, which means that part of the inner organs came out of her genitals, and there was no appropriate treatment for her problem in those days. Even though the family doctor advised her against a third pregnancy, for considering it a risk for her life, she fell pregnant again. The third child of Charles Gerald

FIGURE 8.1 Hermine Marie Quarles van Ufford with her three daughters, around 1903

and Hermine Marie was Maria Catharina Quarles van Ufford, (later she will be known as Mischa Epper), born in Bloemendaal, Holland, on the 18th of August 1901.[4] Because of the fragile condition of the mother, the family expected the birth of Epper with great worries and fears. Indeed, the birth was difficult, and her mother never recovered properly from Epper's delivery.

Charles Quarles van Ufford criticised the doctor who had assisted his wife severely, blamed him for the deterioration of her condition and accused him of killing her. Epper wrote in her notes that the negligence of the doctor was undeniable, and the health of her mother was severely damaged by the delivery. As time went by, the health of the mother deteriorated further, and her condition required intensive treatment. The family decided that she should go to a hospital to be properly treated. This happened two years after Epper's birth, in 1903. Hermine Quarles van Ufford would not leave the hospital until her death in 1908.

Epper described her mother as an extremely tolerant person, Christian in the best sense, amiable, concealing her own suffering and trying to avoid people around her getting upset. She had no memory of her mother at home, because she was too little when she went to be treated in the hospital. In her notes about her mother, Epper considered her as someone who consoled people, even when she herself was suffering. The clearest memories of her mother were those few times in the year when Epper could leave the school to visit her in the hospital. According to her description, the whole atmosphere was grave, and she did not feel well, because she could not express her natural jollity, feeling afraid of the circumstances she was in. In the darkened room of the hospital with her mother, she remembered the scent of her hair and how she spoke quietly about the activities in the school. Epper liked her mother, but she experienced the visits to the hospital as at once both a mixture of solemnity and feeling frightened. After a while she was glad when she could leave the room and go to the sunny outdoors, where she could be a happy child again.

Whilst the mother was still alive, the three children were educated by a nanny at home, whom the children called Juf. Epper described the nanny as an unsatisfied, discontented woman, and retrospectively considered her nanny as somebody distorted by Calvinism. The nanny was usually bad tempered and severe in the way she treated the children, but Epper with her natural gleeful character ignored her moods and was not disturbed by her irritation. However, her second sister, Henriette Reichstein, who was known in the family by the nickname 'Lissy', was more affected by the difficulties caused by Juf, because Lissy was not able to shield herself from the bad temper of the nanny.

Concerning Charles Quarles van Ufford, Epper described her relationship to her father during her childhood as very close. She wrote that she really liked him and considered that among her sisters she was the one most similar to him in character. She played funny tricks with him all the time, and could easily make him do her bidding. She described how her natural cheerfulness helped her father go through the sadness of the loss of his wife, who died when Mischa Epper was around seven years old.

Besides the difficulties at home, Epper's father had considerable demands in his work. In 1897, when the family went back to Holland, he was the owner and director of a trade company. Despite the long and tough time caused by the illness of his wife, he carried on with his business and kept it running well. Epper considered him a hardworking man, serious and fully aware of his duties. He was very successful, but during the time his wife was in hospital he was under intense pressure to make money, because he had to cover the excessive cost of almost five years of intensive care for her in the hospital. In her considerations about her father, Epper noted how much she appreciated him with both his light and shadow side – on the one hand rational and generous, on the other hand explosive and wrathful – suffering under the oppression caused by the prolonged illness and later by the loss of his wife and by the demands of his company.

At home he had emotional outbursts when things did not go in the way he wanted, even if he regretted his behaviour afterwards. But, in spite of his regret, Epper noted that he never considered that he could be the cause of the troubles around him and often blamed others for his mistakes. In her notes, she remembered that he was angry towards her and beat her only once for one of her trickeries. Epper believed that her own susceptibility to emotional outbursts and occasional irrational behaviour was inherited from her father. Remembering her childhood, Epper did not consider her father as a figure of authority, but more as a companion. In general, she considered that she was easy-going in dealing with her surroundings. When Charles van Ufford was in a calm and controlled condition, he had a clear mind, able to consider things from a wider perspective than the rest of the family. In those instances, he was tolerant and generous in his actions. Epper mentioned that in order to support her father in overcoming the loss of his wife, she convinced him to spend the holidays in Switzerland. This led them to spend holidays there every year.

Mischa Epper later became an artist and she and her husband's artworks are important among the Swiss impressionists. She drew and sculpted and some of the motifs in her artwork were inspired by her childhood. Figure 8.2 is an example of one of her drawings that refers to this time with her father.

However, if Epper in her considerations described that she was on good terms with her father, the relationship between her sister, Maggy Reichstein, and their father was almost the opposite. Epper noted that between her sister and her father the contact was very different and much more strained in almost every aspect. Reichstein was, as a child, primarily difficult and gloomy, extremely intelligent and demanding.

A story was told in the family as an example of the gloomy mood of her sister. Epper was told that when Reichstein was five years old, i.e., before the health problems of the mother, she was walking with her parents in the woods and she saw on one oak leaf caterpillars, which formed a white layer over it. For Reichstein, it was a sign of the end of the world and this made a deep impression on her. It triggered feelings of extreme sadness. She had the same impression every year in spring and, according to Epper, this kind of sadness became the pattern

FIGURE 8.2 Daughter and father in Bloemendaal, 1922[5]

of Reichstein's view of the world since her early childhood.[6] Furthermore, she was determined and 'daemonic', with fierce traces of character. She adored her mother and agonised over the extreme patience that her mother showed towards the father. Even as a young child, Reichstein tried to protect her mother from the emotional outbursts of her father and she provoked him to the extreme, up to the point that he beat her. But she reacted to these beatings with cold indifference. In Epper's opinion, the father began to avoid the confrontation with Reichstein, because he knew unconsciously that she had a way to hit him emotionally, causing him to feel guilty for his bad-tempered reactions towards the mother.

Epper considered that her sister saw in the father a kind of rival for the love of the mother. Furthermore, in her description of her sister, she noted that Reichstein was egocentric from the beginning, and that she had an originality and intensity with uncanny strength, which neither the father nor the mother could control. Reichstein had a rational and enlightened approach to life, but her usual way of thinking contained a dark note. In Epper's opinion, her sister was influenced by her birth in Indonesia – this had put her out of harmony with the conventional ways of upbringing in their surroundings in Holland.

Epper mentioned that all three sisters responded in diverse ways to the difficult emotional situation caused by the prolonged illness, absence and, finally, the loss of their mother. The tension among the members of the family increased further when Juf, the nanny, was dismissed after the death of the mother at the end 1908. This was when the paternal grandmother, Anne Quarles van Ufford, whom the children called Mia, assumed responsibility for their upbringing.

Charles Quarles van Ufford saw his mother as a very reasonable woman, and considered the decisions she took as wise and rational. He admired his mother, because after the early death of her husband she brought up her four children alone in very demanding conditions. She had educated him and his siblings with discipline, abstinence, hygiene and a kind of puritanism, too. However, it was mentioned that she allowed them a certain amount of freedom, particularly in sport. Epper remembered that her father told her that he recalled his own teenage years as having been a happy time in his life. Already in those days, when Charles Quarles van Ufford was young, he and his siblings were aware of the demanding conditions that their mother confronted in providing them with a proper upbringing and they admired her for it. Her goal was for her children to be educated, so as to re-establish the wealth of the family, and in this respect Charles Quarles van Ufford was very successful.

Nevertheless, Epper believed that there were aspects missing in the education that Anne Quarles van Ufford provided for her children, such as the lack of spiritual and religious themes and an aesthetic sensibility for the arts and music. Reason and rationality were the most important values in her education. In Epper's perception her grandmother became masculine and authoritarian and expected absolute respect and veneration from her grandchildren too.

As the grandmother assumed the responsibility for the education of the Quarles children, Reichstein began to strongly confront her. She used to ignore the grandmother and demonstrate hate towards her. As time went by, the conflict between Reichstein and the father also increased considerably. The few moments that brought her and her father a little closer again were when, twice a year, the family visited the tomb of the mother in the graveyard.

Besides Epper's description of the situation in her family, she also wrote about the conditions in the surroundings where the family lived. In retrospect, Epper's opinion was that the girls were basically educated for motherhood and to properly attend the expectations and demands that society imposed upon women in those days. Sexuality was not a theme to be discussed, and any question about it was repressed. There was much luxury in mansions with many employees and children all too pampered and spoiled. Epper's description of the manners in which children must learn to fulfil the expectations of the environment runs as follows:

> One was educated to adapt to a hollowed mediocrity, to a colourless convention, [. . .] in which someone gives compliments with an artificial falsetto, from meticulous sentimental cordiality, unreal and hypocritical, from sweet optimisms and dishonest nobility. Men met separately in the smoking room or in the clubs, where women were never allowed, and there the crude business world was discussed without affection, real and concretely, among cigarettes and spirits. In there and in the offices, were

> places where the tough discussions happened. [. . .] The whole of the conventional, social life-style of women was infantile and without *niveau*.[7]

In the notes which followed in her biography, Epper commented about her aristocratic background.[8] She wrote that the father's family (Quarles van Ufford) had almost always belonged to the upper-class society. The family came mostly from England and Scotland, and its roots can be traced back to the 12th century. Part of the family Quarles van Ufford immigrated to Holland in the 17th century.

From her mother's side (van Heel) the family also belonged to Holland's wealthy upper class (the grandfather was director of a sugar company). She described him as an imposing man, authoritarian but fair towards his employees. In Epper's opinion, however, her grandfather treated his wife as if she were a child. According to Epper, this was possibly the reason why her own mother, following the example of her grandmother, was so patient towards her husband. Epper described the relationship between Reichstein and her maternal grandfather as very close, because she had nothing childish in her attitude and both enjoyed music.

As mentioned before, on the other side of the family (Quarles van Ufford) Reichstein's appreciation of music was not well received, because it was considered as 'not hygienic', by which was meant, not adequate for a correct upbringing. Epper criticised this part of her family and considered them as an old upper-class family, with signs of decadence and emotional paralysis, in which the sense of reality had been lost. She described a psychological profile of the father's side of the family as people with a tendency to effusiveness, nervousness and rigidity. Many had nervous symptoms and their opinions were one-sided, to the point of persistent stubbornness. The family had noble ideals, but with a baseless optimism, missing any solid ground. In Epper's opinion some members of the family went mad because of these features. She believed that the whole family was trapped in a neurotic condition, caused by the conventions, the inner conflicts and the preservation of their prestige.

At school, none of the three sisters did well. In Epper's opinion it was because she and her sisters were suffering under the heavy emotional conditions caused by the suffering in the family. The result was that none of the children went on to higher education and had only basic schooling. At the age of eighteen, Reichstein went to Leipzig, Germany, to study. She learned to play piano and was very gifted. She was also very interested in the arts and enjoyed replicating the works of Flemish masters. She liked philosophy and studied the work of Eduard von Hartmann, Kant and Schopenhauer.

Back to Epper, up to this time she considered that she did not have any significant psychic disorder. She observed from a slight distance that the difficulties between Reichstein and the family were growing, but because of her natural jolliness she kept herself away from most of the conflicts. However, Epper wrote that she missed relating to a person with a healthy relationship to the instincts and a normal critical reason in her puberty. If she had had such support, she would have probably not reacted with a neurosis, which began when she was thirteen years old.

Between 1913 and 1914, the tension in the family increased as Reichstein, now approximately nineteen years old, began to have even more serious arguments with the grandmother. Epper considered the moral sermons of her grandmother as merely boring, and she began to question all kinds of authority figures. In this regard, Reichstein's opinion that the grandmother was a hypocrite was only an additional point. Epper described, however, that her neurosis began at that age, because she lost the sense of how to behave. She considered that her father, her grandmother, as well as her other relatives, were not examples of healthy behaviour, and she found the conventions around as suffocating.

She believed that the trigger for her neurosis was when she fell in love with the doctor of the family, a forty-year-old man who was responsible for her treatments when she had any infirmity. She mentioned that she had the wish to be ill, because she would then be close to her doctor. Suddenly her natural cheerfulness and freshness stopped, and this worried the whole family. Her sadness worsened when she fell ill with appendicitis and was sent for surgery in the same hospital as the mother had been.

She mentioned in her memories that her behaviour totally changed. She, who until then had her own personality and did not notice much of Reichstein's quarrels with the father and the grandmother, rapidly adopted Reichstein's position and opinions towards the rest of the family without criticism. However, reviewing those days in her life, she considered that Reichstein's liberation through anarchy was not an adequate model of how to behave either. Epper described her change in her notes as follows:

> It was a transformation of my whole character: from a sportive, bold, active, fond of children and positive (person), I became gloomy, serious, distant from life, melancholic and negative, but mainly hypochondriac. After my appendicitis surgery I went to the same hospital where my mother was treated and the nurse who attended me was the same who attended Maatje (her mother) and she told me stories about her. I searched for the experience of secrecy and of great solemnity, of silent withdrawal and introversion, but for that, unfortunately, I had to be ill.[9]

Epper's illness triggered a severe conflict between Reichstein and the rest of the family. They quarrelled about the better way to treat her. While the family disputed about her illness, Epper was passive through all the quarrels around her and was pampered and fed and in bed most of the day.[10] Epper commented retrospectively that she did not have any somatic illness, but was neurotic and totally passive, that all her psychic energy was gone, and everything had become grey and indifferent. She also wrote in her memories how malicious and repulsive she was in those days, how she used the enormous interest of the family in her condition to get pampered and responded to the attempts of the family with a passive opposition.

Reichstein made a significant effort to bring Epper out of her passiveness and to protect her from the family's influence, particularly against the influence of the grandmother. Epper noted that her sister, who had read Freud and Jung, correctly understood that her illness was caused by a psychic condition, while the rest of the family believed that food and attention would be enough for her healing. Reichstein visited her sister daily, and tried to support Epper's improvement using psychological arguments. Reichstein wrote letters to her sister and invited her to walk by the dunes at the beach.

Looking back at those days, Epper considered that what caused her neurosis was her infantile attitude, i.e., life must be only funny and pleasant, the atmosphere of repressed sexuality, and the dishonesty in ethics and education. But above all the cause of her illness was to be found in the absence of instinctual life. Epper saw that Reichstein, who had a psychological understanding for her condition, searched for a psychological treatment to help. Epper mentioned that her sister was under the influence of a companion called Vic, a young Jew, who was extremely intelligent, a profound student of philosophy and bohemian, totally uncivilised and exceptionally decadent, who instead of a dishonest and hollow ethic chose to live without any ethics and morals.

In Epper's understanding of the conflict about the better way to help her, the dispute was basically caused by the two opposite understandings inside of the family: on the one hand was Mia, the grandmother, who had a hard life after the loss of her husband and the plantations in India; who raised her children alone with hygiene and discipline; who focused on providing a good education for her children and expected from them to work with the trade and the commerce; who aimed to re-establish the wealth of the family; who had an extremely narrow sense of morals, to whom the main principles for the children's upbringing were asceticism and parsimony, and finally who had no interest for the spiritual and religious philosophy and only despised aesthetics, beauty and culture. Therefore, the treatment for her grandchild's illness, she felt, had to follow these lines.

On the other hand, was her sister, Reichstein, who struggled for what she considered the missing parts of their education, who studied philosophy in Germany, who learned how to play the piano, who read Freud and Jung, who appreciated the arts and had a beautiful sense of aesthetics. Epper noted that her sister decorated her room with Indian shawls and carpeting, totally different from the rest of the house. Reichstein knew that her sister had a psychological problem and needed a psychological treatment. In her dispute with the grandmother over the best way to treat Epper, her criticism towards the grandmother became insolent and merciless.

Reichstein's ideas about Epper's illness being of psychic nature were not taken seriously by the father, who did not want to know anything about psychoanalysis. The differences in the family coerced Reichstein to move to a small room in Amsterdam. She took her meals at the *Volksküche*, which literally means 'people's kitchen' or 'folks' kitchen', a place where food was offered for the less privileged parts of the society. This was considered by Epper revolutionary in those days, and an affront by the rest of the family. Such behaviour was not usual for the upper-class society and therefore not expected, for the discrepancy between them and common people was enormous.

From the perspective of the father and of the grandmother, Reichstein's behaviour was unbearable, and they considered her a destructive figure. According to Epper, this view of the family was understandable, because Reichstein's emancipation was also visible in a repulsive masculinisation in her presentation, which excluded any kind of feminine charm and grace, and to an extreme contradiction to the posture of their mother. If the mother were alive, Epper believed that she would have had a compensatory effect on Reichstein. But in the absence of the mother, the balance was missing. She dressed herself in an odd way, walked around with unwashed hair and dirty fingernails and usually had a gloomy face. She had a nervous cough and strong pains, which occasionally caused her to faint.

In Epper's notes, Reichstein developed a kind of 'suggestive-magical' influence on her father, her sisters and grandmother. She appeared as a revolutionary figure, one of the few women who wore trousers in Amsterdam, exceptional in those days.[11] In Epper's eyes, her sister was indeed a revolutionary woman, and her vitality had toughness, perseverance and a piercing force. And these features influenced all the family.

Epper believed that her father, who in her opinion lacked self-confidence, was afraid of confronting Reichstein. He never stood up to her. As we shall see later, when she decided to bring Epper to be treated in Zürich, he allowed them to go, although it was against his own will. Epper recognised that her father cared for his daughters, and even if it was not in accordance with his opinion, he supported them in all cases.

Epper wrote in her memoirs an important passage concerning the way that she believed Reichstein's reaction should be understood in those days. It runs as follows:

> To understand Maggy with her reasons and her positive values it is firstly necessary to have a complete view (of her) in which opposites have their places, opposites that do not tear apart, but that meet each other in a meaningful polarity. If in the rational oriented view of the family, for instance, Freud's dream interpretation is considered 'monkey's sh . . .', and from the whole of the biblical stories only a few moral tendencies (are considered) and the sense of symbolic is denied, then the sense for the development of culture is already destroyed and atrophied; and therefore Maggy, who missed (the sense for culture), was necessarily pushed into a fighting position. And for the fight it is necessary to have masculine attributes, tough energy, consequence and perseverance. [. . .] Even under the guidance of Maatje (their mother), Maggy's mission would have been the same: to

> bring the missing cultural aspect to the family and for this mission the feminine style of Maatje would have not been enough.[12]

Epper recognised the values of her father, such as valuing hard work, rationality and success in business, but saw the problem in his one-sided attitude. In her opinion, Reichstein was compensating it with her open confrontation.

Charles Quarles van Ufford tried to care for Epper, and bring her on his side by making her into a kind of companion. He explained his work and planned a business trip to India with her. The journey, however, was cancelled because of the war, which began in 1914. Thereafter, a fierce dispute between Reichstein and her father for the influence on Epper began. Epper noted that without any reason and under Reichstein's influence she adopted her sister's opinion and subsequently turned against her father as well. Epper later recognised, however, that the connection with her sister was exaggerated. She wrote that Reichstein's influence on her in those days was magical, hypnotic, mysterious and irrational, even if Reichstein used rationality to justify her ice-cold criticism of their family.

According to Epper, Reichstein's femininity was destroyed. She despised both being a woman and the idea of motherhood, and was crude and aggressive in her discussion with men. For Epper, Reichstein was a terrible example, but she followed her anyway, as she brought revolution and movement back to a paralysed world. As Epper's psychic condition deteriorated further, Reichstein took the initiative, and in the winter between 1916 and 1917, against the will of the whole family and during the First World War, she brought Epper to Switzerland for treatment for the first time.

Notes

1 PA – Document no. 8, Jung–Reichstein Letters.
2 Douglas, ed., 1997, p. 7.
3 SA – File PA 979a B5–3 2.
4 NH – Registers.
5 Copyright Museum Epper – Ascona – Switzerland.
6 ME – *Kindheistgeschichte Mischa Epper*, p. 18.
7 Ibid., p. 9.
8 Instead of *aristocracy*, the term *landed gentry* to refer to the family of Charles Gerard Quarles van Ufford would be more appropriate, because they were very wealthy, had links with Dutch nobility, but he himself did not have title of nobility. However, as Jung and the sisters used it, it was kept *aristocracy* in the text. I am grateful to Graham Richards for this information.
9 ME – *Kindheistgeschichte Mischa Epper*, p. 11.
10 Interesting to note that the support of Epper's family resembled Weir Mitchell's method.
11 This information was given by V. Lunin during one of the interviews with the author.
12 ME – *Kindheistgeschichte Mischa Epper*, p. 14.

Reference

Douglas, C., ed. (1997) *Jung, C.G. Visions: Notes of a Seminar Given in 1930–34* (Princeton, NJ: Princeton University Press), vol. 1 and 2.

9

EPPER'S TREATMENT WITH THOMAS HÄMMERLI

In 1917, Reichstein brought Epper to Switzerland for the first time to be treated by Thomas Hämmerli. He was a medical doctor and the chief of a clinic in Zuoz in the canton of Grisons. Although Hämmerli was acquainted with Jung in 1917, it is unknown if Jung participated in Epper's treatment. However, it is interesting to note a remarkable passage which relates Hämmerli to Jung. It is the passage in which Jung had a vision after having a heart attack in 1944 and Hämmerli was the doctor who assisted him in his recovery. Jung described how he saw himself in the outer space and looking down he saw parts of the planet earth. He felt that he was being removed from everything in his life, a painful process. The only thing left was his story, everything he had lived and had done. He was about to enter a stone temple in space when he saw something. He described:

> From below, from the direction of Europe, an image floated up. It was my doctor, Dr. H. or, rather, his likeness framed by a golden chain or a golden laurel wreath. I knew at once: 'Aha, this is my doctor, of course, the one who has been treating me. But now he is coming in his primal form, as a basileus of Kos. In life he was an avatar of this basileus, the temporal embodiment of the primal form, which has existed from the beginning. Now he is appearing in that primal form'.[1]

Jung was angry towards Hämmerli, for he brought him back to life after a painful process of liberation, but at the same time he was worried about him. Jung believed that Hämmerli was at risk of dying, because he saw him in his primal form. He tried to talk to Hämmerli about it, that he should be careful, but he did not understand and did not take him seriously. Jung went further:

> In actual fact I was his last patient. On April 4, 1944 I still remember the exact date I was allowed to sit up on the edge of my bed for the first time

> since the beginning of my illness, and on this same day Dr. H. took to his bed and did not leave it again. I heard that he was having intermittent attacks of fever. Soon afterward he died of septicemia. He was a good doctor; there was something of the genius about him. Otherwise he would not have appeared to me as a prince of Kos.[2]

Returning to Epper's treatment, Hämmerli was not successful in his attempt to help her. She described the treatment with him as follows:

> Naturally I fell hopelessly in love with Hämmerli, which was not reciprocated. He did his best, speaking in a friendly and gentle manner to me, had a beautiful soul and a good sense of aesthetics, but had no idea of my 'demonic' side. He was not an analyst and in his attitude, he was negative towards the treatment of the unconscious (too ugly and awkward for an aesthete). His diagnosis of my condition: sexually abnormal incurable, because I had developed a strong transference towards him. In the trip back to West-Switzerland I had a room in the hotel beside his room and I had a horrible waking dream: 'an unknown man caressed me with a perfumed hand over my face and made me numb', then I woke up with a scream and affirmed that it was not a dream but reality! I could almost not separate from H. and he had such a sweet 'charming' voice, all women were impressed and charmed by him and he was very vain and narcissistic.[3]

Epper saw herself as a malicious, defiant and unsatisfied person in those days. She believed that Hämmerli did not know how to treat her case and he considered her an incurable neurotic. Symbolically, his treatment was described by her as being like a pleasant, numb and terrifying perfume.[4] Another comment in her notes about Hämmerli's treatment was that he did not consider or deal with the tension and problems between Reichstein, the father and the grandmother, and did not see how these aspects affected Epper's condition.

While the sisters were in Switzerland, another important event occurred in the family. After Epper took Reichstein's side, Mia, their grandmother, was deeply disappointed and her reaction was accusative. And then a tragic development occurred: Mia became ill with laryngeal cancer. She grew melancholic, complained that she could barely see the sun and her attitude towards life turned gloomy. She was afraid that she was going increasingly mad. As suffering became unbearable and in the absence of her grandchildren, Mia, calmly and without calling attention to herself, left the house early in the morning, went to a pond close to their house and committed suicide drowning herself in 1917 (Figure 9.1).

The sisters returned to Holland after the first treatment in Switzerland failed and, back at home, the reaction to the suicide of the grandmother was felt differently among the three sisters: Reichstein praised it as a bold act of inner strength; Henriette Reichstein reacted in a dysphoric way, laughing nervously as she heard about it; and Epper was sorry for her grandmother.

FIGURE 9.1 Mia in deep depression and plagued by ghosts, 1927[5]

After Mia's death, the tensions in the family did not decline to considerable extent. Reichstein went on with her emancipated behaviour, inventing stories to tell her father, meeting her boyfriend secretly and confronting the traditional values of her surroundings. Epper described how she went on following her sister's steps, abandoned the positive aspects she had in the world of her father and copied Reichstein's behaviour without criticism and without questioning, as if this behaviour suited her also.

As time went by, Epper's conditions deteriorated further. Her performance in school worsened, she became extremely malicious, and even more melancholic and passive. She isolated herself from others, and used to walk alone in the dunes. She had a vision, which she related to the experience of the divine and linked this vision with the idea of committing suicide:

> I sat at the window and saw how particles of dust shone with the sunlight and disappeared shortly after, forever. [. . .] I thought much on death and found life not worth living. I saw no way out. I had a strange, disturbed way of walking, used darkened glasses and a walking cane, a horrible decadence.[6]

Reichstein took the initiative once more and brought Epper for treatment in Switzerland for a second time, this time to Zürich, where they lived in a pension in the same room. Epper described that she also conflicted with her sister, felt rebellious and had feelings of revenge towards her. Arriving in Zürich, Epper began the treatment with Jung's collaborator Maria Moltzer.

Notes

1 Jaffé, ed., 1989, p. 292. In the protocols of the interviews with Jaffé, Jung mentioned Hämmerli's name.
2 Jaffé, ed., 1989, p. 293.
3 ME – *Kindheistgeschichte Mischa Epper*, p. 17.
4 SB – *Versuch einer Darstellung der verschiedenen Neurosen* – Document PA 979a B 5–3, p. 5.
5 Mischa Epper's drawing – Copyright Museum Epper – Ascona – Switzerland
6 ME – *Kindheistgeschichte Mischa Epper*, p. 17.

Reference

Jaffé, A., ed. (1989) *Memories, Dreams, Reflections, by C.G. Jung* (New York: Vintage Books).

10

EPPER'S TREATMENT WITH MARIA MOLTZER

Epper mentioned that she was sixteen and a half years old when she began her analysis with Maria Moltzer (1874–1944). As mentioned previously, she took notes of the analysis with Moltzer in a diary, in which she wrote her thoughts, dreams and fantasies during the treatment. On the front cover of her diary, which was made with a different paper to the notebook itself, there is a German note written by Epper. This German note was written much later than the notes in Dutch inside the notebook. It runs:

> Treatment Moltzer. Analysis Moltzer from March 1918 until March 1919.[1]

The characteristics of the records in German in the diary are particularly important to note: these are written in blue pen while the passages in Dutch are written in pencil. Comments in German also appear in other passages and, as we shall see, they indicate a later reconsideration and a new interpretation to the contents. In most of these German notes, Epper criticised Moltzer's approach and influence and in retrospect she considered Moltzer's treatment differently from when she had experienced it as a teenager. She wrote that the notes and new interpretations were made with the help of her husband between 1952 and 1957. On the cover, she summarised some of the contents of the diary, as the next passage indicates:

> Period of transference – (emotional) link with father, (emotional) link with Maggy. Dictatorship of Moltzer and (her) fight with Ignaz intensified.

Ignaz Epper, as we will see later, was crucial during and after her treatment. From the dates just mentioned we know that the German comments were made over thirty-five years after the treatment with Moltzer, when Epper was around fifty years old.

Maria Moltzer was a close assistant of Jung and became an analyst under his guidance. In a letter between Freud and Ferenczi, it is noted that Jung and Moltzer had an affair.[2] She was the author of the text *Analytical Collectivity* in which she presented her own view of analytical psychology, different from Jung's own formulations. It was a time when, for Jung and for his collaborators, important concepts in analytical psychology were in development. Around 1915, Moltzer worked close to Jung, as described in a letter that Jung sent to Smith Ely Jelliffe. Jung's letter runs as follows:

> I trusted the cases entirely to her with the only condition that in cases of difficulties she would consult me or send the patient to me in order to be controlled by myself. But this arrangement existed in the beginning only. Later on, Miss M. worked quite independently and quite efficiently. Financially she is quite independent being paid directly by her patients. . . . I arranged weekly meetings with my assistant, where everything was settled carefully and on an analytical basis.[3]

Moltzer broke the cooperation with Jung in June 1918; therefore, her work with Epper was possibly one of the last cases in which the work of Jung and Moltzer was directly linked. Epper described Moltzer in her 'story of my childhood' as a Dutch woman, who was a former assistant to Jung, and distanced herself from him, possibly because she was a woman eager to dominate. According to Epper, Moltzer considered intuition the highest function. Epper's use of the word 'intuition' refers to the psychological type model, which Jung developed and published in his book *Psychological Types* in 1921.[4] Jung gave the credit for the discovery of this function to Moltzer.[5] However, some aspects of Moltzer's ideas about this function, such as the psychobiological tracing of the genesis of intuition and its relation to thinking and feeling, were discarded by Jung in the development of his typology. According to Epper, Moltzer's attitude was opposed to Jung's scientific and research-oriented mind.

When Epper came to Switzerland for the second time to be treated by Moltzer, she was very depressed and barely talking. Because Epper enjoyed making drawings, she got the advice, possibly from Moltzer, that, if she could not talk, it would be good if she could at least create drawings of what she felt (Figures 10.1 and 10.2).[6]

In the following passage from her 'story of my childhood', Epper gave a self-portrait and a portrait of her sister in those days, which gives us an idea about how she perceived their condition. In Epper's opinion, Reichstein looked very decadent, clothed in a bizarre manner. Her sister was very active and intensive in discussion with people and her attitude towards others was always aggressive. Epper saw herself as the opposite of this: she was totally passive, will-less, with empty eyes. Epper considered the way she and her sister appeared as the opposite of femaleness. In the same passage, Epper wrote about her experience of her psychic illness and commented about another aspect of Reichstein's disturbance as follows:

FIGURE 10.1 Deepest introversion: the dance with the mask, 1917

At the time Maggy brought me to Switzerland I experienced a similar hopeless melancholy like Mia (the grandmother) felt, I gazed into a hopeless emptiness. My libido was pressed totally down in the depression and as Jung says: then one must look to what is down there. In me and in Maggy down there exists a dangerous dynamic, which could express itself in an

FIGURE 10.2 Melancholy, 1917[7]

> explosive craziness. In Maggy, the craziness was expressed later, before her marriage, in an unbearable state of anxiety which lasted two months, and came after A. (her future husband) innocently told her about the birth of the child of his colleague. Maggy felt persecuted by the idea of the child and was not able to talk about it with anybody.[8]

In her later considerations, Epper believed that Reichstein, around 1918, protected herself from her melancholy and her compulsive crazy ideas by building up a system of rigid methodical thinking, which had no connection with her psyche and did not have a flowing relationship to the unconscious. Considerations of this kind, however, were not present at the time when she wrote the notes of her analysis with Moltzer.

In her diary, we can find entries about dreams and fantasies and underneath them she wrote associations and interpretations (from herself or, possibly, from Moltzer). Some associations and interpretations have a telegraphic character and their connections with the fantasies or dreams are not always clear. From the notes in Dutch, we can see that the method Moltzer used in Epper's treatment was Jung's mode of interpretation of fantasies, associations and symbols as the following entries from 1918 indicate:

> 2–3 may – Dream
> Hämmerli – the strange unknown, the transcendent [illegible] says that I have influenza, that my intellect is ill – and to heal I must spit up green slime that becomes solid and must be pulverised.
> Influenza – thinking – headache
> Green slime – spinach (fantasies)
> Frog – emerald
> The slime falls into my fantasies and then I create the fantasy of the emerald – this clearly shows that I swallow the emerald instead of rubbing it to dust.
> To solve the thought-problem, fantasies must be expelled first.
>
> **Fantasy of the emerald**
>
> One princess swallows the emerald. As it arrives in her stomach, 7 princes lock themselves to it [lit.: 'him']; then drop it, and they exit through the navel. The emerald falls into the stomach of the princess, so 7 princesses surround it, drop it too and exit through the navel. The emerald leaves the body through the vagina and is coloured yellow by urine. This creates a golden ring. She wears it around her neck and waits until she menstruates. The menstruation turns the emerald red, so that it changes into a ruby. On her right breast there lay a moonstone. On her left breast lay a brilliant. Then a prince arrives (the 7 that have grown into one) and takes the moonstone and puts it in his anus. In a year everything has grown into one big, [illegible] moonstone. A princess comes (the 7 that have grown

> into one) and takes the brilliant that she inserts it into her vagina. After a year she has grown into one big star-shaped brilliant. The big princess now takes the moonstone in her right hand and the brilliant in her left hand. At first they are so heavy that she can hardly bear them. But while she picks them up they become lighter, until she stands straight and holds both stones in the palms of her hand. They are now as big as the ruby. The moonstone receives red light from the ruby and turns into an opal. The brilliant acquires a yellow glow from the gold around the ruby. Then she starts spinning in circles with the three stones, faster and faster.
>
> 7 princes – crab – symbol of introversion
> 7 princesses – starfish[9]
> Urine – drawings
> Menstruation – Red Sea, through which the Jews, led by Moses, walked when they were persecuted by the Egyptians, towards the holy land.
>
> *I am not the princess* – I am above the emerald – swallow it quickly instead of rubbing it to dust – To investigate . . .

The italicized phrase above has beside it a comment in German which indicates the later review of Epper about her fantasies and treatment with Moltzer. She wrote: *Identification (I) wished to play the role of a princess.* The notes in Dutch went on as follows:

> 7 princes – the menstrual function, they must be expelled first – they cannot hold the stone. It is not a function yet, it is still in my stomach, it is not art either, both will be born later. Urine drawing; Jews – masculine materials – Egyptians – Collective unconscious – dried up.
>
> Red Sea – femininity, menstruation,[10] the drawing becomes a masculine function there, also made physical (erection while drawing) and in the femininity dries up – the tr. 7 comes from the collective unconscious, is separated from it and realises itself materialistically physically. But what is the slime that I must spit up because I must do that now too – and the emerald, what is that? I must analyse this.[11]

In the comments about the seven princes, besides the words 'born later' there is a comment in German: *Unsinn* (in English: nonsense). In another part of her diary, she wrote a passage besides the text, which was in German and was also written in blue pen. This time Epper noted the date of her later entry in the notes of her teenage diary, and made clear when she made this comment in German. It runs as follows:

> Nov 1952: Analysis with help of Ignaz. It has to do with the 'end of the world' inside me, a breaking away of the Elementals, caused by the leaving

of the parent's house (17 years old) and the already existing setting out by Maggy of the traditional and conventional milieux, with no religion but only reason, rationality, will and ethics (morality) were valid.

The last associations in Dutch about the Red Sea mentioned before have an arrow linking them to another comment in German. Once more Epper noted *Unsinn* – 'nonsense' – and she wrote further comments, which run as follows:

> Critic very important and essential: in me the unconscious with its endless associations and fantasies, which turns around broad interpretations of princes, princesses, gems; which turns around again and again as a wonder-working mystic of self-adulation, is the purest polyp and devouring mother which by my lack of consciousness dazes my relation to reality in a typical escaping thought in (mental) masturbation – this was supported in the worst way by Ms Moltzer.[12]

The preceding comments in German show that Epper later reviewed the problems she had in her teenage years. She clearly criticised the way Maria Moltzer interpreted her fantasies. Her criticism of the treatment with Moltzer can also be found in other documents. Epper went in analysis with Jung's collaborator Marie-Louise von Franz in 1956, and her analysis with Moltzer was a recurrent topic in their long correspondence. For instance, in 1957, in a letter to von Franz, Epper wrote about the time with Moltzer as follows:

> During the puberty I was in a kind of enchantment, [. . .] I was totally under Maggy's influence and, like her, rejected father and family. I adopted her attitude and sank in a complete apathy and melancholy. Only through Maggy's action and energy I came into analysis with Moltzer, but it meant a new enchantment. And I was near insanity when Ignaz came and took me out of this new hold. [. . .] Since my sister and Moltzer were just like goddesses and sorceresses (for me), negative mother figures, I was impotent in front of the unconscious and totally engulfed. I was completely devoured by my unconscious.[13]

And Epper continued her criticism of Moltzer in a later passage in the same letter, as follows:

> It is a morbid, decadent, squiggling, highly sneaky unconscious, qualities which Moltzer, and the experiences I had those days, had a lot. My sister was highly infected (by it) and in my opinion until now she is not conscious about how much she should be grateful for Jung's treatment, that she was able to marry.[14]

Later, in 1976, Epper noted the following about the treatment with Moltzer:

> I would not forget what Maggy did for me, when I was 17 years old and was considered incurably neurotic. [. . .] She imposed her conviction against the will of our father and the family, because she was convinced that healing was possible using Jung's theory and brought me to Maria Moltzer, who really made the unconscious fluid, but she made the mistake of giving too much power to intuition, without developing enough the function of reality.[15]

In the preceding note it is clear that, although she criticised the treatment with Maria Moltzer, Epper, in her later evaluations, also had consideration for a positive aspect thereof, namely, how the treatment made the unconscious fluid. The technique Moltzer used for 'making the unconscious fluid', as we shall see next, besides the analysis of dreams and fantasies, was also the technique Jung developed in his self-experimentation, which he later called active imagination.

In October 1918, Epper mentioned that she began to have conversations with the unconscious. Epper's case is probably among the first known cases in which the technique Jung developed in his self-experimentation was used by another analyst in the treatment of a patient. It is an indication that Jung was already teaching his new method to his closest collaborators, such as Moltzer, before 1918 when his self-experimentation was still going on.

It also shows that Epper went on with her treatment with Moltzer after June 1918, when she left the Psychological Club and the collaboration with Jung. The reason for the break of Moltzer and Jung can be followed in the records of the meetings. In the protocols of the Psychological Club in Zürich from the 1st of June 1918, Emma Jung, the president of the club, read the letter from Moltzer, in which she gave her reasons for leaving the club. Most of the members regretted her departure. Jung also regretted Moltzer's leaving, but his comments show that he disagreed with the reasons she gave, namely, that the club was too obsessed by the quarrels about typology, which he considered a theoretical problem. Moltzer also criticised what she considered the intellectualism in the club. Jung contested that intellectualism was a vital interest for some people. He admits that there were intellectualistic discussions of the club, which should not always be the case, but this could be improved. It was questionable, however, that one must talk about love in the club, because this was one of the reasons why the club was founded. If Moltzer had realised that, she would not have left it. A member of the club pointed out that Moltzer was influenced by some of her patients against the club. To this Jung answered that it was highly possible that the patients exerted a certain degree of influence on Moltzer, particularly because she was not present much at the club.

Back to Epper's conversation with the unconscious – the first passage in her notes runs as follows:

First conversation with the unconscious – Fantasy: Wednesday 2nd of October 18

> I go to Epper and bring him a burning candle. He takes the candle in his right hand and waves it above his head three times, and does the same with his left hand. From here I lose reality and identify [illegible] with the unknown stranger; reality changes into [illegible]. A blue, sweet smelling mist develops in the room, like incense. Then he blows out the candle and we are sitting next to each other in the dark, in the blue mist, on the sofa. His genital starts glowing red, it starts burning and gives off yellow flames. The room is lighted again by the glow that the candle gave. When the phallus [vallus] is burned up it gives off a blue vapour that rises into my vagina. The womb and my whole body is shrouded in a purple mist, that hangs around me like a cloak. I have been completely turned into purple mist, only my head is still grey and solid. Now I get up and look at Epper. His whole body is shrouded in smoke, but he remains solid. His eyes are glowing yellow. He is death, but I am not afraid of him and go and talk to him.

To this passage Epper wrote the following associations:

> Candle – middle ages – mysticism/churches
> Phallus [vallus] – also candle.
> Purple mist – velvet – curtains at crematorium [illegible]

And Epper noted an interpretation of her fantasy as follows:

> Everything is a transition from the real Epper to the imaginary Epper. It has nothing to do with Epper himself, it is the unconscious that performs in the form of Epper, later of death.

The conversation began as follows:

- What must I do to get my body back?

  'Write a book like the "Kleine Johannes"'.[16]

- But I can't do that.

  'Yes, you can'.

- How must I start then?

  'With me, when I appeared to you like Epper'.

- What must I write about Epper? Must it be like the Kleine Johannes? Isn't that a book about the transition of a boy to manhood poured into a fantastical form?

'You must write about the development of your relationship with Epper from when you met him up until now, in the shape of a fantasy'.

- That's nonsense, I cannot do it. How must I present it?

'In the form of a conversation, like the one you are now having with me'.

- With whom must I have that dialogue?

'With Miss Moltzer'.

- How can that be? With Miss Moltzer in reality or with Miss Moltzer in thought?

'In thought'.

- What shape must she take then?

'That of a sphinx'.

- I don't understand. Must I ask the sphinx questions?

'No'.

- What must I do with the sphinx then?

'Nothing – Think about the sphinx and then write about Epper. Epper and you will then become symbols and will assume a new and fantastic form'.

- Why do you have yellow eyes?

'I bring you light'.

- Why are you death?

'I cannot tell you yet'.

- Why not? What and who are you?

'I am a fantastic shape and bring you light'.

- What must I do now to be able to leave this emptiness?

'Write, as I have told you. If you have any questions, you may always come, I will answer you as far as I am able to'.

- I just don't understand how you can be death and bring light at the same time.

'It is impossible for you to comprehend it yet, and I cannot tell you. Trust me and do as I tell you'.

- Must I do more than write?

'Continue drawing if you must, and continue writing'.

- May I see Epper himself?

'Yes, but you may not tell him about me, you may only tell Miss Moltzer about me'.

- Will you always come when I call you, and will you tell me what I must do?

  'Yes. At least if you do what I tell you, and if you believe me'.

- I am still a little afraid of you. Who are you?

  'I am the unconscious inside you'.

- Will you always appear to me in the shape of death with your yellow eyes? And in your black cloak?

  'Yes, in your case I will come this way'.

- Do you appear to others?

  'I will tell you later. For now, do as I tell you and don't be afraid that you won't be able to do it, *but do not speak to other people about it. Only Moltzer. Not even with Epper*'.[17]

- Why can I not tell Epper?

  'Only when the fantasy of you and Epper has been completed'.

- So that is what I must do first?

  'Yes, and no complaining!'[18]

The preceding passage '*but do not speak to other people about it. Only Moltzer. Not even with Epper*' has below it a note written in German, which was added later in the same manner as mentioned in the note of November 1952. The passage runs as follows:

> Moltzer's dictatorship: horrible – through it she had always more power over me.

Similar later criticism towards Moltzer's treatment can be found in other parts of her conversations with the unconscious as the following passage shows:

'Child, why do you avoid me?'

- I don't know. I am scared. Will I get the flu?[19]

  'Of course not. Your fear of the flu is a way of avoiding me'.

- But what will happen to me?

  'You have to start by not seeing Epper for a while. I know it's hard, but you must do it anyway. You will not be empty, but you will talk more to me. I will make sure that there will be no emptiness. You *must* start taking more notice of me, and stop avoiding me'.

- You were with me Friday night too, weren't you?

  'Yes, that was me'.

After this passage, Epper wrote another comment in German. It runs as follows:

> The only contact with reality will be prohibited by the dictatorship of the unconscious – Moltzer is a gruesome, devouring and swallowing mother. Besides – this dictatorship is unbearable! A healthy instinct would have finished it.

Epper described that the fantasies came from time to time in the form of overwhelming images of the unconscious. They appeared as voices; in the image of a doctor or a dictator with a prophetic air.[20] The figures demanded from her to fantasise specific situations or to paint images in a certain way, as this passage shows:

Wednesday 9 October

- What should I do? What have I done wrong?

  'You don't want to paint, or write, or fantasise'.

- What should I do first?

  'Make a fantasy about Ascona'.[21]

She also had inner dialogues discussing the meaning of the fantasies with the inner figure as well. The fantasies and dialogues seem to have occurred very frequently and the inner figure was very demanding, as the following example shows:

Monday evening 14 October[22]

  'Child, you are avoiding me again'.

- Have you truly arrived again at last?

  'Yes, how do you want me to come if you are continually avoiding me?'

- I don't understand. When have I been avoiding you?

  'Yesterday afternoon when Epper was here, this morning, this afternoon and tonight'.

- But I was looking for you and I wanted to have you so badly.

  'That's what you thought: you feared what I had to tell you'.

- What is that then?

Tuesday morning

'First of all, make a fantasy about the red lake that I showed you last night.'

- Yes, but I wanted to ask you something first.

'No, first the fantasy. If you ask me something now I will not answer.'

Another note in German follows this passage in which Epper later commented: *The most terrible dictatorship by Moltzer.* And she also added in German:

> One should just not ask questions about one's fantasies – the dictatorship of the uncs.

The note about the dictatorship of the unconscious has parallels to the way she described the treatment with Moltzer, which she also perceived as a dictatorship. One could hypothesise that Epper established an equivalence between the figures of her fantasies and the way Moltzer treated her. Epper's later criticism points to one important question concerning depth psychology theories, namely, the transferential process. As we shall see later, this central issue was also important in Jung's treatment of Epper's sister, Maggy Reichstein. Epper's conversation with the unconscious went on as follows:

'Listen child, if you are going to walk away every time, and are looking for distraction, then I will leave [lit.: "let you walk"] and you'll have to find your own way. I am aware that it is very hard what I am now asking of you, but you have to put up with it [lit.: "bite through it"] the sooner the better, the sooner you will be able to draw, paint and write again'.

- Yes, but what is this all for, and where is that prediction of yours?

'You are fully capable of knowing that yourself, but you only half believe me. You doubt me, and if you do, I can only help you a little, and if you will not believe in me then I will leave, and you can be sure that you will not find your way alone. And when I have left you will not easily find me again. You must surely stay with me all day tomorrow'.

- Yes, I will do that of course.

Here again is a later comment in German from Epper. It runs as follows:

> Dominance of the blind belief in intuition with the increasing sense of loss of reality.

The passage in German previously mentioned indicates the criticism of the way in which Moltzer worked. Epper reproached the focus Moltzer gave to intuition as the main instrument in analysis in detriment to the reality function.

On the next passage there is another comment in German under the date. It reads: '*Fantasy with an exit – Alchemical transformation process!*' The comment indicates that Epper experienced change through the process. From other notes in her diary, we know that it was the time when Ignaz Epper, who as we shall see was an important figure in Mischa Epper's life, increased his criticism towards the way Moltzer was treating Mischa Epper. The passage runs as follows:

> **Wednesday, 16 Oct. 1918**
>
> I see a black mountain with a yellow crater. I climb the mountain and stand on the edge of the crater. Then I fall into the crater face forward, and hit my head on a funnel-shaped opening. I slide through a long brown, slippery tunnel. The tunnel becomes more and more narrow and darker and ends with a closed wall. I want to go back, yell out and almost choke because of shortness of breath. But I cannot turn around, I writhe with my arms and legs and suddenly the wall moves, and I enter a large yellow room. There lays a mattress and I am tired and go to sleep. When I awake, the room is a fiery red and dark. I can see almost naught; all the yellow light has gone. I feel oppressed and want to leave but I am left standing in front of closed walls. I bang on all the walls, and finally I find a door opposite to the one I used to enter. Then I walk through a winding yellow hallway and enter a blue-green lit room. There is blue transparent water that I swim in. The water is being moved much and changes into a very dark blue (Pariser blue) then into violet (Pariser blue mixed with cinnabar with blue as the main shade). I am having trouble keeping myself up. Suddenly a wall opens, and the water quickly runs out. It is then left dark blue again. It is running through a brown wall, arrives in a bullet-round red room, where it spreads again and is forcedly sent through a very narrow canal. Now I am in the free open air on the beach, in front of me the endless sea, dark blue, and where the red sun sets, casting violet rays on the sea. The sky is a pale yellow. I stand there and fall asleep.

To the preceding fantasy Epper wrote the following comment in German:

> This fantasy leads to the outside, to a bigger world after constricted stages of the unconscious.

The notes in Dutch went on as follows:

> **Thursday**
>
> - What now?
>
>   'First write Epper of course, I've told you that – *do you really have to talk to me in writing?*'

There is a line crossing the page with a pencil, i.e., it was done when Epper wrote her diary. It shows a kind of separation of the preceding contents from the lines below.

- What kind of fantasy?

  'No fantasy'.

- What then?

Another German comment to this passage adds the following:

> Fantasy of incest – in struggle with Maggy and the father.

The fantasy in Dutch runs as follows:

> Incest – then I see Pa[23] lying next to Ma [lit.: Maatje: little mother] in a half-dark room. Pa has had intercourse with her. She's lying quietly [lit.: dead quiet] and as white as a ghost [lit.: dead body]. *She has died and suddenly I am in her place.*[24] She is now lying under the bed and black men come and carry her away. (Pinocchio-fairy tale – snow white, appendicitis). Then Pa stands up and I am alone. I am now an infant born out of the navel of my dead mother. I scream and sister Sedel[25] comes and gives me a drink, but she is hard and ugly, and I push her away.
>
> In her place stands Mia now [illeg.] and hurts me and she has no milk. Then Pa comes and lays his hand on my neck so that I almost choke and whispers in my ear that he will get his revenge later for what I have done. 'Just wait until you are older' he says. Then Maggy comes, and takes me to her warm room and gives me a drink. But Maggy becomes skinnier and skinnier and in the end, becomes a skeleton and I grow, strong and grown-up. I hide Maggy in the closet and wait, scared, in the room until Pa will come to fetch me. Now Pa enters, large, red and ugly, and wants to fetch me. I am scared to death but say in fear: 'In the closet is something better to fetch, have a look'. Pa opens the closet and I lock him in it. Pa takes revenge on Maggy who dies completely now. Now he has become so strong that he breaks open the closet, he picks me up and throws me in. He locks me up and leaves me there without food or drink for 7 days. Every night he comes and tells me that I will have become so weak that he can now abuse me. I become very weak but feed on Maggy's skeleton which makes me very hard. When he comes, I am very skinny, but strong as metal. This scares him, and he walks away from me. I find him and wrap my arms of steel around him, so he chokes and becomes skinny and pale. He turns greyish-brown and then I release him.
>
> Analyse this one especially well.

This fantasy could be linked with Epper's mother's illness after giving birth and her death. It also shows a fantasy in which the relation to her sister (Reichstein) made her stronger against the demands of the father figure. As we shall see later, in the treatment with Jung the fixation to the father figure was a crucial point.

The next passage has a different quality from other writings in her diary. It was made with a black pen and it is not identical with the notes in blue pen that Epper added later to her diary. It is also in Dutch, which could be an indication that was written at the same time around the fantasies, namely in 1918. However, the reason why she wrote it differently is not clearly known. It runs as follows:

> DO NOT READ – tis a prediction about my art in the future that I would rather not have you read
>
> Little girl, you have to trust me more. It has been very good of you to stay with me, but although you believe me, you believe too little in my power. *I will give you an unheard of great Schöpferische*[26] *power, do you understand?*[27] You will be able to do what you cannot even dream of now, you cannot understand it now, you are too young to understand. But you must trust in my power, the Schöpferische power, and wait and believe. You are already laughing because you cannot understand. Of course not; you will have to understand so much more about me and about yourself, but you must believe in your powers now. [. . .] You're a half child still and you are full of too much unnecessary contempt, also aimed at yourself. In the future you will lose that habit. Do not cross over to the other extreme, if you are doing very well, because you will [do very well] if you stay with me. Much more will happen to you than you may ever expect it to; thank God you are not one who has great expectations of oneself. You may never have that; only faith!!

This passage is underlined and there are exclamation signs in blue pen, which indicates that Epper was later on particularly impressed by what she wrote here in her analysis with Moltzer. Above this passage the following comment in German is added:

> The voice of intuition promises the same as the catholic church or any other faith – a miracle – This voice gets me too as it says that I am excessively 'modest' but through the faith I will do very well!!

And the text in Dutch follows:

> Are you satisfied now, little child, I have told you a lot this evening. I will come to you often, as long as you remain silent about me. *You may always confide in Miss Moltzer about me, and as little as possible in other people.*

This passage was underlined with the following comment in German:

> She breeds the wonder child with exorbitant megalomania.

The text in Dutch went on as follows:

> And start writing about the colours now, the ones that emerged today, and write down what you have noticed of people. I will keep treating you like a child for now; you are partially no more than just that. I shall give you orders continually. Good night!

Under this passage there is the following comment in German:

> The creative Animus is effectively a fountain of energy, but it is in detriment of every adaptation to reality and it breeds a grotesque megalomania and a sense of privilege that are fatal to the character and leads to the total loss of reality. Ignaz was a projection of what I have in me, my own creative-artistic (side) upon him, but the natural feminine relationship was missed out by the megalomania – besides it is catastrophic, because it (her creation) is not work but it happens through intuition.

Epper's fantasies went on in the same style. In dialogues with her inner figures they told her about the sequence she would have to follow and how she should relate to them to get better: A passage which demonstrates it runs as follows:

> When you have accepted all these fantasies and have analysed them well, your fear of throwing up will cease and you can go on with the later fantasies about menstruation and birth and sexualverkehr,[28] in your 13th and 14th and 15th year. Then you will arrive at the relationships of Dr. van Veen,[29] Api[30] and Hämmerli, about those you also must fantasise and analyse and then you will be free, and you will be able to draw, and paint, and focus on your book.

However, in the second half of October 1918, apparently a disturbance changed the development of the analysis. As we shall see next, it is related to a conflict between Moltzer and Ignaz Epper, which caused the problem.

Saturday 19 Oct.

- In God's name, what have I done that is so wrong?

  'A lot'.

- Now what?

  'First of all, you have to write to Epper immediately. I have said enough about what you have done wrong there. Do it now'.

- Do I have to send the letter?

  'Yes of course, stupid [lit.: chicklet]. And immediately'.
  'Do you know what this is about? You wrote in your first letter that you were berühigt[31] because you would not see each other when you went out riding. But you found it terrible not to see him when you went out riding'.

- Should I write this to him now?

  'No, you needn't. You would only hurt him that way. It is enough if you accept it and think about it'.

After this passage there is a comment in Dutch in black pen with Mischa Epper's handwriting, which runs as follows:

> This isn't either. It was because of a conflict with Epper and a letter – you can't understand it without the letter.

The reason for this different note in her diary is unknown and it is also not known when she wrote this comment, whether it was written in 1918 or later, as the other blue ink comments. The Dutch comments in pencil went on:

> Now you have to put the problem of Epper aside. You know what it is about now. That is why you feel so bad now, because those two problems are now threatening to become confused, and that would lead to a great conflict, that would lead to your [illeg.] downfall. You must do as little drawing as possible. I have been telling you that all along, but you have not been listening, because you haven't understood me yet.
>
> Make those 6 fantasies tomorrow in God's name and take them to Frl. M.[32] It is urgent. Now you must work hard and carefully, and cut yourself off from all else. Then you truthfully walk to the door and see if there is nothing of Epper's there. I command you, as harshly as I can command you, leave the Epper problem alone. Forget everything about it, and think *only* of your fantasies. It will cost you a lot now to get associations for them, but you *have* to. You *must*!

What follows is an important comment in German, because it presents in a resumed way the opinion that Mischa Epper in her later review had about herself and her condition in those days, the aetiology of her suffering and the connection between the inner voice and Moltzer:

> Reality: a teenage girl – bossy, pretentious and headstrong, but truly talented artistically, (who) failed in the school for neurotic reasons, she ran away from the normal confrontation with the father, grandmother and

> relatives and sister and became apathetic, neurotic, melancholic, sick and rootless. (She) sits alone as 17 years-old in a room in Zürich with no contact, with the sister as the only contact. The priest-like relationship to the analyst Ms Moltzer and to the artist Ignaz Epper, (and he) constitutes the only link to human reality: from him she will even be cut off by 'the voice' – medium from Ms Moltzer. The voice promises her the 'chosen-one-likeness', if she follows completely what he designates to her – thus the direct way to madness.

The preceding comment indicates that Mischa Epper considered the inner voice in her fantasies during her teenage years as an expression of Moltzer's opinions about how she should behave. It is clear, however, that during the treatment with Moltzer, Epper did not have this kind of criticism. She went on with the conversations and fantasies, very often with sexual contents, which she considered as part of her psychological disturbance. In another passage from her diary she wrote of her recollection of moments from her childhood and teenage years, and described how she saw the conflict she lived in on the one hand, she had the advantages of being ill; on the other, she had the wish to get better. In such passages, she recognised the effort of her sister to support her in her recovery.

In the late autumn of 1918, a disagreement between Moltzer and Ignaz Epper led Mischa Epper to stop her analysis. In a note on the front cover of her diary Mischa Epper mentioned that on the 10th of November 1918 there were heavy arguments between Moltzer and Ignaz Epper about her treatment. As mentioned before, Ignaz Epper was a central person and played a decisive role in Mischa Epper's recovery. She mentioned that when she was confronting insanity, Ignaz came and took her out of its clasp.

Mischa Epper met Ignaz Epper (1892–1969) in April 1918 when she was around 17 years old and already in treatment with Moltzer. He was her teacher for drawing techniques and gave her the important emotional support during her illness and throughout her life.[33] She wrote that before she met Ignaz Epper she walked around using a walking cane with a silver head, and it was Ignaz Epper who threw the cane in the lake saying she was too young to use such a thing. In retrospect she mentioned that he helped her against the flood of the unconscious, against the influence of other people and gave moral support when she was ill.

In one of the undated letters to Marie-Louise von Franz[34] she described how, around 1917, she was psychologically completely exhausted, thoughtless and unable to handle life, hypnotised by her unconscious. Then Reichstein brought her to be analysed by Moltzer and in this treatment, the unconscious produced an immense amount, but the analysis missed any kind of common sense or critical thinking, up to the point of insanity. Then Ignaz came as a rescuer, who helped her out of that condition. With his help, her angry feelings towards her family and Reichstein disappeared; the relationship to her sister became normal and friendly.[35] According to Orsoni, Mischa Epper considered that Ignaz Epper was more important for her recovery than either Jung or Moltzer.[36] They married in September 1919, and later in that same year, Epper's father married for the second time.

Shortly before the end of her analysis with Moltzer in March 1919, Epper noted in her diary how much she valued her development and the need to assume responsibility for her own life, independent from the influence from others. The passage runs as follows:

> **7 February[37] – No dream**
>
> I and I alone am responsible for my life and no one else. Further: I am not alive, I am living a sort of vegetative, plant-like life and if I continue like this I do not have a Lebensberechtigung.[38] I must think of this: Until now I have given the responsibility for my life away to: Maggy, Miss Moltzer, Jung, Ignaz. They have all tinkered with me, and taught me much that is useful.

The mentioning of Jung's name in the list of people to which Mischa Epper had given responsibility for her own life and helped her with her difficulties suggests that Mischa Epper may have had contact with Jung during the analysis with Moltzer. The passage went on as follows:

> And yet no other person carries the responsibility but myself. If I make of my life a plant-life, then I have no right to live, and I will not live long. But no one carries responsibility for this but me and me alone. Now is the question: how do I get to the 'stokkingspunt'[39] the quickest? How do I get to that point where the trouble lays, and which causes me to live a vegetative existence? My great passivity rests in a large part on this: that I keep waiting for an influential person to come from the outside. No, I must be that influential person myself. I do not have to be afraid of confronting others. [lit. bumping into others] Also I should for once not point my actions outwards, but apply them to myself.

As just presented, Epper considered the analysis with Moltzer as a dictatorship and, according to her opinion, lacking contact with reality, which brought her close to insanity. In her later considerations about Moltzer's treatment, Epper mentioned that it had also helped her to understand the reason why she adopted Reichstein's attitude against the family without questioning it. Furthermore, she realised that she did not develop her own position in the conflict. She believed that the conflict was caused by the pampered style of life she had had in her childhood, always running away when difficult issues arose. For her, in her teenage years, life should have been sunny, beautiful and pleasant, and achievement should have come without effort. Epper wrote that her education had kept at a distance any shadowy aspect, and it was not shown to her how she would need to confront her own burden and that one should do it well and with courage. She missed, in her education, an attitude towards life, which would have allowed her to deal with the blows of destiny.

Notes

1 ME – Mischa Epper notes of her analysis, front cover.
2 Shamdasani, 1998, p. 57.
3 Ibid.
4 Jung, 1921, CW 6.
5 Shamdasani, 2003, pp. 70–71.
6 This information was given to the author in an interview with D. Mirolo, director of Museum Epper in Ascona, Switzerland.
7 Mischa Epper's drawings. Copyright Museum Epper – Ascona – Switzerland.
8 ME – *Kindheistgeschichte Mischa Epper*, p. 18.
9 There is an arrow in her notes pointing to the word *introversion*.
10 Here there is the comment written in blue pen: *nonsense*.
11 ME – Mischa Epper notes of her analysis, p. 3.
12 Ibid.
13 SB – Document PA 979a B 5–1 5, letter from Mischa Epper to M.L. von Franz from 21.6.1957, p. 1.
14 Ibid, p. 2.
15 Ibid.
16 Famous Dutch children's book written by the psychoanalyst Frederik van Eeden.
17 Passage underlined in blue pencil by Epper.
18 ME – Mischa Epper notes of her analysis, pp. 4–7.
19 This was the time when the Spanish flu was causing many deaths in Europe.
20 ME – *Kindheistgeschichte Mischa Epper*.
21 Ascona is a city in the Italian part of Switzerland. Mischa Epper and her husband built a house there in the 1930s.
22 1918 – Next to this date there is again the German note – *Dictatorship*.
23 Father.
24 Underlined with blue pen.
25 The identity of sister Sedel is unknown.
26 This word written in German means 'creative'.
27 Underlined with blue pen, i.e., it was done in her later review of the text.
28 Epper wrote the word in German, which means sexual intercourse.
29 Dr van Veen was possibly the forty-year-old doctor with whom she fell in love when she was twelve.
30 The identity of Api is unknown.
31 German word for 'calmed'.
32 Frl. M. – Abbreviation in German to *Fraulein Moltzer* – Miss Moltzer.
33 This information was given to the author by Mrs Margrit Orsoni, who lived with Mischa Epper in her house in Ascona for about three years, from 1969 until 1972. She was a companion for Mischa Epper after the death of Ignaz Epper, in 1969.
34 Epper noted 'possibly around 1955', indicating that she rechecked this letter.
35 SB – Document PA 979a B 5–1 5, letter from Mischa Epper to M.L. von Franz from 1955, p. 2.
36 Interview with the author.
37 1919.
38 The original note in German '*Lebensberechtigung*' means 'right to be alive'.
39 The meaning of the word '*stokkingspunt*' it is not clear. However, it could possibly mean 'sticking *point*'.

References

Jung, C.G. (1921) "Psychological types" in *The Collected Works of C.G. Jung* (London: Routledge), 1989, vol. 6.

Shamdasani, S. (1998) *Cult Fictions* (London: Routledge, New Fetter Lane).

——— (2003) *Jung and the Making of Modern Psychology: The Dream of a Science* (Cambridge: Cambridge University Press).

11

EPPER'S TREATMENT WITH C.G. JUNG

After one year in analysis with Moltzer, Mischa Epper wrote to Jung asking for treatment. In a letter to von Franz from 1976, Epper wrote that it was her husband who convinced her to leave her analysis with Moltzer and begin the treatment with Jung.[1] It was a condition that Ignaz Epper required if he was to marry her. In the collection of the Museum Epper there are fragments of a document written by Epper, which seem to be the reproduction of the letter she wrote to Jung asking for treatment. The date of the document is unknown. However, Epper noted at the top of the paper: *letter to Dr Jung asking for treatment April/May 1919.* The text seems to be her recollection of the letter she wrote to Jung and it has a note at the margin of the paper with the remark 'essentially'. The text has parts in German and parts in Dutch. The German part runs as follows:

> Dear Dr Jung
>
> I am a patient of Ms. Moltzer. I took 2-months vacations in the mountains and during this time the problems in me became very active. I repressed it for a long time until up to the moment that I suddenly exploded. I had a dream in which I was surgically operated upon by a man. After that I had a fantasy in which a man stopped a crazy, galloping white horse (symbol for my unconscious), put it under control and started riding it. Both times I considered that you were this man. When I do not pay attention to myself, I feel worst. Now I am in a critical situation. I have the entire material ready, but I cannot, and I must not analyse it. I have a very clear talking unconscious, which functions very sharply. When I do not follow it, I feel incredibly bad. I always followed inevitably the path that it showed to me. Otherwise I have been immediately attacked by the most severe symptoms. That's the way I am now. I think that I necessarily must go to you for analysis and I would like to ask you to write

> to me saying if you have the time. I don't think that I need a long treatment. It seems to me that one month at the longest (should suffice).
>
> I am 17½ years old and was since March last year in analysis with Ms Moltzer.[2]

The text stops abruptly and is not signed. At the end of the paper there is a note in Dutch. The passage runs as follows:

> Yes, girl – that is a difficult struggle. The worst thing is when you imagine the injustice to an extent that makes you lose contact with reality and me of course. That makes your situation very dangerous. You must accept that you will have to give in to him now. If he knocks now, you may not close your door.

The preceding comment, written in Dutch, does not seem to be related to the letter she wrote to Jung and is written with Epper's handwriting. Although the reason why she wrote it in this way is not clearly known, it could be hypothesised that it was a similar process to that which she experienced in her conversations with the unconscious, in which an inner figure talks to her, enabling a kind of inner dialogue. The fragment shows another example of how Epper's fantasies affected her behaviour.

Epper was in treatment with Jung for a very short time, only nine hours. Notes or documents about the treatment with Jung were not found, and therefore little is known about the way Jung worked with her. In an interview of Mrs Orsoni with the author she described that Mischa Epper told her that whilst in therapy with Jung he asked her to draw and to tell him her dreams. However, much later, in a letter to Aniela Jaffé from the 18th of July 1977, Mischa Epper wrote briefly about her analysis with Jung from 1919. She wrote to Jaffé about the story of her husband and how she met him. The passage runs as follows:

> Then I saw his xylography and I was enthusiastic about it, I was 17 years old. I met him, and we fell in love with each other and I began to make drawings under his guidance. But I was too chaotic (I was suffering from depression, the reason why I was in treatment with Maria Moltzer). He recommended me to go in treatment with Jung. After only 9 hours Jung said: 'Get married. Now life begins!', typically Jung.[3]

At the end of the treatment, after approximately three months, Epper wrote Jung a letter which runs as follows:

> 20th May 1919
>
> Dear Dr Jung
>
> I must write to you to say how terribly grateful I am towards you, because you helped me so carefully. I feel happy that I finally have become a totally

> normal healthy person. And I know that I must be thankful primarily to you and the analysis. Otherwise I would have been still walking about like a repulsive demon. I must just yell and laugh for pure happiness. I hope I can stay so genuine and spontaneous otherwise I just need to think about how much the last hour with you triggered in me.
>
> Yours, Epper Quarles

Although no notes referring to Epper's treatment with Jung were found, there is a record in the protocols of the meetings at the Psychological Club in Zürich, which offers us a few hints about how Jung understood her case. In the notes of the meeting from the 17th of March 1922, in which Jung was present, there was a discussion on topics related to theoretical issues, among others – themes such as persona, anima and the intuitive function. While the group was discussing the father-imago, Jung made comments using examples from one case that, most probably, refers to Mischa Epper. The notes have a telegraphic character and the meaning of the sentences is not always clear. The passage runs as follows:

> The Father imago can be dissolved, and (nevertheless) fixation can still be present. What does then stay in the transference? (Man, same gender, humanity, collectiveness, God).
>
> These cases have a part in the depth of the nature and are determined by a mysterious fate, such transference becomes a strong event.
>
> Young woman, father from Holland, lived in the colonies (the father?), not born in the tropics (the young woman?).
>
> Neuroses through love to an older musician. Normal childhood until 8, then after felt not well. Introverted; strange fantasies; (came) into treatment not voluntary; (had a) revelation, (she) saw suddenly the father, embraced him, wanted to kiss him. He moved the head back. When he finally kissed her, she saw a basilisk gaze. (She) fainted. The father has a snake inside. The snake poisoned her. (She got) the mission to a great peregrination (illegible). In a wide plane area (she saw) the rest of the animals from before the diluvium, frozen bodies of primitives, among them a young man, who she can warm. He kisses her. That was the solution. Because the father namely holds her (illegible), what he communicated to her. She began to make drawings, beautiful Malayan drawings. In these figures were what the father gave her and what she experienced with the musician. (The) father was ascetical as (he was) young. Therefore, (the) primitive female must unconsciously affect! (him?) Introverted! The not lived instinct must be lived by the daughter. Only after she liberated (the) love from the primitive, was (the) father overcome. The fixation in the analyst stopped then too. But not totally, because the primitive was still not over. The relation to man was also not adequate. Only when the primitive-problem was solved, was the fixation totally overcome.[4]

Considering that Jung in this passage is most probably referring to Epper's case, it may give us hints about how he interpreted and worked with the material she brought to him. His comments indicate that, for him, Epper had an unconscious link to her father and unconsciously lived part of her father's blocked instinctual life. Concerning the technique Jung used, it also showed that Epper used drawings to express her fantasies, and that Jung worked with them, which led to her liberation not only of fixation to the father, but also from the transference to him.

Although the man mentioned in the fantasy was called a musician, it is most probably a reference to Ignaz Epper. Although speculative, it is possible that Jung mentioned musician instead of painter, the real profession of Ignaz Epper, to disguise the information about the patient. The relationship with this 'man' transformed her 'frozen' condition and liberated her from the instinctual, primitive aspects of her fantasies.

Like in his analysis of the text of Frank Miller, Jung considered in Epper's case the importance of the father-imago and its influence in her relationships. Another similarity between these two cases was his consideration of the significant role of the ego in dealing with the inner images. Jung considered in his evaluation about Miller that her ego was not able to cope with the contents of her unconscious and concluded that it was the cause of her psychic breakdown. In the case of Epper, from her criticism of Moltzer's approach and her feeling that Jung brought her back to reality, one can deduce that his attempt was to prevent the ego from being dazed by the contents coming from the unconscious. This argument can be corroborated with the passage mentioned earlier, when Epper began to write the story of her own neuroses and Jung told her that if she felt uncomfortable once confronted with the material, either written or in paintings, she should leave it and let it rest for a while.

Another interesting point to note is Jung's consideration of Epper's transference and his remarks on the case of Keller-Jenny. He was aware of the transference of both women and considered that Epper's transference was not completely over. As mentioned, he suggested Keller-Jenny to write letters to him, but without necessarily sending them. Epper wrote and occasionally sent her letters to Jung.

As mentioned, Epper felt cured after her treatment with Jung. In a letter from 1976, she described to von Franz her experience of how she had been helped by him as follows:

> Then I went 9 hours to Jung and those hours I will never forget, because it meant to wake up from an evil scary dream. After that, at 18, I got married.[5]

Following Epper's treatment with Jung, the sisters moved to Switzerland definitively on the 7th of June 1919.[6] Reichstein liked the atmosphere of Zürich and the distance from the aristocratic surroundings of her family in Holland. And, after her sister, Reichstein (Figure 11.1) went into analysis with Jung.

FIGURE 11.1 Reichstein at the age of 26

The precise date when she started her analysis with Jung is not clearly known. In a letter from Reichstein to Jung dated just with the year (1942) she mentioned that she did not clearly remember when her treatment began, but believed it was sometime between the end of 1919 and the beginning of 1920 (Reichstein was twenty-five years old in 1919). In the same letter, she mentioned her own notes dating to the years 1921, 1922, 1923 and 1924. Unfortunately, the notes of her analysis with Jung mentioned in this letter were not found. This indicates, however, that she was in treatment with Jung until at least 1924.[7] The first available letter from Jung to Reichstein is dated 15th of June 1924,[8] in which he offered her an appointment and apologised that she had to wait so long for it. Reichstein was then 30 years old. Around this time, she met her future husband, Adam Reichstein, whom she married in October 1925.

From the letters in the pictures archive of the C.G. Jung Institute in Zürich, we know that after 1924, Reichstein kept in contact with Jung through letters and met with him occasionally. She wrote to Jung about her dreams, psychological insights and difficulties, sent him her paintings and embroideries and discussed with him her ideas on his writings. In his answers, Jung showed interest in Reichstein's health and psychological condition, interpreted psychic conflicts and dreams and debated theoretical aspects with her. She was deeply involved in Jung's theory and, after her analysis, she went on with her studies in Jungian psychology. She helped Jung in the translation of his work into Dutch and worked occasionally as a lay analyst with a few patients. Besides, she attended seminars at the Psychological Club in Zürich, where she was subscribed as a guest between 1929 and 1966.[9]

Later in her life, around 1957, Reichstein was also in treatment with one of Jung's collaborators, Marie-Louise von Franz. This time it was her sister, Mischa Epper, who was worried about her condition and she supported Reichstein's treatment, giving information to von Franz about their stories, and her opinion regarding Reichstein's problems.

Unfortunately, further details of Reichstein's life after her treatments with Jung and von Franz cannot be presented, because additional notes or documents were not found. However, we can follow the life of Mischa Epper after her treatments in the notes she left.

Notes

1 SB – Document PA 979a B 5–1 5, letter from Mischa Epper to von Franz from 13 June 1976, p. 2.
2 ME – Fragments in the collection with no identification.
3 SB – Document PA 979a B 5–1 4, letter from Mischa Epper to A. Jaffé from 18.07.1977.
4 Note in the protocols from the 29th of March 1915 to the 12th of October 1922 at the Psychological Club, Zürich.
5 SB – Document PA 979a B 5–1 5, letter from Mischa Epper to M.L. von Franz from 13.06.1976, p. 2.
6 NH – Registers.
7 PA – Document no. 18, Jung–Reichstein Letters.
8 PA – Document no. 6, Jung–Reichstein Letters.
9 I am grateful to Mrs Georgina Seel for this information.

12

EPPER'S LIFE AFTER THE TREATMENTS

After the treatment with Jung and with the support of her husband, Mischa Epper recovered from her psychic disturbance. She described that for many years after the treatment she felt psychically very well and cared for her physical conditions by training and practising skiing. From February to June 1922, she took dance lessons in Dresden, Germany, with Mary Wigmann (1886–1973), who was a dancer and choreographer, one of the most prominent figures in the dance scene in Germany and Europe, and a pioneer of expressionist dance and dance therapy. Later, between 1923 and 1930, she also took classes on goldsmithing techniques and in carving.

When she realised that some unconscious conflicts were present, she illustrated her fantasies based on the situations she was in, like she had done during the treatments with Moltzer and Jung and her conversations with the unconscious. Many drawings were of half-human, half-animal figures which expressed the conflict.

The couple Mischa and Ignaz Epper lived in Zürich during those days. She had the flair of an 'enfant terrible' in society. Epper described that they lived unconventional lives. In accordance with her husband, they lived a marriage without restrictions in their sexual lives and without lying to each other. She mentioned that she enjoyed a 'nymph freedom' and fell in love with artists and sculptors. She wrote about her confrontation with conventions that put a barrier against the expression of one's own nature and of the instinctual life.

Epper criticised the aristocracy as the origin of repressions and mentioned that she and her sisters wanted to choose their husbands freely and not exclusively from the aristocracy, as did other distant members of the family. The sisters were ashamed of their aristocratic background and Reichstein was their leader against it, but they all had their inner motivation to go against the narrow prison they lived in and from which they wanted to liberate themselves.

Around 1926, when Epper was 25 years old, she had a series of health problems and believed that the illness was caused by psychic factors. She spent months in the house of her second sister (Henriette Reichstein). Initially, her husband and her sister Reichstein advised her to go back to treatment with Jung, but she did not want it. She described that she had fantasies with an inner figure of a doctor, who was also a prophet. With time, this inner figure began to tyrannise her. She sought help with Schmidhauser,[1] who was a philosopher of religion, but his support did not work well. Mischa Epper wrote that two prophets, namely Schmidhauser and her inner prophet, could barely find agreement with each other. She mentioned that she had read Jung's 'The Relationship between the Ego and the Unconscious' and her husband convinced her that she should go into treatment with Jung once again and, this time, she accepted it.[2] Unfortunately, no notes of this second treatment with Jung were found.

In the following years, Epper occasionally sent Jung her dreams and he interpreted them in his answers. Around 1930, Mischa Epper was ill with a pulmonary disease and she believed that her illness had a psychological component once again. In an unpublished letter from the 17th of April 1930, she presented her situation to Jung and asked for the interpretation of a dream and a fantasy. Her letter runs as follows:

> Dear Dr. Jung!
>
> I would like to ask you for advice, although I have waited too long to write to you. I waited, because I wanted to deal with the troubles myself, and because I know that you are flooded with letters and have the right to rest in your vacations. I would like to put two questions to you: I am in Arosa for two months, ill with pulmonary catarrh, etc. I do not doubt that my psychic disposition was responsible for it, too, and I wanted to be fully on my own, which is for me fruitful and necessary, i.e., to be distant from my husband. Now, there is the trouble; my husband fell in love with another woman and he is on a journey with her at the moment. But, in fact, this is not dramatic and will have its meaning and the expected uneasiness in the situation is healthy for me too. However, what is disturbing for me is the terrible uncertainty with him, which I would like to get rid of. I resist it with my willpower, reason and conscience, but it does not help, because the unconscious is stronger and close-knit with him. It has to do with an experience that has a strong influence in his life and surely, he has a lot to learn from it. But why do I need to go along with his development instead of being just a simple observer?
>
> I had the following fantasy: I work in a basement (my 'birth' basement, where the fountain of my creativity lies) I need to put it in order, reading and sorting books, dissecting bodies, etc., I do it with the help of an assistant and of a religious man, who helps me to excavate a shining core (flower), which I had lost in life and found here again. Suddenly, my husband comes in and kills the religious man to be together with a foreign woman. After that, a terrible confusion, a disorder erupted in the

basement, because I cannot organise it without the help of the religious man and I cannot find the core. This fantasy I wrote before I knew that my husband had travelled with his girlfriend. A few days later I got a letter from him writing about his travelling and that he was in a condition that was productive, but very confusing, in which he could not recognise himself (had lost his track). And now I am not moving, I dream nothing and there is disorder just like in the fantasy. I feel impotent. It really unnerves me, because it is his experience and not mine. I would like to be an observer and not involved.

I would like vehemently to get myself free from this involvement, but I did not get it. My mental attitude is surely wrong, and I want to force it with my will and have a mistaken obsession for independence, but I realise that I am cramped and am stiff. I cannot find a correct attitude and would be glad if you could give me advice.

And could you please tell me what the following dream means? In a garden there is an elephant, which has been totally devoured by worms and other creatures in such a way that the bones are already partially exposed. A totally unknown person tells me: I should observe the elephant carefully, because it is a symbol for the process that is going on in my lungs. This dream must really be associated with my illness. What does the elephant mean?

A similar tenseness, like I have towards my husband, I also have in my posture towards you. It comes from last year when I depicted both of you with 'small wings of angels' in heaven (you remember the drawing I did for you, with the *I* in the middle). There is no possibility for a human relationship if personifications are still happening in 'heavenly principle' or in 'devilishly principle' (because I put my relatives in hell with devilish grimaces), because I value some as highly superhuman and others as deeply subhuman and therefore I don't allow life and people to interact with me, because a narrow judgement of value disturbs me.

I hope I did not bother you too much.

Yours faithfully[3]

The letter was reproduced in full length, because it gives us a frame to understand Jung's answer, which is the only published letter between them. The name of Mischa Epper was not revealed, and she was presented anonymously as Mrs N. The letter gives us an example of Jung's understanding of her problem with her husband and of his interpretations in Epper's case. It is a letter from the 26th of April 1930 and it runs as follows:

My dear Mrs N

It is obvious that you have inwardly coalesced with your husband. Formerly, he assimilated so much of you that you yourself are now in him too. Nothing is so binding as affects and unconscious states let loose on the other person.

Now you must suffer your husband as he has suffered you. You must take it for granted that you'll have to endure everything that affects him. Naturally he is now confused and disoriented because his unconscious side is coming up. The whole situation is turning around.

He wrote to me recently and accused me of teaching psychology instead of living. I know this accusation. All those people make it who misuse psychology to shirk their own life. He has lived too long *through you* instead of through himself. But now it has caught him by the scruff of the neck. He has, as a matter of fact, killed the old man (in me) since he has thrown out the baby with the bathwater and no longer gets any benefit from psychological insight. That comes from misuse. I have answered him but have mislaid his address. Perhaps I had an unconscious resistance to answering him because his letter didn't tell the truth. I enclose my answer. You can send it to him if you wish. Your dream: The elephant is the largest animal. It represents the crushing weight of the unconscious life in you. It has to decompose, that it is to say you mustn't let yourself be driven to extremes any longer by the unconscious, but must act according to your conscious insight. This transformation process expresses itself in your body. It is the same process your husband is going through, only in reverse. It is a dangerous crisis and you must cling with might and main to consciousness. You need insight and understanding in the highest degree, for only this can ensure that the animal will decompose in you in such a way that you are not too much affected by it. It's a question of becoming human. Man is distinguished by the supremacy of consciousness, but the animal is the victim of instincts, impulsive moods, affects and illusions.

Your husband has still to experience all this in his own body. Until now he has been much too reasonable because for him you have represented too much of his own unreason. Now the boot is on the other foot. You can be absolutely sure of my discretion.

With heartfelt sympathy,

Very sincerely – C.G Jung[4]

In an unpublished letter from the 3rd of May 1930, Mischa Epper answered Jung. Her answer runs as follows:

Inner-Arosa 3.5.30

Dear Dr. Jung!

Thank you indeed for your letter, in which you brought the main aspect of the problem to the point. Through your letter, the difficulties between me and my husband from last summer and autumn became clear too, because the reversal of the attitude has been going on for one year.

I am too accustomed to be loved, understood and guided by him. Now I need to become a loving and comprehending person, and the spoiled

> child (in me) complains and would like to stay emotional and irresponsible. He needs an independent woman, who can act by herself, and hates the child who pushes him to be active as a father, and by which he is forced in the role of a psychologist that damages his artist-side [. . .].[5]

She also mentioned in her answer the criticisms of Ignaz Epper to Jung. She wrote:

> I did not read his letter to you, but if he wrote that you teach psychology instead of living, I do not agree with it, because you always pushed me back to life! In every analysis there is for the patient the risk of running away from life, because the neurotic tends to stay away from difficulties. You have the opposite effect on me.[6]

Jung's answer in the letter of April 1930 indicates one of the disagreements he had with Ignaz Epper. Another example can be seen in a letter Jung sent to Mischa Epper from the 29th of May 1930.[7] Jung mentioned a correspondence exchange with Ignaz Epper, in which he wrote that artists do not see their work as handcraft any longer, as was the case during the Middle Ages. Jung thought that contemporary artists had therefore lost their basis and felt a social resentment, a problem which he also observed in Ignaz Epper. Jung believed, however, it was a problem of the contemporary artist, and he could not blame Ignaz Epper for feeling in this way. He further added that he considered that Ignaz Epper was not able to apprehend his (Jung's) ideas properly. Mischa Epper noted that this letter caused a strong reaction against Jung in her husband.

The Eppers lived in Zürich until 1932, when Mischa Epper's father supported them to build a house in the Italian part of Switzerland, and Epper started a new phase in his paintings. He modified his xylography, by which he became well known as an expressionist, and began to paint colourful gardens, motifs quite different from his xylography. According to Orsoni,[8] Jung would then have told him that he did not paint well, that he did not need to search for a new phase in his art, and that he should be satisfied with what he did, i.e., what Jung said was that Ignaz Epper was over with his art. This comment offended Ignaz Epper, who was annoyed with him. But Jung was not alone in his consideration of Ignaz Epper's art. Hansjakob Diggelmann, who wrote a booklet to the Museum Epper presenting the art of Mischa and Ignaz Epper mentioned that after the 1930s the expression in Ignaz Epper's *oeuvre* lost its strength. Diggelmann mentioned that it was known among their friends that Ignaz Epper suffered from a severe depression. Mrs Lunin added that Ignaz Epper had a melancholic character, possibly as a result of the severe difficulties he had in his childhood.[9] In spite of differences and disagreements, the Eppers and Jung kept a friendly contact throughout their lives.

Mischa Epper went on to have conversations with her inner figures in the way Jung described in his technique of active imagination. One of her figures was 'the fool'. She listened to the advice of this inner figure when she built her house. For instance, the fool told her that an olive tree in the terrain should not be cut off for the construction, so the house was built around that olive tree. Like her father, Epper played a good hand in the stock market and in dealing with her investments. Epper noted many times that she followed the advice of the fool, apparently with satisfactory results.

Between 1933 and 1934, she learned sculpting at the *Academie Scandinave* in Paris with Charles Despiau (1874–1946), a French sculptor who worked with Rodin, and in 1937 she began to work with the development of marionettes for presentations at the theatre of marionettes in Ascona.

Epper's interest in Jungian psychology remained throughout her life and in her library in Ascona she had many of Jung's books and of the publications of the conferences in Eranos. In her notes about her neuroses, she also wrote about how Jung's ideas helped her to relate to her cultural background. She considered that the psychology of Jung would aid the improvement in the conditions of the aristocracy in Holland, particularly in the court, where she was acquainted with some members (a school friend of Epper gave ceramic lessons to the princess). Epper described Holland as a country which had had colonies for 300 years. Many members of the upper class, her countrymen, ruled and lived in the Eastern colonies such as India and Indonesia as engineers, executives, businessmen, doctors and technicians, without consciously considering the spiritual influence these foreign cultures had upon them. For her, the influence was present in the people of Holland with mixed blood and in the number of followers of Indian-mystical movements and sects such as anthroposophy, which were opposed to the rational trade-man type and the intellect influenced by Calvinism.

Epper saw in the development of her life two different periods with opposite characters, and she saw that these opposites were also presented in the Dutch society: on the one hand there was a period when an aesthetic-spiritual side dominated with a severe abstinence, which was the fruit of the influence of Calvinism; and on the other, a period when Eros ruled, when faithfulness was not considered, not in fantasies, nor in the interchange of partners. This opposition, out of pure unconsciousness and lack of psychological knowledge, ended in neurosis.

Epper saw the aristocracy under the influence of a rigid Calvinistic orientation with a strong logical intellect. She considered that the Queen[10] was a serious protestant, a religious person, but with the typical Dutch innocence and lack of awareness about the dark forces (inside the psyche). For Epper, the conventions of the aristocracy led them to marry among themselves to keep the line in their race, a kind of racism. This was one of the reasons why she and her sisters went against the barriers of conventions. Reichstein was the leader in the Quarles' children against those rules. According to Epper, it was the influence of the intellect formed by Calvinism, which also influenced Reichstein's rationalism and led her to destroy her femininity.

Although Mischa Epper clearly gave much value to Jung's ideas, she also wrote notes in which it is demonstrated that her appreciation of Jung was not without criticism. She mentioned the conversation with a colleague about how much she was grateful to Jung's ideas. The man, however, argued with irony and sarcasm, considering Jung's ideas were of no use and that he was a kind of wizard. To this respect Epper wrote:

> If I consider what comes out of Jung's mouth, I will not assume that he is a kind of saint, and that he would never fall to his Mephistopheles' impulse, but most important in his great personality is his real dedication to the idea of searching for new paths and knowledge, for his passionate search, and ultimately for his wish to help mankind.[11]

FIGURE 12.1 Epper's sculpture of C.G. Jung in Museum Epper

Ignaz Epper went into analysis with Jung in 1951,[12] but it seems that it did not work well. For how long Ignaz Epper was in analysis with Jung is not known and notes of his analysis with Jung were not found. Mrs Mirolo said that Jung helped Mischa Epper with her psychic difficulties, but he did not achieve the same improvement with Ignaz Epper.[13]

Around 1955, Mischa Epper proposed to make a sculpture in gypsum of Jung as a homage, and he accepted, sitting as a model for her. But Ignaz Epper, while transporting the sculpture from one room to another dropped and broke it. Thereafter, Jung refused to stay as a model for a second time. Epper made a second sculpture of Jung (Figure 12.1), this time from memory, and considered the second sculpture much better.

Jung, however, did not like the sculpture. He wrote his opinion about the sculpture in a letter from the 25th of July 1956 as follows:

> Dear Mrs. Epper
>
> Please forgive me for the delay in my reply [. . .] I have the impression that since I saw the bust at your place you had much work done, which somehow fatally changed the face expression and the shape. The forehead is no longer correct, and the mouth is not correct either, and there are some spasmodic traces which came in the face which were not there before. Somehow, I think that you missed the point. I got the impression that you put too much of your own subjectivity in it. Please forgive me my open criticism. I cannot cope with the idea that I look like a conqueror attacking the clouds, or like the eagle of Zeus, which did not catch Ganymede. I look like someone who strives after the highest goal in vain. The expression here is too intellectualist. I have for me my own judgment, which I always take with scepticism and let be confirmed by others, because I do not want to be unfair to your work, in which you invested so much effort and attentiveness [. . .] I suggest you leave it for at least half a year, and then to take it up again.
>
> Yours faithfully
>
> C.G Jung[14]

The letter shows the friendly contact and openness in the relationship between Mischa Epper and Jung. It is not known if Epper modified her work after Jung's letter, but we have the sculpture, which can found in the Museum Epper.

The Eppers attended lectures in Eranos, where Jung and other scholars presented papers on topics related to Jungian psychology. Occasionally, Jung spent some time in their house in Ascona and Mischa Epper had sporadic sessions with Jung.[15]

In the 1960s, Ignaz Epper had a stroke, and he was not able to continue with his artwork for a while. He was afraid of the risk of having more strokes, which would lead to him to give up work. According to Mrs Lunin, Epper said that if he could not work, he would prefer to die. He committed suicide in January

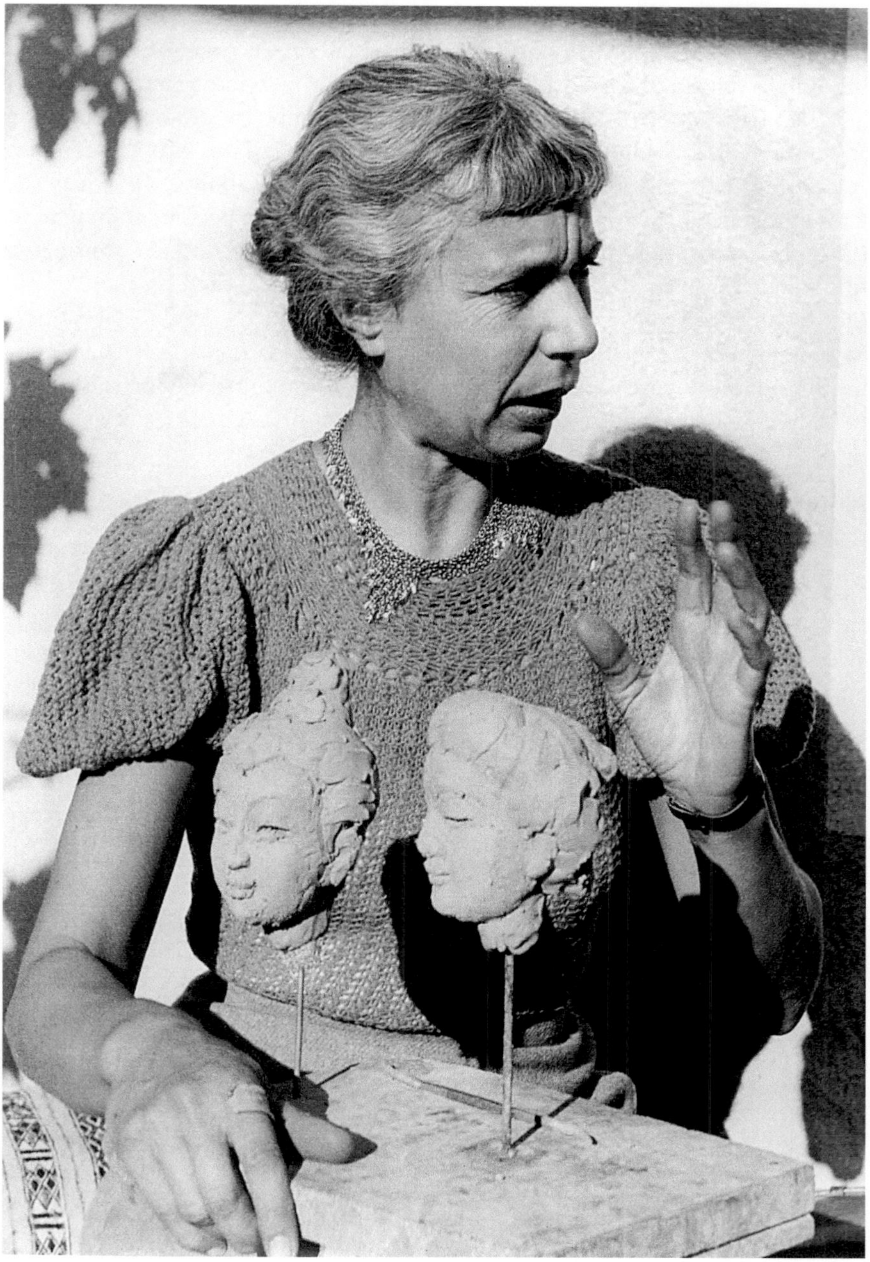

FIGURE 12.2 Mischa Epper around 1970[16]

1969. Ignaz Epper is nowadays considered one of the most prominent figures among Swiss expressionists.

After the death of her husband, Mischa Epper began a sequence of paintings related to the passion of Christ, and according to Mrs Mirolo the paintings helped her in the mourning process caused by the loss of her husband. Afterwards, she invested her time and energy in organising and cataloguing the work of her husband, with which she carried on until the end of her life. Mischa Epper had the idea of transforming her house into a museum and established a foundation, which exists today as the Museum Epper. According to Orsoni, Epper never had a relapse of her illness in the way she had experienced it as a teenager, but she was a singular person, and an artist through and through. Jung left a deep impression on her, and she considered him a man larger than life. Mischa Epper (Figure 12.2) died on the 22nd of October 1978.

Jung did not use the material from the case of Mischa Epper in his own publications. However, as we shall see next, Jung wrote an introduction to a Dutch book in which he mentioned her case mistakenly.

Notes

1 Mischa Epper possibly meant Julius Schmidhauser (1893–1970), who was a Swiss philosopher.
2 Fragments in the collection with no identification.
3 SB – Document PA 979a B 5–1 4, letter from Mischa Epper to C.G. Jung from 17.04.1930.
4 Jaffé, ed., 1973, p. 103.
5 SB – Document PA 979a B 5–1 4, letter from Mischa Epper to C.G. Jung from 03.05.1930, p. 2.
6 SB – Document PA 979a B 5–1 4, letter from Mischa Epper to C.G. Jung from 03.06.1930, p. 2.
7 SB – Document PA 979a B 5–1 4, letter from C.G. Jung to Mischa Epper from 29.06.1930.
8 Mrs Orsoni interview with the author.
9 Mrs Lunin interview with the author.
10 The date Mischa Epper wrote her notes is not clearly known; however it is possible that she refers in this passage to Queen Juliana (1909–2004), who reigned from 1948 to 1980. It was during her time as Queen that Indonesia became independent in 1949.
11 ME – *Kindheistgeschichte Mischa Epper*, p. 28a.
12 ETH – Letter from Mischa Epper to C.G. Jung, 31st of May 1956, Code: HS 1056 22 548.
13 Mrs Mirolo interview with the author.
14 ME – Letter of C.G. Jung to Mischa Epper.
15 ETH – Letter from Aniella Jaffé to Mischa Epper, 23rd of February 1955, Code: HS 1056 21861; and letter from Mischa Epper to C.G. Jung, 29th of September 1956, Code: HS 1056 22 547.
16 Photo from Mischa Epper. Copyright Museum Epper – Ascona – Switzerland.

Reference

Jaffé, A., ed. (1973) *C.G. Jung: Briefe* (Olten und Freiburg im Breisgau: Walter-Verlag), Band 1 und 2.

13

JUNG'S MISTAKEN INFORMATION ON THE CASE OF MISCHA EPPER

In May 1954, Jung wrote the preface for the book written by the Dutch psychiatrist R.J. van Helsdingen, *Images from the Unconscious – A Case of Jung's*. The book described the case of a Dutch patient treated by Jung in the early 1930s. In a footnote to the preface, Jung wrote as follows:

> This case is not to be confused with the similar case – the patients were in fact sisters – discussed in 'The Realities of Practical Psychotherapy' appendix to *The Practice of Psychotherapy*.[1]

The case presented in the 'The Realities of Practical Psychotherapy', as we shall see later, was the case of Mischa Epper's sister, Maggy Reichstein. But from the signatures of the drawings in the pictures archive of the C.G. Jung Institute in Zürich, we know that the patient mentioned in van Helsdingen's book was not the case of Mischa Epper, but another Dutch woman. Jung's comment is mistaken.

In his book *In de ban van Jung*,[2] Van den Berk mentioned this Dutch patient of Jung's, calling her 'Claire', because the family required that her real identity should not be revealed. He also interviewed van Helsdingen, questioning him about the book, and presented the case, which Jung thought referred to the sister of Reichstein. Van Helsdingen mentioned the conversation with Jung in 1952, in which Jung had said that he forgot most of the information about the patient and that his notes about it were lost. Therefore, it can be concluded that Jung's memory about the case was no longer accurate.

The failures in Jung's memory about the case are corroborated by information from another source. In a private interview in 1950 with Suzanne Percheron, Jung gave a description which indicates the confusion of information between the cases of Reichstein and the Dutch patient in van Helsdingen's book.

Percheron had asked Jung about his patients, and he answered the following related to the cases mentioned here:

> An English girl of nobility, titled, is born in India. Wealthy parents. Her aya (nanny) takes full charge of her and she is nourished morally by Asia – tales, legends, atmosphere, plus the influence of the land where she is born. Then she is sent to France to an aristocratic boarding school. She becomes unbalanced, dissociated, cannot live, cannot adapt. She does not want to acknowledge to herself that she has the background of an Asian peasant. She comes to see me and makes no progress. Of her dreams I cannot manage to understand a good third. I tell her: 'Go see someone else, I cannot . . . ' 'No', says she, 'at least you listen to me. I can talk to you. With others I don't even have that' 'Good, let's try and continue'. She arrives one day: 'I have dreamt of a golden scarab'. At that precise moment something knocks on my windowpane. The noise attracts my attention, I turn around. Against the glass there is a golden scarab, that is its name. I pick it up and put on her knees. 'See!' Coincidence, synchronicity, which principle?[3]

This passage shows that Jung's memory was mistaken, and that he confused information from the cases of Maggy Reichstein and the Dutch patient in van Helsdingen's book. Firstly, the woman was not English, all the persons involved were Dutch; secondly, it was the patient in van Helsdingen's book who was sent to an English (not French) boarding school, and not Reichstein, who was in Holland in her school years; and finally, the story of the scarab mentioned by Jung, as we shall see later, is related to the case of Reichstein, not to the case of the Dutch patient. Therefore, in the interview, Jung fused elements pertaining to the stories of the two cases. But in order to properly understand Jung's confusion, it is important to present the similarities and differences in the stories of these two women. Following are the passages of van Helsdingen's book which may contribute to an understanding of the circumstances of Jung's mistaken information about the identity of the patient.

In the introduction, Jung mentioned that van Helsdingen asked him to write a preface for the book. In his text, Jung praised the technical quality of the drawings, which are of high artistic value and uncommonly expressive. The high artistic quality of the drawings is an aspect, which may have contributed to confounding Jung: the Dutch patient presented in van Helsdingen's book was an artist like Mischa Epper. Both women painted and sculpted to an elevated level. Furthermore, they have a similar technique and style in their drawings and in some pictures both women use similar motifs.

In the preface, Jung wrote about the drawings of the Dutch patient that they communicate their frightening, daemonic content to the beholder and convince him of the terrors of a fantastic underworld.[4] He commented on the pictures and material presented, gave his understanding of the case and the goal of his therapeutic use of the drawings. It runs as follows:

> The pictures in this book show us imaginative activity unleashed in another form: the Indomalaysian phantasmagoria of pullulating vegetation and of fear-haunted, stifling tropical nights. Environment and inner disposition conspired to produce this series of pictures which give expression to an infantile-archaic fear. Partly it is the fear of a child who, deprived of her parents, is defencelessly exposed to the unconscious and its menacing, phantasmal figures; partly the fear of a European who can find no other attitude to everything that the East conjures up in her save that of rejection and repression. [. . .] The pictures not only illustrate the phase of treatment that brought the contents of her neurosis to consciousness, they were also an instrument of treatment, as they reduced the half conscious or unconscious images floating about in her mind to a common denominator and fixated them. Once an expression of this kind has been found, it proves its 'magical' efficacy by putting a spell as it were, on the content so represented and making it relatively innocuous. The more complex this content is, the more pictures are needed to depotentiate it. The therapeutic effect of this technique consists in inducing the conscious mind to collaborate with the unconscious, the latter being integrated in the process. In this way the neurotic dissociation is gradually remedied.[5]

The influence of the East in the case of Reichstein and the Dutch patient is another element that contributes to the confusion. As we shall see later, the Eastern background in the case of Reichstein was a crucial element for Jung's understanding of her case, as it was in his consideration about the case of the Dutch patient.

Van Helsdingen mentioned that years before he had met Jung's patient by chance. She showed him a series of paintings that she had done during the treatment with Jung around thirty years ago, when she had suffered a severe psychic breakdown. He was impressed by the paintings and wanted to make them available to the interested public. The date given to the case is another indication of the confusion of the cases, because Mischa Epper was in analysis with Jung first in 1919, and for a second time around 1926. The Dutch patient was in analysis with Jung between 1930 and 1931, when she drew the images presented in the book. It is interesting to note that during the same period, Mischa Epper was subscribed as a guest in the Psychological Club in Zürich – between 1930 and 1931.[6]

The conditions in which the patients made the drawings were also different. Van Helsdingen described the way the Dutch patient drew her pictures as follows:

> The drawings were conceived spontaneously in time of great psychic tensions. The patient felt the urge to draw, and then drew 'from her feelings',

> without having a distinct idea in her mind's eye. She did not know what she would draw, did not think of anything while drawing, and often she did not understand the bizarre likeness she came up with. Nonetheless, she worked with feverish speed, in the grip of great emotion. Only when the drawings were finished she noticed that a feeling of great loosening/relaxation came over her. The act of drawing was a form of emancipation (liberation), a psychocatharsis. She knew that this was a way to temporarily release herself from her tensions and had thereby found a form of auto (self) therapy. However, after some time, the emotions and the fears returned, so that again she was forced to draw. The drawings themselves held no great interest for her. Only later, under the influence of her psychotherapy, was her attention drawn to the deeper symbolic meaning of these drawings, which one rightly may call 'images out of the unconscious'.[7]

Van Helsdingen's comments indicate that the drawings were made under tension and in a spontaneous way, differently than in the case of Mischa Epper, who did not paint in such a condition. Furthermore, many of her drawings were made in the treatment and under the guidance of Moltzer and, possibly, of Jung himself. Comparing the original pictures which are kept in the pictures archive of the C.G. Jung Institute in Zürich with the dates given in the book, we know that van Helsdingen slightly altered the chronology of a few drawings.

In his description of the story of the patient, Van Helsdingen further wrote that 'The patient whose drawings are the subject of this book was born in Indonesia as a daughter to educated parents'.[8] From the story of Epper, we know that she was born in Bloemendaal, Holland, on the 18th of August 1901.[9] It was her older sister, Maggy Reichstein, who was born in Indonesia in 1894.

In van Helsdingen's book, the patient lived in the grandparents' house where 'Aunt Anne' took care of the children. She was described as puritan and perverse in the way she treated them. In the following passages in van Helsdingen's book we have descriptions of the kind of treatment 'Aunt Anne' gave to the Dutch patient.

> The grandparental house was run by the younger sister of the patient's mother, Aunt Anne, an unmarried woman, who was about 35 at that time. She was a masculine woman with a harsh voice, a leader of boy-scouts, and very strict with the children. [. . .] (She) dismissed the child as a 'dreamer' and the latter was very afraid of her. The aunt loved rough games, which always involved hurting the patient. She must have had sadistic tendencies. In one of the 'games' the Aunt would lift the child and then drop her, legs apart, on the hard arm of a chair, so that the child's genitals would be bruised. When she cried the aunt called her childish. The aunt was strongly religious and would often speak to the children about her beliefs. The patient saw in her aunt the sadistic side of religion,

> without any compensatory beauty. There were times when she (the aunt) would dress in a long white robe, close the curtains, lie on the sofa, eyes closed, and hands folded in prayer and then make the children come in to look at her. This would greatly unsettle them. When the child was even a little bit naughty, she would be locked up in Grandfather's dark study, the one with the weapons on the wall. She would always hear voices, thinking it might be Momok, the Indonesian ghost feared by all children there. The relationship between the grandparents was very tense, but Aunt Ann and Grandfather got along very well. The patient hated them both deeply.[10]

Here we have similarities but also clear distinctions from Mischa Epper's story. As noted before, Epper grew up in the house of her parents and her family had a nanny who was rude and puritan too, but there is no report in Epper's family of the kind of punishments that the Dutch patient went through. Furthermore, in Epper's family it was not an aunt who cared for them while the mother was in hospital, but the grandmother. Coincidentally, both the aunt of the Dutch patient and Epper's grandmother were named 'Anne'. In both cases, the mother was absent. The absence of her parents was described in van Helsdingen's book as follows:

> Beginning at the tender age of four, the patient was sent to an English boarding school, together with the other children of the family, for the usual reasons of health and proper upbringing. The mother returned to her husband in Java.[11]

Epper's mother was in the hospital from 1903 to 1908, when she died. During this time, Epper and her sisters had limited contact with her. Here again we have similarities, but also clear distinctions between the stories: Epper's mother was very fragile with her health problems, and in the Dutch patient's story the mother figure – the grandmother – was also described as fragile. Van Helsdingen's description runs as follows:

> Grandmother was of fragile character, always in her dressing room, which was very feminine with lace and a scent of lavender.[12]

Another similarity is that both patients felt that their mothers were too submissive to their father. And, concerning the father; in Epper's case, he was present over the course of Epper's childhood, but this was not so in the case of the Dutch patient.

In both cases, the grandparents played a significant role in the education of the children. As mentioned in Epper's story, the grandfather died much earlier, and the grandmother assumed the education of the children. In van Helsdingen's descriptions, the rude education of the patient was not just coming from 'Aunt

Anne' alone, but also from the grandfather, who was violent with the children. He is described as follows:

> Grandfather had a very masculine constitution. [. . .] When she was small Grandfather would terrorise her by making her come to him when he was sitting in his armchair and then crushing her between his knees – tremendously strong because he was a horseman. She was always filled with dread when she came to wish him good-night in his sombre English study with its war trophies, including swords and sabres, on the wall. Sometimes, just to increase her fears, he would make her lie down on his sofa and would brandish the sharp weapons closely over her. The child was then stiff with terror.[13]

Van Helsdingen wrote that the patient went to a boarding school in England and described that during her childhood she was an outsider, lacking self-esteem. Her personality in her childhood was described in the book as follows:

> In this learned (intellectual) family she, who was both sensitive and emotional, always felt an outsider, which bred a lack of self-esteem. Later in her life she developed a fear of intellectualism, even conceiving the notion that she could be 'raped' by it [. . .]. As the youngest of the children she was coddled and spoiled. Nonetheless she must have lacked love in such a collective setting. The school was very strict. [. . .] Every Sunday the children had to go to church. The patient developed an unconscious repugnance for this compulsory and conventional church attendance. [. . .] She would faint. [. . .] Nonetheless (she) was required to continue going to church.[14]

Again, there are similarities, but also clear differences in both stories. As mentioned before, Epper's personality in her childhood was outgoing and cheerful, and therefore opposed to the Dutch patient. But the link with England (Epper's family had ancestry in England) and the difficulties related to sexuality are present in both cases. The attitude towards the church was the opposite. Epper's family was not religious at all and, in the case described, attending church was obligatory.

In both cases, it was during the teenage years that a severe neurosis broke out. However, in Epper's case the main symptom was paralysing depression, while with the Dutch patient it was anxiety and persecutory ideas. In van Helsdingen's book it was described as follows:

> In Indonesia she had her first menstruation [. . .] and [. . .] the first symptoms of a persecution complex. She had not had any sexual education. [. . .] However now she imagined that the 'djongos', the beautiful and powerfully built native servants, wanted first to rape, then to kill her. She was very fearful, but did not confide in anyone; instead she became quieter and quieter, ate little and slept less. Each night she expected them to come a step closer. Finally, the family doctor discovered her secret fears

> and she was sent to live with a cousin who owned a tea plantation in the mountains of central Java. In this tranquil and beautiful environment, she entered a wonderful period. She rode through the plantation, calmed down and gained weight. She said of this time: 'My nerves were isolated by the fat, though in reality this was not a solution'. The rainforest motifs in her drawings are rooted in this period. [. . .] During this period, she also visited Brahmin Temples, including the complex of Tjandi Sewoe, with its enormous and beautifully sculpted statue of Nanda, the world-cow.[15]

Both women went through treatments in their teenage years. Epper had the treatment with Moltzer and Hämmerli and the Dutch patient with the doctor of the family. But Epper was in Holland, the Dutch patient in Indonesia. The description of the patient in van Helsdingen's book goes on as follows:

> At the age of seventeen she returned to Europe with her parents. She lived for a few months in Geneva, and then returned to her English boarding school. After graduation she wanted to attend art school, but her father stipulated that she had first to complete one year of academic study. She chose biology, passed her exams, and then could devote herself to her art. During this time, she was free from fears. [. . .] Much later, when she was twenty-six, she met her future husband, who could subdue her uneasiness. However, during the honeymoon, she was overwhelmed by her old fear-psychosis. Sexual contact was impossible. She saw faces behind every tree, and felt she would be murdered. On the train she felt everybody looked at her and feared a conspiracy. [. . .] A friend of the family, a psychiatrist, found her in tears as she was packing up her husband's luggage and suggested that she enter treatment with him, though he lived in another country. Her husband agreed and so, between twenty-eight and thirty, she lived in a pension in that foreign country and saw the psychiatrist every day. He treated her psychoanalytically, by Freud's method, but the patient felt this was not the way to the source of her problems and that he did not understand her at all. Although she protested continuously, she nonetheless accepted all his interpretations. He awakened her sexuality, but forbade her to draw, saying 'she could really become crazy then!'[16]

Here we have another difference in the cases: Epper's treatments were not based on Freudian theory: firstly, with Hämmerli, who Epper did not consider as a psychotherapist, and then with Moltzer, based on Jung's theories and techniques. According to van Helsdingen, the patient's contact with Jung happened when she was around thirty years old, when the patient had developed anxiety symptoms and had an urge to draw again. Van Helsdingen wrote:

> When she was thirty-two she returned to Holland, and was again caught in the grip of unknown terrors. In one week, she drew all the drawings

> referring to the 'Cathédrale engloutie' and within a few months followed all others in the series, including those of 'The Nuns'. *A lady-friend* showed her drawings to Professor Jung, who said: 'if she wants to come, she should do so immediately!' And so, in her thirty-third year, the patient came under Jung's care, who – in contrast with her previous psychiatrist – urged her to draw. To aid the interpretation of her dreams he encouraged her to speak with the persons and animals in the drawings[17] (I italicised).

Here we have a situation that is possibly the origin of Jung's confusion of the cases: the lady friend (the part that I emphasised) in van Helsdingen's book, who brought the Dutch patient in contact with Jung, was Maggy Reichstein.[18] The two women knew each other, and Reichstein and the Dutch patient both attended a seminar Jung gave in 1930.[19] The technique used in both cases is the same: conversations with the unconscious, or what Jung called active imagination. Another similarity was the outcome of the treatment: both women felt that they were helped by Jung. Dr van Helsdingen wrote at the end of his book:

> After her treatment, the patient never again felt the need to give expression to any 'images from the unconscious', although she continued to unfold as an artist. She has been in full health for more than thirty years![20]

From Epper's notes, it is known that she knew the Dutch patient from Jung and they kept in contact throughout their lives. In 1957, Epper wrote to Jung that she visited the Dutch patient in Holland and she told Epper about the book that van Helsdingen would publish about her treatment with Jung.[21]

Jung's mistaken information to van Helsdingen's in 1952 about the Dutch patient as the sister of Reichstein, and the confusion in his report about the case stories in his interview to Percheron indicate that in the 1950s his memory about his treatments was no longer precise. This is important to note because, it seems, Jung did not take notes of treatments systematically. Nevertheless, van Helsdingen's presentation of Jung's treatment of the Dutch patient gives us another example of Jung's use of his techniques in his practice. Further, it gives us another example of Jung's use of case material to support his postulations. As we shall see later, he asked Reichstein in a letter in 1949 about her dream with the scarab and about the details of the event, because he did not write notes when it happened.

To conclude this chapter, I would like to point out that the stories of Epper and Reichstein give us their reasons for coming to Zürich and for the encounter with Jung. It shows that key issues related to Epper's treatment were the condition of aristocracy, the pampered style of life, the illness of the mother, the conflicts inside the family and in their upbringing, the importance of religious and cultural issues, the search for spiritual values and the quest of women regarding sexuality and emancipation.

Concerning Epper's analysis with Moltzer, we can conclude that, although the treatment helped her in making the unconscious more fluid, Epper considered that the connection with reality was missing, and the exaggerated focus on intuition almost made her insane. Concerning Epper's short treatment with Jung, one can say that it was focused on her unconscious connection to her father, and on the confrontation with the realities of life.

Notes

1 Jung, 1954b, par. 1254, footnote, CW 18.
2 Van den Berk, 2014, p. 360.
3 Percheron, 1982, pp. 56–57.
4 Jung, 1954b, par. 1252, CW 18.
5 Ibid., pars. 1253–1254.
6 I am grateful to Mrs Georgina Seel for this information.
7 van Helsdingen, 1957, p. 3.
8 Ibid., p. 2.
9 NH – Registers.
10 van Helsdingen, 1957, pp. 4–5.
11 Ibid., p. 4.
12 Ibid.
13 Ibid.
14 Ibid.
15 Ibid., p. 5.
16 Ibid., p. 6.
17 Ibid.
18 I am grateful to Tjeu van den Berk for this information.
19 PA – List of those present at the 1930 Seminar of C.G. Jung.
20 van Helsdingen, 1957, p. 5.
21 ETH – Letter from Mischa Epper to C.G. Jung from the 26th of July 1957, Code Hs 1056 23 919.

References

Jung, C.G. (1954b) Foreword to "Beelden uit het Onbewuste – een Geval van Jung"(1957) van Helsdingen, Dr. R.J., Van Loghum Slaterus-Arnhem, in *The Collected Works of C.G. Jung* (London: Routledge), 1993, vol. 18.

Percheron, S. (1982) "Interview Jung to Suzanne Percheron" in *C.G. Jung, Emma Jung, Toni Wolff* (San Francisco: The Analytical Psychology Club of San Francisco, Inc).

Van den Berk, T. (2014) *In de ban van Jung – Nederlanders ontdekken de Analytische Psychologie* (Zoetermeer: Uitgeverij Meinema).

Van Helsdingen, R.J. (1957) *Beelden uit het Onbewuste* (Arnhem: Van Loghum Slaterus) Pages No. from Internal translation for the C.G. Jung Institute: Zürich by Marianne Wysma.

PART 3

Maggy Reichstein

14

JUNG'S DESCRIPTIONS OF REICHSTEIN'S CASE IN THE LITERATURE[1]

> It is unbelievable what familial severity lays on the Quarles children. But I learned a lot from you, which will help other people. Therefore, I always think of you with gratitude.
>
> Yours Faithfully,
>
> C.G. Jung[2]

After the presentation of their story, we can understand Jung's first sentence in this passage from his letter to Reichstein from February 1929. But the second sentence is more intriguing, for it engenders an important question: what did he learn from Reichstein? And, as we will see next, he used her case as an example in different passages; therefore, what happened in Reichstein's treatment that led Jung to mention her case in some of his presentations?

What follows is an investigation into these questions, presenting what Jung wrote regarding her case, and describing his contact with Reichstein, a person with whom he debated his ideas in depth. It is the case of a woman known in some Jungian circles as 'the Mandala Lady', and who appeared in many of Jung's writings.

The first time Jung mentioned Reichstein's case was on the 8th of October 1932, when he gave a seminar on Kundalini yoga. Jung's presentation followed the seminars given by the Indologist Wilhelm Hauer, at the Psychological Club in Zürich. Hauer's presentations were entitled 'Yoga, especially the meaning of the chakras'. Jung focused his presentation on the psychological meaning of the symbols in the process of awakening the Kundalini, and on the differences between Eastern and Western approaches to spirituality. These seminars by Jung are known in the literature as the Kundalini Yoga Seminars.[3]

In his comments, Jung thanked Hauer for the presentation in which he explained the symbolism of the chakras and added that he had a different approach to them, mentioning how he first met the symbolism of Kundalini in a patient. Jung said that he had no chance of getting a teaching of the chakras before and that its symbolism had no relationship to the Western mentality. He reported then about a very difficult case he had, a European girl born in the East, who had no idea about such Eastern symbolism. She had great trouble in adapting to the European conditions, was against everything and became very neurotic. She was treated by two analysts before, whom she 'exploded', and Jung was not able to understand her dreams, which had a peculiar Eastern psychology. He described her condition as follows:

> She developed an entirely new set of symptoms, beginning with a dream which made a tremendous impression on her: that out of her genital organs came a white elephant. I was completely bluffed, I had never heard of such nonsense – and yet she was so impressed that she began to carve the elephant in ivory. Then organic symptoms appeared: she had ulcers in the womb, and I had to send her to a gynaecologist. [. . .] She developed polyuria, an impossible amount of fluid; she could hardly hold the urine. [. . .] With that there were acute attacks of diarrhoea – again floods of water with apparently no provocation; it just happened. At the same time, she really loved a man but could not think of marrying him. And then the thought entered her head that I, or circumstances, might persuade her to marry and have a baby, but that was impossible. For a whole year she fought against this idea, until she developed an entirely new symptom. She felt as if the skull had become soft on the top, as if the fontanelle was opening up – like a child with an open skull – and that something like a bird was descending from above with a long beak and going into her through the skull, meeting something that was coming up from below. When that happened, the whole thing cleared up, and she married and had babies.[4]

Jung added that he was only able to understand the symptomatology of the case after he read the Avalon's book *The Serpent Power* and found the parallels to the chakras. He wrote:

> You see, first was the elephant in muladhara, second was svadhisthana, the water region, and after that the emotional center, manipura; and then it did not go on continuously – something came from above, and this brought the dissolution. At first it was absolutely dark to me; I could not understand what had happened. But subsequently I understood that this was the awakening from above, and she could then disentangle herself from the maze of the exotic jungle. She could objectify the Indian psychology that had been grafted upon her with the milk she drank from the ayah and through the suggestion of her surroundings. She became liberated by the objectifying and could accept European life. And, quite naturally, she objectified her whole development in the most beautiful mandalas.[5]

I have quoted Jung's commentary here rather extensively, because in it, we find his description of Reichstein's conditions and his understanding of her case. In this context, it is important to briefly present the book mentioned by Jung, *The Serpent Power.* Its author, Arthur Avalon, alias Sir John Woodroffe, published the book in 1919. Woodroffe translated and commented on the two Sanskrit texts 'The Description of an Investigation into the Six Bodily Centres' (Sat-Cakra-Nirupana) and 'The Five-fold Footstool of the Guru' (Paduka-Pancaka). These texts address a form of tantric yoga, referred to as Kundalini yoga. The aim of practicing Kundalini yoga was to enable the raising of a divine cosmic energy, which lays dormant in the lower body at the base of the spinal column, in the imaginary shape of a coiled snake. Woodroffe referred to Kundalini as 'the serpent power'. The yoga exercises aim to awaken the Kundalini, leading it to higher chakras, the centres of consciousness. On its way through the chakras, the Kundalini develops the consciousness of the yogi and gives him psychic powers.[6]

In a different context, Jung gave another description of her case, in 1937, in his paper 'The Realities of Practical Psychotherapy'. In this text, Jung wrote that psychogenic disturbances are untypical and individual, and with the many variations it is difficult for the doctor to give a diagnosis. He further noted that, if the treatment took the form of an analysis, its development would be unique. Jung also mentioned the similarities among people, which facilitate the communication between doctor and patient, but once the differences in their personalities appeared, a dialectical process was necessary. Jung described two conditions that might cause trouble in the treatment: the first was when the analyst was neurotic or unconscious of his own issues. This phenomenon was, according to Jung, one of the main causes for problems in the countertransference. The second condition, which might cause troubles in the treatment was the lack of knowledge of the doctor, i.e., when the doctor did not know how to understand the material brought by the patient. In such a case, the lack of knowledge had the same effect as the mutual unconsciousness. Jung then described Reichstein and her condition as follows:

> I remember a case that caused me no end of trouble. It concerned a 25-year old woman patient, who suffered from a high degree of emotivity, exaggerated sensitiveness, and hysterical fever. She was very musical; whenever she played the piano she got so emotional that her temperature rose and after ten minutes registered 100° F. or more. She also suffered from a compulsive argumentativeness and a fondness for philosophical hair-splitting that was quite intolerable despite her high intelligence. She was unmarried, but was having a love affair which, except for her hypersensitivity, was perfectly normal. Before she came to me, she had been treated by an analyst for two months with no success. Then she went to a woman analyst, who broke off the treatment at the end of a week. I was the third. She felt she was one of those who were doomed to fail in analysis, and she came to me with pronounced feelings of inferiority. She didn't know why

> it hadn't worked with the other analysts. I got her to tell me her somewhat lengthy anamnesis, which took several consulting hours.[7]

Jung mentioned that she had two analysts before him and he described the problem in the first analysis was due to the inability of the doctor to interpret a dream Reichstein had had, in which she needed to cross a frontier, did not find the way to do it and got lost in the dark. For Jung, it was a failure of the doctor to identify the unconscious state of identity in the treatment. Jung added:

> As a matter of fact, a few years later this analyst gave up psychotherapy altogether because of too many failures and personal involvements.[8]

Concerning the problems of the second treatment, which lasted for one week, Jung mentioned:

> Early in the second treatment, the dream of the frontier was repeated in the following form: *She had arrived at the same frontier station. She had to find the crossing, and she saw, despite the darkness, a little light in the distance showing where the place was. In order to get there, she had to go through a wooded valley in pitch-blackness. She plucked up her courage and went ahead. But hardly had she entered the wood than she felt somebody clinging to her, and she knew it was her analyst.* She awoke in terror. This analyst, too, later gave up her profession for very much the same reasons.[9]

It was not possible to identify the names of the two analysts. Yet, considering the treatment of Reichstein's sister, it is possible that the analysts, as in the case of Mischa Epper, were Maria Moltzer and Thomas Hämmerli. This hypothesis is particularly probable concerning Moltzer, because Moltzer and Reichstein had the same mother tongue (Dutch). Unfortunately, no documents to check this hypothesis on the treatments she had before Jung were found up to this date. In his text from 1937, Jung described how initially his treatment was not successful. The turning point came as he connected Reichstein's symptoms with the Eastern symbolism of the Kundalini yoga, which led to the positive development of the case.

A third presentation of her case was also given by Jung in 1950, in 'Concerning Mandala Symbolism', a text based on a seminar Jung delivered in Berlin in 1930. Jung presented three of her paintings, in the text drawings no. 7, 8 and 9, and gave the following comments on them:

> Figure 7 – Flower motif with cross in the centre. The square, too, is arranged like a flower. The four faces at the corners correspond to the four cardinal points, which are often depicted as four deities. Here they have a demonic character. This may be connected with the fact that the patient was born

in the Dutch East Indies, where she sucked up the peculiar local demonology with the mother's milk of her native ayah. Her numerous drawings all had a distinctly Eastern character, and thereby helped her to assimilate influences that at first could not be reconciled with her Western mentality. [. . .] Brought up in the East Indies until her sixth year, she came later into a conventional European milieu, and this had a devastating effect on the flowerlike quality of her Eastern spirit and caused a prolonged psychic trauma. Under treatment her native world, long submerged, came up again in these drawings, bringing with it psychic recovery.

Figure 8 – The flowerlike development has got stronger and is beginning to overgrow the 'demonishness' of the faces.

Figure 9 – A later stage is shown here. Minute care in the draughtsmanship vies with richness of colour and form. From this, we can discern not only the extraordinary concentration of the patient but the triumph of Eastern 'flowerlikeness' over the demon of Western intellectualism, rationalism.[10] (See Figure 14.1.)

From Jung's preceding texts we can conclude that in presenting her case he focused on the impact caused by Reichstein's birth in the East, and saw it as the main cause for her disturbance and lack of adaptation. He stated that only after he became acquainted with Eastern symbolism was it possible for him to understand and treat the case properly. I will discuss Jung's presentations of her case in relation to the topics mentioned in the subsequent chapters.

FIGURE 14.1 Mandala figure no. 9[11] (See Plate 1)

Notes

1 A short version of this text was published in an article in the *Journal of Analytical Psychology*. See de Moura, 2014.
2 PA – Document no. 8, Jung–Reichstein Letters.
3 Shamdasani, ed., 1996.
4 Ibid., pp. 104–106.
5 Ibid.
6 Woodroffe, 2003.
7 Jung, 1937, par. 546, CW 16.
8 Ibid., par. 546.
9 Ibid., par. 547.
10 Jung, 1950b, pars. 657–659, CW 9i.
11 Copyright by Foundation C.G. Jung and C.G. Jung Institute – Zürich.

References

de Moura, V. (2014) "Learning from the patient: The East, synchronicity and transference in the history of an unknown case of C.G. Jung" in *Journal of Analytical Psychology* 59:391–409.

Jung, C.G. (1937) "The realities of practical psychotherapy" in *The Collected Works of C.G. Jung* (London: Routledge), 1993, vol. 16.

——— (1950b) "Concerning mandala symbolism" in *The Collected Works of C.G. Jung* (London: Routledge), 1991, vol. 9i.

Shamdasani, S., ed. (1996) *The Psychology of Kundalini Yoga: Notes of the Seminar Given in 1932 by C.G. Jung* (London: Routledge).

Woodroffe, J. (2003) *The Serpent Power* (Madras: Ganesh and Co.).

15

REICHSTEIN'S CASE AND JUNG'S CONCEPTS OF TRANSFERENCE AND COUNTERTRANSFERENCE

After 1914, Jung went on differentiating his understanding of the concepts of transference and countertransference, which is vital in analytical treatment. Freud, who published his papers about it mainly between 1911 and 1915,[1] suggested that transference and countertransference are primarily related to the patient: the doctor got the projection of the patient's former important relationships (transference), and he was affected by it unconsciously (countertransference). Freud recommended analysis for the analyst and argued that the doctor must become aware of this phenomenon.

For Jung, however, there was a mutual collaboration in the analytical relationship. He wrote in 1929:

> For two personalities to meet is like mixing two different chemical substances; if there is any combination at all, both are transformed. In any effective psychological treatment the doctor is bound to influence the patient; but this influence can only take place if the patient has a reciprocal influence on the doctor. [. . .] It is futile for the doctor to shield himself from the influence of the patient and to surround himself with a smoke-screen of fatherly and professional authority.[2]

Two years later, in 1931, Jung mentioned the dream of a patient in a lecture named 'The Practical Use of Dream-Analysis', published in 1933, to illustrate how dreams can reflect the attitude of the patient to the doctor.[3] Four years later, he would discuss the reciprocal influence of patients and doctors in a series of five lectures known as the Tavistock Lectures, which he held in London between September and October 1935. In these lectures, he talked about his understanding of psychology, which was for him a science concerned with consciousness and the products of the unconscious; presented some of his concepts and mentioned the differences and similarities between his and Freud's approach. In the fourth lecture, Jung said the following:

> I consider my contribution to psychology to be my subjective confession. It is my personal psychology, my prejudice that I see psychological facts as I do. I admit that I see things in such and such a way. But I expect Freud and Adler to do the same and confess that their ideas are their subjective point of view. So far as we admit our personal prejudice, we are really contributing towards an objective psychology.[4]

Jung's comment pointed out that he had his individual view of psychology and that the analyst cannot be free of his personal views in treating the patient. Therefore, in his understanding, the ideas, values and personality of the analyst have a major influence on the psychological treatment.

Later, in May 1937, during a lecture entitled 'The Realities of Practical Psychotherapy' in Bern, Switzerland, Jung postulated the differences between two ways of treatment. In the first, the doctor followed one specific method, in which the individuality 'would mean little more than a disturbance of the method employed'.[5] In the second, he described a way of treatment in the form of analysis, which never followed a typical course. The first method was successful when 'the premises of the method coincide with the problematical situations of the patient'.[6] For the doctor convinced by this art of working, failures in the treatment would be considered as failures of the patient. Jung, however, stated that he preferred the second way of working, staying away from methods and diagnoses, working with a minimum of prior assumptions, because 'the assumption that I myself am will determine my method: as I am, so will I proceed'.[7] These statements clearly indicate Jung's opinion of how his own personality was the base for the treatment he offered to his patients. He called his approach a dialectical procedure, an encounter between his premises and those of the patient.

In his lecture from 1937, Jung made a particularly important remark about treatment which came to a standstill or was discontinued due to problems in the process of transference–countertransference (Jung wrote about an unconscious identification) and added 'this state of unconscious identity is also the reason why an analyst can help his patient just so far as he himself has gone and not a step further'.[8] He added that the lack of knowledge from the analyst would have exactly the same effect as unconsciousness.

The case Jung used in 1931 in 'The Practical Use of Dream-Analysis' to illustrate how dreams can mirror the attitude of the patient to the doctor, and the case in 1937 in 'The Realities of Practical Psychotherapy', to illustrate his postulations on the mutual influence between the patient and the doctor, which was not previously identified, were both based on the case of Reichstein. As mentioned, formerly he presented the case of a woman who had been unsuccessfully treated by two analysts before she came to see him and described the dreams of the patient and her symptoms, which he did not understand. The treatment with

Jung was also unsatisfactory, and he was bored. His description of the event went on as follows:

> Once I lost patience with her because I felt she wasn't making any effort. 'So here are the personal reactions coming out', I thought. The following night I *dreamt that I was walking along a country road at the foot of a steep hill. On the hill was a castle with a high tower. Sitting on the parapet of the topmost pinnacle was a woman, golden in the light of the evening sun. In order to see her properly, I had to bend my head so far back that I woke up with a crick in the neck.* I realised to my amazement that the woman was my patient. The dream was distinctly disturbing, for the first thing that came into my head while dozing was the verse from Schenkenbach's 'Reiterlied':
>
> She sits so high above us, no prayer will she refuse.
>
> This is an invocation to the Virgin Mary. The dream had put my patient on the highest peak, making her a goddess, while I, to say the least, had been looking down on her. The next day I said to her: 'Haven't you noticed that our work is stuck in the doldrums?' She burst into tears and said: course I've noticed it. I know I always fail and never do anything right. You were my last hope and now this isn't going to work either'. I interrupted her: 'This time it is different. I've had a dream about you'. And I told her the dream, with the result that the superficial symptomatology, her argumentativeness, her insistence on always being right, and her touchiness vanished.[9]

Jung understood his dream as compensation for his attitude of looking down at her. It was an important turning point in her treatment, which made him look at her in a new light. But this was not the only dream Jung had with Reichstein that shows that he was caught in countertransference with her. In an unpublished letter from the 7th of December 1926 Jung wrote the following:

> My dear Mrs Reichstein
>
> Three weeks ago, I had an unsettling dream about you (a day before you should have come). Then you did not come, [. . .] you did not come either. [. . .] nothing bad happened. Please, let me know soon, what happened. I am seriously worried about you.
>
> With best regards
>
> Yours faithfully
>
> Dr. Jung.[10]

From this note, it is clear that Jung had a genuine interest in Reichstein's condition and that he at least occasionally communicated his dreams to her. It shows that in the analysis with Reichstein, Jung acted as he postulated theoretically in the countertransference, namely, that both analyst and patient interact with their full personalities. The case of Reichstein shows Jung's development of his understanding of the process of the transference–countertransference. His dream led him to evaluate his approach to the case and to assume a different attitude towards her. But not only his 'looking down on her' changed, he considered his lack of knowledge as also causing troubles in the treatment. He took the mutual influence as an element in the search for understanding the process in both the patient and himself.

Mischa Epper was present in the audience at the lecture Jung delivered in May 1937. She took notes of his presentation and much later, in a letter dated the 13th of March 1963,[11] she sent her notes of Jung's presentation to Reichstein. Epper underlined the passages which seemed especially important to her, which were mostly related to the individual character of the psychological illness, and, in the case of Reichstein, the fantasies, which Jung did not understand until he had read Avalon's work on Kundalini yoga. For Jung, the oriental background in Reichstein's life was one of the most interesting factors in her treatment, because it called forth his attention and, as we will see, led him to deepen his studies of the relationship between Eastern and Western psychology.

Notes

1 Leitner, 2001, p. 209.
2 Jung, 1929a, par.163, CW 16.
3 Jung, 1933a, pars. 307–311, CW 16.
4 Jung, 1935a, par. 275, CW 18.
5 Jung. 1937, par. 542 CW 16.
6 Ibid.
7 Ibid., par. 543.
8 Ibid., par. 545.
9 Ibid., pars. 549–551.
10 PA – Document no. 7, Jung–Reichstein Letters. Parts of this letter are lacerated.
11 PA – Document no. 4, Jung–Reichstein Letters.

References

Jung, C.G. (1929a) "The problems of modern psychotherapy" in *The Collected Works of C.G. Jung* (London: Routledge), 1993, vol. 16.

——— (1933a) "The practical use of dream-analysis" in *The Collected Works of C.G. Jung* (London: Routledge), 1993, vol. 16.

——— (1935a) "Analytical psychology: Its theory and practice; The Tavistock Lectures" in *The Collected Works of C.G. Jung* (London: Routledge), 1993, vol. 18.

——— (1937) "The realities of practical psychotherapy" in *The Collected Works of C.G. Jung* (London: Routledge), 1993, vol. 16.

Leitner, M. (2001) *Ein gut gehütetes Geheimnis: die Geschichte der psychoanalytischen Behandlungstechnik von den Anfängen in Wien bis zur Gründung der Berliner Poliklinik im Jahr 1920* (Giessen: Psychosozial-Verlag).

16

REICHSTEIN'S CASE AND JUNG'S UNDERSTANDING OF EASTERN AND WESTERN PSYCHOLOGY

In 1928, Jung began to work on the psychological commentary of the Chinese treatise 'The Secret of the Golden Flower' with the sinologist Richard Wilhelm. At that time, Jung was unsatisfied with the extent to which he had managed to substantiate his claims about the collective unconscious and his efforts seemed to be inconclusive. In the work with the text just mentioned, Jung saw an opportunity to find historical support for his ideas. He mentioned that when he received the text from Wilhelm it did not seem of any importance to him that, besides being a Taoist text, it was also an alchemist treatise. He declared that it was only later that he made the connection between the text and the processes of the collective unconscious that he had observed in the modern man. Jung emphasised that the text put him on the right track.[1]

In his commentary, Jung wrote that the scientific mind of the West had its own merits, but a scientific approach alone was not enough to properly understand the wisdom present in the text. It was genuine and had grown out of the Eastern way of life and its deepest instincts, rooted in the ancient cultural life of China. Therefore, it was inaccessible to people in the West and impossible to imitate. Jung considered that the problem regarding a proper understanding of the text was rooted in the intellectual one-sidedness of the Western mind. For him, the Eastern way of thinking, as presented by the principles of Yin and Yang and the search for balance between the polarities, was 'a sign of cultural advance, a widening of consciousness beyond the narrow confines of a tyrannical intellect'.[2]

The one-sidedness was important for the development of the intellect in the West, but this development happened with too much focus on reason. Consciousness became relatively independent from instinctual behaviour, but, acquiring more independence, it suffered from *hybris mit y*, i.e., an inflation which had led to a psychic collapse. The collapse manifested itself in the form of a breakdown, felt in the psyche as an irreconcilable conflict. It could only be solved by considering both the conscious and the unconscious elements. Jung saw in the Eastern approach, in its conciliation between the opposites, a parallel attitude which could lead to a new level of consciousness and to a new perspective on the conflict. However, this new perspective was not to be attained through rational thinking. The psychic development expressed itself in symbols, and these also had effects on the person who has experienced them.[3] The symbol of the union of the opposites would mainly appear in the shape of a mandala, such as the golden flower in the original Chinese text.

In the biography of Jung's pupil Peter Baynes, alias Helton Godwin Baynes, who was an analytical psychologist and translated some of Jung's work, it is mentioned how Jung's interest in Eastern psychology began. In a dialogue between Baynes and Jung, in which they were discussing the influence of the anima, the conversation about this issue was presented as follows:

> Jung made a very fine contribution to appease the storm (a relationship Baynes had with a woman) and got the thing on the level again. He told of how he had himself been caught by a countertransference to a beautiful aristocratic girl and how he had a dream in which she was enthroned very high on an Eastern temple, high above him. And this explained how all his knowledge and interest in Oriental ideas and feelings had developed out of his transference to the girl. He had, as he said, to cut off his head and learn to submit his ignorance to his patient.[4]

The countertransference process in which Jung was caught was the case of Reichstein. But before presenting Reichstein's role in the development of Jung's relation to the East, it is necessary to critically consider the quotation mentioned before that 'all his knowledge and interest in Oriental ideas and feelings had developed out of the transference to the girl'.

As illustrated in his publications, Jung's interest in Eastern ideas existed before 1919, i.e., before his first meeting with Reichstein. He demonstrated it by using Eastern mythology to amplify the symbols related to the symbolism of the mother figure and to rebirth in his *Transformations and Symbols of the Libido* from 1912, in which he mentioned the Chinese and the Hindu mythologies.

Another example was mentioned in the seminar given in 1925. Jung described that during his time as a practitioner at the Burghölzli between 1900 and 1909 he dreamt of a medieval house, where he went down to the cellar and found the entrance to a cave, in which he uncovered prehistoric pottery and bones. He mentioned that he was impressed by the dream and searched for where archaeological excavations were being made. However, he noted:

> But of course that did not satisfy me. My thoughts then beginning to turn to the East, I began to read about excavations being made in Babylonia. My

> interest went to books, and I came upon a German book called *Mythology and Symbolism.*[5]

Furthermore, in one of Jung's fantasies portrayed in *The Red Book* there is also evidence which suggests an interest in the Eastern attitude of searching for balance between the opposites. In the humorous dialogue between Ammonius and the red one (the old monk and the devil) it is possible to recognise the attempt to find balance between the opposites in Jung's fantasy, and in the following passage he made an interesting remark, possibly related to the Eastern attitude. Jung wrote:

> I am alone, but I fill my solitariness with my life. I am man enough, I am noise, conversation, comfort, and help enough unto myself. And so I wander to the Far East. Not that I know anything about what my distant goal might be. I see blue horizons before me: they suffice as a goal. I hurry toward the East and my rising – I will my rising.[6]

Jung also noted that even before the meeting with R. Wilhelm he had been interested in oriental philosophy and around 1920 had begun experimenting with the *I Ching.*[7]

The preceding passages point to Jung's general interest in Eastern mythology. But from the conversation mentioned in Jansen's book, it is clear that the material that Jung faced in Reichstein's case fuelled his interest.

In 1932, in his seminars on Kundalini yoga, Jung's interest was specifically focused on the parallels between the process of awakening Kundalini and his postulations on the individuation process. As mentioned before, the case he used to illustrate it was the case of Reichstein. He understood her symptoms and the images in her dreams symbolically, relating them to the activation of the chakras. However, Jung was of the opinion that people in the West did not have the patience to follow the process described in the yoga tradition, and that this path was not appropriate for the Western mind.

In 'Yoga and the West' (1936) Jung wrote about the physiological and philosophical aspects of yoga and considered it a method developed and embedded in Eastern tradition for over four thousand years, a period in which the necessary spiritual conditions were created. For Western people, the practice of yoga could even be considered dangerous, because it could lead the practitioner to get lost in foreign symbolism and bring him close to madness. Jung believed that, in the course of the centuries, the West would produce its own kind of yoga. Interesting to note, however, is that during his self-experiment Jung practised yoga to calm down his emotions, when he realised that he was too impressed by the images.[8]

According to Jung, the highly scientific and severe criticism of the philosophical ideas of the Western mind led to a disposition that separated religion and science and therefore important concepts of yoga were not accurately understood, for 'either it falls into the trap of faith and swallows concepts like prana, atman, chakra, samadhi etc., without giving them a thought, or its scientific critique repudiates them one and all as "pure mysticism"'.[9] Mentioning, for instance, the understanding of the concept of *prana*, which literally means *breath*, he affirmed that the Western mind would understand it in a completely different way than the Eastern mind. For a yogi, *prana* expresses much more than just *breath*, because it is related to the rich metaphysics and symbolisms of the East. In this way 'the European only imitates and learns ideas by rote, and is therefore incapable of expressing his subjective facts through Indian concepts'.[10]

The crucial point in Jung's criticism, therefore, is *who* is applying the method. In his final remarks in the text of 1936, he stated:

> If I remain so critically averse to yoga, it does not mean that I do not regard this spiritual achievement of the East as one of the greatest things the human mind has ever created. I hope my exposition makes it clear that my criticism is directed solely against the application of yoga to the peoples of the West. [. . .] Western civilization is scarcely a thousand years old and must first of all free itself from its barbarous one-sidedness. This means, above all, deeper insight into the nature of man. But no insight is gained by repressing and controlling the unconscious, and least of all by imitating methods which have grown up under totally different psychological conditions.[11]

Jung was also sceptical towards movements which combined Western and Eastern traditions, such as Theosophy and Anthroposophy, movements which were very popular in the beginning of the 20th century. One of the main figures of the movement in Switzerland and Germany was Rudolf Steiner (1861–1925). His teachings were basically a generous amalgam of Indian mysticism and sublimated Christian values and symbolism, seeking a higher truth beyond rationality. Steiner used concepts introduced by German philosophers and authors such as Hegel, Kant, Goethe and Nietzsche's cult of life, with a conservative German background. In his writings, he presented what he considered the truth of the spiritual world against materialism, and he had answers to everything which happened in one's life.[12] These movements were considered by Jung as a result of the religious disorientation in modern society, an 'amateurish, indeed barbarous imitation of the East'.[13] For Jung, the only difference between the materialistic and the theosophical view of the world was that the first reduces everything to physiology, whereas theosophy reduces everything to Indian metaphysics.[14]

In Jung's description of Reichstein's case in the seminar of 1932, he postulated that her rebellious attitude towards European conventions was the result of her unconscious assimilation of the experiences during her childhood in the East. Therefore, the crucial point from the preceding notes is Jung's postulation that Reichstein's psychic conflicts were related to her difficulties in adapting the European mentality to her Eastern background.

It is correct that Reichstein herself considered that her birth in the East had partially influenced her character. But Jung's presentation of the case must be considered critically. As described in the notes on her story, Reichstein's rebellious youth was marked by the conflicts between her and other members of the family, and her emancipated attitude in the aristocratic surroundings. Emancipation and the movement for women's rights were among the most important movements in Europe in the turn of the 19th to the 20th century. They changed the very core of society, namely, the relationship between men and women. At the end of the 19th century, women activists fought for their rights and brought women's emancipation to public debate. Women began to assume roles which were typically occupied by men. The most important feminist movement in those days was the fight for women's right to vote, and women who went to the streets for their civil rights and for participation in the political decisions were called suffragettes. Women's growing assertiveness and political engagement put men's understanding of masculinity and of their role in society in question. Throughout Europe, women were having fewer children and were increasing their participation in work outside the home. As women became more assertive and earned money, their economic dependence on men consequentially changed, and as a result, the traditional role of men as the breadwinners for the family was fundamentally questioned. With machines assuming most of the heavy work and women becoming independent, many men were increasingly confronted in their role in the society.[15] Therefore, it can be postulated that Reichstein's attitude was also part of the spirit of the time in Europe, of the *zeitgeist* present in the women's movement for emancipation as well as the opposition to aristocracy in the beginning of the century. Jung, however, did not consider these aspects of Reichstein's story in the presentation of her case, and postulated that her Eastern background was the main point in the aetiology of her illness.

Besides, Reichstein's rebellion was against the aristocratic milieu in which she lived. She believed that the psychic illness of her sister was caused by the repressive and dull ambiance of her surroundings. As we know, Reichstein's family was very aristocratic and the role of aristocracy around those days allows us to grasp an important aspect of her background. Until around the 1870s, except for France and smaller republican nations, such as Switzerland and the Netherlands, the political decisions in the most influential countries were taken mainly by noblemen of monarchies. By the turn of the 19th to the 20th century, however, the *status quo* in politics was changing rapidly. All over Europe, the influence of aristocracy, which until then had significant political and economic power, was undergoing a rapid change.[16]

Another important element in Reichstein's story, which was not mentioned in Jung's description of her case in the seminar of 1932, was the passage in which he wrote 'that out of her genital organs came a white elephant. (. . .) Then organic symptoms appeared: she had ulcers in the womb, and I had to send her to a gynaecologist'.[17] As mentioned earlier, Jung associated the white elephant with Eastern symbolism, but we know from her story that Reichstein's mother had a severe problem during the birth of Mischa Epper, the cause of her fragile condition and of her death in 1908. In her sister's notes about their childhood, it was described how Reichstein had strong anxiety states after the comment of her husband mentioning the birth of a child of one of his colleagues. The idea of giving birth was distressful for Reichstein, to which she reacted with panic attacks. She had strong anxiety when she became pregnant despite the use of a contraceptive method and she told her father and his new wife that she thought of her pregnancy as if it were a tumour in her belly. Mrs Lunin mentioned in the interview with the author that her mother discovered the positive feelings of motherhood only in her second pregnancy. The prolapse of her mother and her absence in her childhood were crucial turning points in Reichstein's life, and the importance of these personal facts was not mentioned in Jung's interpretation of her symptoms and fantasies.

Like in the cases of Helene Preiswerk and Frank Miller, Jung highlighted some elements to support his theorising and did not mention others. These were, nevertheless, important biographical elements for the understanding of the cases.

The problem of doing amplification without considering the personal story of the patient was stressed by Fordham in 1967 in his paper on active imagination. He wrote about the importance of considering the events during childhood once using Jung's method of amplification, because only then the symbolism in the case can be properly understood. Historical parallels can be supportive for the patient, indicating that he is not alone in his experience, but the meaning gained out of it is fragile. After presenting the case material Fordham writes:

> All the cases showed that it was essential to relate the patient to his personal and individual development from birth onwards. Concurrently with using the historical analogic method went a blind spot about the personal history, a feature to be observed in the literature; there is also to be found an inability to scrutinise the patient's imagery so that the roots of the symbolism are ignored. [. . .] Here the symbol becomes used defensively and the concept of the objective psyche gives support to defences against the reconstruction and integration of those parts of infancy and childhood without which the patient is more or less at a loss.[18]

Although in his writings Jung did not mention the illness of Reichstein's mother in relation to her symptoms, it does not necessarily mean that he did not consider these elements of her story during her treatment. Unfortunately, Reichstein's diary of her analysis was not found up to this date, and it was not possible to evaluate the approach which Jung took to these issues.

One of the techniques which Jung used in the treatment of her symptoms was constituted by drawings. His suggestion to Reichstein to draw can be related to his own self-experimentation and, as seen in other cases, became one of his most used psychotherapeutic techniques. His understanding of her symptoms and the use of drawings in Reichstein's case can be seen in the following passage:

> Psychologically, the symptom meant that something had to be 'ex-pressed'. So I gave her the task of expressing by drawings whatever her hand suggested to her. She had never drawn before, and set about it with much doubt and hesitation. But now symmetrical flowers took shape under her hand, vividly coloured and arranged in symbolic patterns. She made these pictures with great care and with a concentration I can only call devout.[19]

Reichstein's devotion to her drawings and embroideries was emphasised by her daughter too. The family has a kimono in silk on which Reichstein worked almost daily for four years. Mrs Lunin mentioned that her mother made embroidery in a kind of meditative state.

Jung observed that the symbolism in Reichstein's drawings had an Eastern character, and in his description of the case he mentioned the image of the bird descending into the fontanelle coming from above (Figure 16.1).

However, Jung's comment that she never drew before is not correct, because from her story we know that Reichstein enjoyed copying the work of Flemish masters. Furthermore, he wrote mistakenly in 'The Secret of the Golden Flower'

FIGURE 16.1 Bird in the fontanelle[20] (See Plate 2)

about her drawings that 'All the pictures were done independently of any Eastern influence'.[21] As we know from Reichstein's case, this is not correct, since Reichstein lived in the East until about the age of four and Jung himself noted in his text 'Concerning Mandala Symbolism', 'her numerous drawings all had a distinctively Eastern character, and thereby helped her to assimilate influences that at first could not be reconciled with the Western mentality'.[22]

Another interesting aspect of the connection of Reichstein with the East can be seen in her later correspondence with Jung. Around 1957, Reichstein reviewed a book on the Indonesian religion from S.H. Rakosa for Jung. Rakosa mentioned Jung's ideas in the book, but he considered that the author misunderstood him as a philosopher. In the only published letter to Reichstein from the 2nd of August 1957, Jung expressed his criticism of the book and of the Eastern philosophy being applied to the Western mind as follows:

> Dear Dr. Reichstein
>
> Thank you very much for the great trouble you have taken in working through Sumantri Hardjo Rakosa's book on 'The Conception of Man in Indonesian Religion as a Basis for Psychotherapy', and for furnishing such a clear report of its contents. [. . .] You are right in supposing that the author hasn't grasped much of my thinking. [. . .] He mistakes me as a philosopher, which I am quite definitively not. I am a psychologist and an empiricist, and for me the meaning of life does not lie in annulling it for the sake of an alleged 'possibility of transcendental existence', which nobody knows how to envisage. We are men and not gods. The meaning of human development is to be found in the fulfilment of this life. [. . .] And not in detachment of this world. How can I fulfil the meaning of my life if the goal I set myself is the 'disappearance of individual consciousness'? [. . .] Even what I have called 'self' functions only by the virtue of an ego which hears the voice of that greater being. I fear I have saddled you with a thankless task in working through this book. That you have discharged it with such a patience and lucidity was a very great help.
>
> With best regards,
>
> yours sincerely
>
> C.G Jung[23]

Finally, Jung gave attention to one symbol in Eastern tradition, the mandala, and he used Reichstein's drawings as examples. In Sanskrit, mandala means 'circle' or 'magic circle'. The mandala is commonly painted in a regular schema: a geometrical form, like a square or triangle, surrounded by a circle. Paintings in the shape of mandalas have been found in all cultures and religions, in many variations. For Jung, the mandala is a symbol of unity, totality, of the union of the opposites, as well as compensation for chaos and confusion. It is interesting to note that Jung deepened his understanding of mandalas only after 1920,[24] i.e., contemporaneous to Reichstein's treatment. As presented before, some of her mandalas were published by Jung in 'Concerning Mandala Symbolism' (Figs. 7, 8 and 9),[25] in 'Commentary on "the Secret of the Golden Flower"' (Fig. A1)[26] and in the 'The Philosophical Tree' (Figs. 2, 30 and 31).[27]

As mentioned before, Reichstein's case was known in some circles as the 'Mandala Lady'. She wrote a text explaining what the process of drawing was like and it was supposedly written for an exhibition.[28] Although the text and the mandalas are not dated, she described how she drew the mandalas approximately 45 years ago. Based on Reichstein's description, the drawings were probably made during the time she was in analysis with Jung (around 1920).

Reichstein wrote that when she drew her mandalas, Jung was at the beginning of his discovery of the collective unconscious, and she did not accept his comments about her drawings for personal reasons. She described how she had difficulties in dealing with the negative experiences in her youth and had sought refuge in the philosophy of Schopenhauer, Kant and Hartmann. However, she was so centred on her rational thinking that she felt completely dried out and she could no longer go on with her life in the same fashion. She decided then to allow herself to be completely passive, receptive to the images from her unconscious, and accept whatever would come out of it. Her condition improved only after she gave up her overinvestment in the intellectual side and allowed herself to be led by her inner instincts.

Considering Jung's specific interest in Reichstein's case related to Eastern symbolism we can summarise it as follows: in *Transformation and Symbols of the Libido* (1912), while analysing the case of Ms Frank Miller, Jung was interested in the parallels between fantasies and the primordial images present in different mythologies, but he did not treat Miller personally. Then, in his self-experimentation, Jung focused on his subjective experiences and saw parallels between his fantasies and Eastern ideas. Reichstein's case was, in fact, one of the first cases which gave him the possibility of treating a modern patient linked to the symbolism of the East.

Interesting to note is that the overwhelming influence of rationalism and its relation to the instincts and irrationality were elements that Jung considered crucial in his analyses of Reichstein's case and in other cases like those of Morgan and Pauli. These elements were also crucial in Jung's self-experiment. As mentioned in the case of Miller, Jung considered that whilst analysing her fantasies, he was also analysing his own fantasy-function, and that in his elaboration of Miller's morbidity into myths he assimilated the Miller side of himself. One may postulate that Jung's understanding of the conflict between the rational and the irrational in Reichstein's and other cases was possibly the result of his considerations for himself, out of the insights he gained from his self-experiment.

Notes

1 Jung, 1929b, p. 4, CW 13.
2 Ibid., par. 7.
3 Ibid., par. 31.

4 Baynes-Jansen, 2003, pp. 244–245. See also Shamdasani, 1996, p. xxv.
5 McGuire, 1990, p. 23.
6 Shamdasani, ed., 2009, p. 277.
7 Jaffé, ed., 1989, p. 373.
8 Protocols, p. 381
9 Jung, 1936, par .867, CW 11.
10 Ibid., par. 872.
11 Ibid., par. 876.
12 Blom, 2008, pp. 208–215.
13 Jung, 1931, par. 188, CW 10.
14 Jung, 1921, par. 594, CW 6.
15 Blom, 2008, pp. 219–248.
16 Ibid., pp. 92–121.
17 Shamdasani, ed., 1996, p. 105.
18 Fordham, 1967, p. 62.
19 Jung, 1937, par. 553, CW16.
20 PA – Picture 019-ASAB. Copyright by the C.G. Jung Institute – Zürich.
21 Jung, 1929b, par. 56, CW13.
22 Jung, 1950b, par. 656, CW 9i.
23 Adler, ed., 1975, p. 381.
24 Shamdasani, ed., 2009, p. 206.
25 Jung, 1950b, CW 9i.
26 Jung, 1929b, CW 13.
27 Jung, 1954a, CW 13.
28 PA – Document no. 44, Jung–Reichstein Letters. The information about the exhibition was given to the author in an interview with V. Lunin, Reichstein's daughter, on 21.06.2011.

References

Adler, G. ed. (1975) *C.G. Jung: Letters vol. 2 1951–1961* (Princeton, NJ: Princeton University Press).

Baynes-Jansen, D. (2003) *Jung's Apprentice: A Biography of Helton Godwin Baynes* (Einsiedeln: Daimon Verlag).

Blom, P. (2008) *The Vertigo Years: Europe, 1900–1914* (New York: Basic Books).

Fordham, M. (1967) "Active imagination: Deintegration or disintegration?" in *The Journal of Analytical Psychology* Jan;12:51–66.

Jaffé, A., ed. (1989) *Memories, Dreams, Reflections, by C.G. Jung* (New York: Vintage Books).

Jung, C.G. (1921) "Psychological types" in *The Collected Works of C.G. Jung* (London: Routledge), 1989, vol. 6.

——— (1929b) "Commentary on *The Secret of the Golden Flower*" in *The Collected Works of C.G. Jung* (London and Henley: Routledge & Kegan Paul), 1981, vol. 13.

——— (1931) "The spiritual problem of modern man" in *The Collected Works of C.G. Jung* (London Routledge), 1991, vol. 10.

——— (1936) "Yoga and the west" in *The Collected Works of C.G. Jung* (London: Routledge), 1991, vol. 11.

——— (1937) "The realities of practical psychotherapy" in *The Collected Works of C.G. Jung* (London Routledge), 1993, vol. 16.

——— (1950b) "Concerning mandala symbolism" in *The Collected Works of C.G. Jung* (London: Routledge), 1991, vol. 9i.

——— (1954a) "The philosophical tree" in *The Collected Works of C.G. Jung* (London and Henley: Routledge & Kegan Paul), 1981, vol. 13.

McGuire, W. (1990) *C.G. Jung: Analytical Psychology Notes of the Seminar Given in 1925* (London: Routledge).

Shamdasani, S., ed. (1996) *The Psychology of Kundalini Yoga: Notes of the Seminar Given in 1932 by C.G. Jung* (London: Routledge).

———, ed. (2009) *The Red Book: Liber Novus/C.G. Jung* (New York: Norton & Company).

17

REICHSTEIN'S CASE AND SYNCHRONICITY

In a passage in *Memories, Dreams, Reflections*, Jung wrote about phenomena, which called his attention as follows:

> Time and again I encountered amazing coincidences which seemed to suggest the idea of an acausal parallelism (a synchronicity, as I later called it). So fascinated was I by these experiments that I altogether forgot to take notes, which I afterward greatly regretted. Later, however, when I often used to carry out the experiment with my patients, it became quite clear that a significant number of answers did indeed hit the mark.[1]

Nevertheless, Jung also experienced events in his life which he considered as acausal parallelisms between the events and his psychic condition. One example was the well-known passage about his conversation with Freud in 1909 about occultism, in which they talked about precognition and parapsychology in general. Jung described how Freud's materialistic view of the world disturbed him and he had a hot physical sensation in his diaphragm. Shortly after a loud report in the bookcase alarmed them. Jung then affirmed it was a so-called catalytic exteriorization phenomenon and predicted that it would occur again, what indeed happened.[2]

Another example, as mentioned before, was in 1913 when he was overwhelmed by the events he did not understand and he initially thought that he was in the process of developing a psychic disturbance. But after the outbreak of the First World War, he considered his visions as precognitions. He commented:

> As a psychiatrist I became worried, wondering if I was not on the way to 'doing schizophrenia', as we said in the language of those days. [. . .] On July 31st, immediately after my lecture, I learned from the newspapers that

> war had broken out. Finally I understood. And when I disembarked in Holland on the next day, nobody was happier than I. Now I was sure that no schizophrenia was threatening me. I understood that my dreams and my visions came to me from the subsoil of the collective unconscious. What remained for me to do now was to deepen and validate this discovery.[3]

Therefore, after the outbreak of war, Jung took his fantasies not as something that would happen to him, but to Europe, and considered that his fantasies were precognitive of a collective event.[4] As mentioned before, because precognition is included in his postulations on synchronicity, it is possible that Jung may have considered the event with Freud in 1909 and visions and dreams he had around 1913 and 1914 in the elaboration of a concept referring to acausal parallelisms.[5]

The concept of synchronicity is one that challenges traditional scientific thinking. It does so because synchronistic events, by definition, do not fall within the principle of causality, cannot be repeated and therefore are impossible to replicate. The term is used (and misused) by many, and it is highly controversial. Jung postulated the concept in his seminars in 1928 and in his memorial address for Richard Wilhelm in 1930.[6] However, only much later, in 1952, did he publish on the concept in his article 'Synchronicity: an acausal connecting principle'[7] in the German volume of the '*Studien aus dem C.G. Jung Institut – Zürich – Naturerklärung und Psyche*'.[8] He proposed the concept of synchronicity as an acausal principle connecting two or more simultaneous events, where meaning is the linking factor. His definition of synchronicity runs as follows:

> I am therefore using the general concept of synchronicity in the special sense of a coincidence in time of two or more causally unrelated events which have the same or similar meaning, in contrast to 'synchronism' which simply means the simultaneous occurrence of two events. Synchronicity therefore means the simultaneous occurrence of a certain psychic state with one or more external events which appear as meaningful parallels to the momentary subjective state and, in certain cases, vice-versa.[9]

Jung wrote that he considered three categories for the phenomena. The first category was a correspondence of a psychic state in the observer with an external event in which a causal relationship was not conceivable; the second, a more or less simultaneous event perceived by the observer but outside his field of perception and only verifiable afterwards; and the third, a psychic state corresponding to a future event, which, likewise was only open to verification afterwards.[10]

Jung's three categories of the phenomena could be related to the fields of research in parapsychology. For instance, Jung's first category could be linked to cases of telepathy, the second category could be linked to remote viewing (also known as remote perception) and the third category to cases of precognition.

Jung's delay in publishing his ideas on synchronicity was possibly due to his awareness of the difficulties that such a concept would evoke. In the foreword to the text he referred to the great difficulties of the problem and its presentation. He considered the field, although obscure, of foremost importance and that his presentation was an attempt to present the problem and reveal some of its manifold aspects and connections.[11] Later in the text, Jung relativised the term synchronicity, noting that it explained nothing, but was an assumption about some kind of principle or property of the empirical world.[12]

The controversy around the concept of synchronicity could be linked to the implications and claims it presents. It is taken up enthusiastically by some, and sarcastically dismissed or simply disregarded by others. Those who accepted it take the postulation as approaching a range of phenomena, which were marginalised but present in the popular view of the world, but also as a reaction to the one-sided reason-based approach which rules in science. For those who dismissed the concept, it is only an expression of an old tendency to superstition present in the Western culture.[13]

To sustain his assumptions in the concept of synchronicity Jung searched for support in different areas, such as the experiments of Joseph Banks Rhine (1895–1980). In his library, Jung had the following of Rhine's works: *Extra-Sensory Perception* (1934), *New Frontiers of the Mind* (1939), and *The Reach of Mind* (1948) as well as the German translations of Rhine's texts. In his books about parapsychology, Rhine researched what later would be called psi factors. His goal was to scientifically test the assumptions presented by the psychical researchers, because before him (around the 1920s) the studies were based on natural-historical observations, rather than on clear statistical-empirical methods.

One remarkable example of the studies before Rhine's time was the research by E. Gurney, F.W.H. Myers and F. Podmore presented in the book *Phantasms of the Living* in 1886.[14] The authors collected and reported cases of telepathy and checked their veracity with witnesses. Besides this, they conducted experiments with the telepathic transmission of images. The claim of the book was that telepathy exists, and that the reports about apparitions of a dying person to a loved one at the moment of death were the result of something beyond chance. For the authors, their experiments and the spontaneous cases proved the action of one mind on another at a distance. The book, supported by the Society for Psychical Research, presented over 850 cases mainly on the transmission of thoughts and feelings from one person to another by means other than the recognised channels of the senses. From the notes on the first page of the book in Jung's library, we know that the Society for Psychical Research sent a copy of the two volumes in English to Jung in 1897 at the request of one of the authors, Edmund Gurney.

Back to Rhine, the *novum* in his experiments was the attempt to use scientific methods to approach the phenomena. His studies on telepathy and clairvoyance were conducted at Duke University (USA) and first published in his book *Extra-Sensory Perception* in 1934. Rhine used special cards designed by Dr Karl Zener, who worked at Duke University and mainly studied the psychology of perception. He developed for Rhine's studies a set of five cards which were easily distinguished and easily remembered – a circle, a rectangle, a plus sign, a star and wave lines – known as the Zener cards. The goal was to demonstrate the possibility of telepathy in the communication between two subjects, the agent and the percipient. The results were analysed in comparison with results that would be expected to occur by chance.

In Rhine's experiments the subjects were tested in different settings. In some telepathy experiments, the subjects were in the same room, in others they were distant from each other, and in a third setting the subjects were tested at various times. According to Rhine's reports, these different settings did not affect the results, which were above chance expectations. His experiments led to impressive findings that apparently proved the existence of the psi factors.

But the studies in parapsychology were, and still are, controversial in academic research. Many critics do not take psychical studies seriously, considering them unscientific.[15] They pointed out that studies such as those presented in the *Phantasms of the Living* are impossible to replicate and that Rhine's studies contained mistakes such as the loose control in some of his experiments and the omission of background information for his statistical calculations. To resume: critics consider parapsychology a pseudoscience. Therefore, even with promising results, Rhine failed in making parapsychology acceptable in the scientific community, but his work was close to the experimental-mathematical tradition, an original approach in this area. His results were considered a breakthrough by the researchers on psychical phenomena, and set new standards for the development of parapsychology.

Jung used Rhine's studies as corroboration for his ideas and commented on Rhine's results in his experiments with different settings, noting that

> we have no alternative but to assume that distance is psychically variable, and may in certain circumstances be reduced to a vanishing point by a psychic condition. Even more remarkable is the fact that time is not in principle a prohibition factor either. That is to say, the scanning of a series of cards to be turned up in the future produces a score that exceeds chance probability. [. . .] In these circumstances the time factor seems to have been eliminated by a psychic function or psychic condition which is also capable of abolishing the spatial factor.[16]

Besides Rhine's studies, Jung made an attempt to support his assumptions in the concept of synchronicity with a historical basis, referring to the alchemical notion of the *Unus Mundus* in his book *Mysterium Coniunctionis*.[17] By this is meant a unity between psyche and the external, material world, which would therefore be aspects of one and the same thing.

The *Unus Mundus* in alchemy is expressed in a famous saying which runs 'what is inside is also outside'. Jung suggests with the concept of synchronicity that there is a connection between one's psychic state and an external event, as if it would be the manifestation of a factor that goes beyond the psyche. He wrote in a letter from 1955 to M. Fordham that 'Synchronicity tells us about the nature of what I call the psychoid factor, i.e., the unconscious archetype (not its conscious representation!)'.[18] This factor would be behind the connection between psychic and non-psychic events, and would indicate the dual nature of the archetype.

For Jung, a synchronistic event suggested that there was something more than just an interpretation of meaning. His postulation of the psychoid nature of the archetype presented the possibility of an organisational factor outside the psyche. According to Jung, synchronicity would show an aspect of the archetype *per se*, and not just its psychic aspects. In his understanding, beside the triad of the classic physics which explains the events observed in nature (time, space and causality), synchronicity would add a missing dimension. And he wrote:

> The advantage, however, of adding this concept is that it makes possible a view which includes the psychoid factor in our description and understanding of nature – that is, an a priori meaning or equivalence.[19]

To present the use of the concept in an analytical treatment, Jung wrote about the events that affected his patients which were impossible to explain by the natural laws of causality and required another principle of explanation. As an example, he mentioned the analytical hour with a patient during which a scarab-like insect appeared in the consulting room after the patient had presented a dream with the insect in it. His description of the incident runs as follows:

> A young woman I was treating had, at a critical moment, a dream in which she was given a golden scarab. While she was telling me this dream I sat with my back to the closed window. Suddenly I hear a noise behind me, like a gentle tapping. I turned round and saw a flying insect knocking against the window-pane from outside. I opened the window and caught the creature in the air as it flew in. It was the nearest analogy to a golden scarab that one finds in our latitudes, a scarabaeid beetle, the common rose chafer (Cetonia Aurata), which contrary to its usual habits had evidently felt an urge to get into a dark room at this particular moment. I must admit that nothing like it ever happened to me before or since, and that the dream of the patient has remained unique in my experience.[20]

The patient Jung mentioned, who has not been previously identified, was Reichstein. In a letter from the 13th of July 1949 Jung asked Reichstein about the details of the event during her analysis, possibly for publication. His letter runs as follows:

> Dear Mrs Doctor Reichstein
>
> I would be grateful, if you could inform me when you had the dream with the golden scarab and when you told it to me, as the rose-chafer came

flying in the room. Unfortunately, I did not note the event when it happened. I thank you in advance and with my best wishes

C.G Jung[21]

In her answer to Jung, which is dated July 1949, Reichstein wrote that she received his letter while she was in Holland and she did not remember exactly the date when it happened. However, once back in Zürich, she would check the information in her dreams diary and would tell him later. Unfortunately, Reichstein's dream diary was not found until this date. The event was possibly impressive to Reichstein, too, because she made an embroidery with the figure of the scarab (Figure 17.1) which is today in the collection of her family.[22]

Jung described the impact of the event on Reichstein's treatment as a changing factor in her rationalistic approach to her problems, the importance of the appearance of this image and the synchronicity of the rose-chafer coming in the practice room during the session as follows:

> It was an extraordinarily difficult case to treat, and up to the time of the dream little or no progress had been made. I should explain that the main reason for this was my patient's animus, which was steeped in Cartesian philosophy and clung so rigidly to its own idea of reality that the efforts of three doctors – I was the third – had not been able to weaken it. Evidently something quite irrational was needed which was beyond my powers to produce. The dream alone was enough to disturb ever so slightly the rationalistic attitude of my patient. But when the 'scarab' came flying in through the window in actual fact, her natural being could burst through the armour of her animus possession and the process of transformation could at last begin to move. Any essential change of attitude signifies a psychic renewal which is usually accompanied by symbols of rebirth in the patient's dreams and fantasies. The scarab is a classic example of a rebirth symbol.[23]

The scarab symbol in the dream and its appearance during the hour with Reichstein may have possibly impacted Jung for another reason: Jung himself described the appearance of the symbol of the scarab in the beginning of his 'confrontation with the unconscious'. He described on the 12th of December 1913 how he was in great psychic confusion and a fantasy occurred: he was in a dark cave and he saw different things like a red stone and snakes, and heard voices. In the dark stream of water in the cave he also saw a black scarab.[24] He interpreted its appearance in his comments about this fantasy in the layer [2] of *The Red Book* that the black scarab was a symbol of the death which is necessary for renewal.[25] The event of the scarab in the session with Reichstein possibly reminded him of his own experience.

Furthermore, the manifold aspects related to the symbolism of the scarab for Jung was stressed by Main in 'Myth, synchronicity and re-enchantment'. In his paper, Main pointed out that Jung related the appearance of the scarab to the

FIGURE 17.1 Embroidery of the scarab made by Reichstein (See Plate 3)

symbol of rebirth, but it could be possibly related to Jung in many ways. For instance: a) the scarab as a synchronicity not only for the patient but for Jung himself, because Jung also saw it as meaningful for the treatment; b) the scarab as part of a living myth, as part of a re-enchantment of the world; c) the scarab as meaningful to Jung's relationship to Freud, who had many figures of the scarab in his office; d) the scarab as a symbol in alchemy known, but not mentioned, by Jung in this paper and finally e) the scarab as a heroic element, fairy-tale-like, between Jung and the patient, which assumes the role of a helper against the up-to-this-point fruitless analysis and helping him to break the imprisonment of her rationalism.[26]

As mentioned, Reichstein's case was relevant to Jung in terms of transference and countertransference and it could be postulated that the connection between Reichstein and Jung was particularly intense. The link between synchronistic events and the transferential process has been stressed by Main, who suggested that there was a special bond between Jung and the patient, who had the event with the scarab during the analytical hour. He wrote that an intense emotional connection occurs in transference, particularly when it is an archetypal one, and that such a process facilitates the occurrence of synchronistic events. He postulated that Jung's prompt and effective reaction as the rose-chafer came in the room suggested that he was in harmony with the patient and acting out a well-judged countertransference feeling.[27] But the event of the scarab, which is one of the most well-known examples in Jung's literature on synchronicity, was by no means the only one that occurred during her treatment. In a letter just with the note in the envelope '*1930 an Dr. Jung*' Reichstein described another strange happening before her first pregnancy in one of the sessions with him.[28] Her description of the event in the letter runs as follows:

> Dear Dr. Jung
>
> I must tell you about things that appear very strange to me. Can you still remember, what happened before I got pregnant for the first time? I came to tell you about a very impressive dream: I dreamt that I lay in bed ill and your spirit appeared to me. It bowed down to me and kissed me. In this kiss *your spirit from the afterlife held something vital for me, which would lead to an improvement of my condition.*[29]
>
> With this dream I went to see you. As I told you about the dream, you said that the following had happened to you before I came: you had a patient with you and suddenly, without any reason, you felt the irresistible urge to send the patient away and, as this urge became too powerful, you did it. When you were alone, you were forced to go to the bookshelf, to get by chance one of the books in there. In the book you read the story about an ill man, to whom the spirit of his beloved appeared. Beside her stood the phantom of a man, who had the mission to guide the woman from the afterlife to the ill man.
>
> The similarities between my dream and the story were clear enough. After you had told me this story, we fell silent for a while, sitting next to each other, and you smoked your pipe. Then, shortly after this happened,

> you gave me your hand and fell asleep. As you woke up, you told me that you had concealed something from me: before you read the first story, you had been forced to read another one, which revealed the following: An ill woman and her husband went to see a clergyman, and asked for help. The clergyman felt helpless and did not know what to tell her. After the couple had left and the clergyman was alone in the evening, he constantly thought about the ill woman, and in what way he could help her, until he suddenly *was forced to sleep*. The next day, the ill woman wrote him a letter, in which she thanked him for his help. *He had appeared to her in spirit, and his appearance* had caused a very strong sense of well-being.
>
> After you had read this story, you felt uneasy, probably because you had a presentiment of what would happen with me in the next hour, you quickly decided to read another story. Shortly after this occurrence, I had a dream announcing the birth of Miriam.[30]

In the sequence of this letter, Reichstein reported another dream that for her announced the pregnancy of her second daughter. It was not possible to identify in Jung's library the book which is reported in this letter of Reichstein. Andreas Jung, who is the administrator for Jung's library, informed me that since Jung's time the book could have been lost. Although not identical, however, the passages mentioned here by Reichstein (apparitions of ghosts) are similar to the reports of extra-sensory perceptions found in the book mentioned before, Gurney, Myers, Podmore's *Phantasms of the Living*. Interesting to note is that Jung mentioned this same book in his paper from 1952 on synchronicity in a footnote,[31] a few passages before the passage about Reichstein's scarab.[32] Jung did not publish this occurrence mentioned earlier in his writings, but it shows that besides the incident with the scarab-like insect, Reichstein's treatment included more than one occurrence that called forth Jung's attention. One may conclude that Jung's previous comment, that nothing like it had ever happened to him before or since, refers not only to the event of the scarab but also to some synchronistic events which occurred during her treatment.

Also interesting to note is that Jung affirmed that the incident with the scarab-like insect was a turning point in the patient's analysis; in other words, he interpreted the synchronistic event as an indication of her need to accept the irrational, and as an event that changed the rationalistic approach of the patient to her problems. However, Jung commented in another of his presentations, namely, in his Kundalini yoga seminars, that it was the parallels between the symbolism of the East and Reichstein's symptoms which had enabled him to understand the case and became a turning point in her treatment.

A third comment of Jung's that could be put in the same category of a 'turning point' in Reichstein's treatment could be when he told her his dream in which he saw her high above, as mentioned in his lecture of 1937 about the topic of transference–countertransference. Jung noted that Reichstein's superficial symptomatology, argumentativeness, her insistence on always being right, and her touchiness vanished thereafter.

One could argue that her treatment had more than one turning point. Nevertheless, the way Jung presented the three events in relation to the same patient (the telling to her of his dream, the synchronicity of the scarab and the Eastern symbolism) as turning points in the same treatment, indicate how Jung shaped the clinical material of his practice to reinforce the theoretical postulation he was presenting.

Notes

1 Jaffé, ed., 1989, p. 374.
2 Ibid., p. 155.
3 Shamdasani, ed., 2009, p. 201.
4 Ibid., p. 202.
5 Ibid., p. 220.
6 Jung, 1984, pp. 44 and 417. In his memorial address, Jung praised Richard Wilhelm for his work with the *I Ching*, which, Jung summarised, was based on the principle that whatever is born or done at one particular moment of time has the quality of that moment of time, i.e., it was based on a synchronistic principle. Jung, 1930, pars. 77–82, CW 15.
7 Original in German: *Synchronizität als ein Prinzip akausaler Zusammenhänge.*
8 Jung published his concept together with papers of Wolfgang Pauli.
9 Jung, 1952, pars. 849–850, CW 8.
10 Ibid., par. 984.
11 Ibid., par. 816.
12 Ibid., par. 995.
13 Main, 2004, p. 2.
14 Gurney, Myers, and Podmore, 1886.
15 Mauskopf and Mc Vaugh, 1980.
16 Jung, 1952, pars. 835–836, CW 8.
17 Jung, 1955/56, pars. 661–662, CW 14.
18 Jung, 1955, par. 1208, CW 18.
19 Jung, 1952, par. 962, CW 8.
20 Ibid., par. 843.
21 PA – Document no. 25, Jung–Reichstein Letters.
22 Interviews of the author with Verena Reichstein-Lunin in Zürich: 17.02.2011 and 21.06.2011.
23 Jung, 1952, par. 845, CW 8.
24 Shamdasani, ed., 2009, p. 237.
25 Ibid., p. 239.
26 Main, 2013, pp. 129–146.
27 Main, 2004, pp. 24–25.
28 Reichstein's first daughter was born in 1927.
29 Reichstein's underlined passages.
30 PA – Document no. 10, Jung–Reichstein Letters.
31 Jung, 1952, par. 830 footnote, CW 8.
32 Ibid., par. 843.

References

Gurney, E., Myers, F.W.H. and Podmore, F. (1886) *Phantasms of the Living* (London: Trübner and Co.).

Jaffé, A., ed. (1989) *Memories, Dreams, Reflections, by C.G. Jung* (New York: Vintage Books).

Jung, C.G. (1930) "Richard Wilhelm: In memoriam" in *The Collected Works of C.G. Jung* (London: Routledge), 1990, vol. 15.

——— (1952) "Synchronicity: An acausal connecting principle" in *The Collected Works of C.G. Jung* (London: Routledge), 1991, vol. 8.

——— (1955) "Letter on synchronicity" in *The Collected Works of C.G. Jung* (London: Routledge), 1993, vol. 18, par. 1208.

——— (1955/56) "Mysterium coniunctionis" in *The Collected Works of C.G. Jung* (London: Routledge), 1992, vol. 14.

——— (1984) *Dream Analyses: Notes of the Seminar Given in 1928–1930 by C.G. Jung* (London, Melbourne and Henley: Routledge and Kegan Paul).

Main, R. (2004) *The Rupture of Time: Synchronicity and Jung's Critique of Modern Western Culture* (New York: Brunner-Routledge).

——— (2013) "Myth, synchronicity, and re-enchantment" in *Myth, Literature and the Unconscious* (London: Karnac Books).

Mauskopf, S.H. and Mc Vaugh, M.R. (1980) *The Elusive Science* (Baltimore London: Johns Hopkins University Press).

Shamdasani, S., ed. (2009) *The Red Book: Liber Novus/C.G. Jung* (New York: Norton & Company).

18

THE LETTERS ON PSYCHOLOGY AND RELIGION

In his articles from 2015 on the history of psychoanalysis, Falzeder mentions the differences in the way Freud and Jung disseminated their theories. He wrote that while Freud often advised his followers how to conduct their work but seldom taught, explained, or expanded upon his theoretical concepts in his letters, Jung was almost the opposite of this in his correspondence. He wrote a vast number of letters, created and maintained a network through correspondence, and was occupied in explaining himself and his theories, correcting misconceptions.[1]

Most of Reichstein's letters to Jung have personal motives, such as, for instance, comments on some event in her life, asking for an appointment or for Jung's interpretation of her dreams. As to the content of Jung's letters to Reichstein, there are personal notes, such as when he congratulated her on the birth of her daughter. But beyond the personal topics mentioned previously, there are letters in which he requested her support for the publications and texts in Dutch, which indicates that Jung trusted Reichstein's ability to evaluate texts related to his psychology; and there are also letters which confirm Falzeder's description of how Jung taught and explained his theories in his correspondence. In the letters to Reichstein this is particularly observed in those letters after 1940.

As pointed out before, Reichstein went on with her studies in Jung's psychology after her analyses with him. She attended lectures in the Psychological Club in Zürich and at the *Lesezirkel Hottingen*, a traditional literary circle in which discussions on arts and scientific themes took place.[2] Jung himself delivered a lecture there entitled 'Archaic Man' in October 1930, which was published in English in 1933.[3] In these circles, Reichstein discussed Jung's ideas and occasionally asked him for clarifications on her conclusions. Furthermore, she debated and criticised what she considered some of his unclear formulations. What follows are passages from these letters, in which we can see that Jung considered Reichstein as someone who understood his ideas in depth. I will present some letters in detail, because it allows us to follow the debates adequately. The most relevant topics in these letters were those related to religious motifs such as God, Christ and Buddha, and their relation to theoretical issues such as individuation and the Self.

It is important to mention that Reichstein did not usually date her letters and, when the date is noted, it is mostly only the year on the envelope as if she had dated them at a later point. Also, it is important to note that many of the available letters from Reichstein are the drafts of the letters she sent to Jung. The answers from Jung are originals.

The first available letter that indicates Jung's consideration of Reichstein's opinion about theoretical issues is from September 1940. Jung wrote to Reichstein thanking her for a book she had sent to him. Jung wrote as follows:

> Dear Mrs Doctor
>
> Accept my gratitude for the surprising beautiful present: the bound book. The cover is beautifully done and the way it is done makes sense. It made me also happy to hear that the content of the book was important for you. It seems that very few people can grasp it properly. At least, this is the conclusion I drew from what I have heard from people.[4]

It is not clear which book Jung is referring to. It is possible, however, that he referred to the book he published in German in 1940, *Psychology and Religion*.[5] In a part of the letter Jung wrote that he would like to see her embroidery once more and discussed an appointment with her. From the preceding notes, it is clear that Jung considered Reichstein among those who could understand the themes he wrote about in a satisfactory way. As we shall see, it indicates that Jung considered her opinion on difficult topics and discussed her views and opinions about them, even though Reichstein had no formal academic education (her title 'Mrs Dr. Reichstein' came from her husband, Adam Reichstein).

The next available letter in which we can find a discussion on religious and theoretical topics is from 1943.[6] Reichstein wrote to Jung the following:

> Dear Mr Doctor
>
> It is about one year since I visited Küsnacht to bring my last work to you. Meanwhile I have reached a sense of certainty in my understanding that, it seems to me, I could neither strengthen nor correct [. . .] I would like to give to you this outline to get this time an approval from you and, if necessary, corrections as well. [. . .] In order not to bother you that much I turned to those topics in which the abstract introverted Intuition is most settled and therefore in the direction which I considered to be the most developed, and thereafter, to the realm of experience which I considered related to it, but to which I did not find the validation that I searched for. On the contrary, many issues were not only not grasped and consequently wrongly discussed, but also *totally misconceived*, with the result that I frequently began to doubt

in desperation, and questioned how it is possible while reading the same thing to get so many different results at the end. It relates no more, no less to the relationship between God and Man and God and the World, and finally to the ultimate question of life and death. [. . .] Afterwards I present what I believe that I need to contrast with, using your standpoint and based upon the many images you presented of *the unconscious, of the archetypes and God, of imagination, of the goal and the way of Buddha and Christ.*[7]

What follows in this long letter was Reichstein's understanding of Jung's ideas on religious motifs. She wrote that this topic had become vital for her after a dream she had had with the figure of Christ. She added a mandala she painted and asked for Jung's opinion. To this letter Jung answered the following:

1st October 1943

Dear Mrs Doctor

Please accept my apologies for answering your long letter only today. It came exactly when I was doing a piece of work which it was impossible to postpone and which I could not stop for anything else. Accept my sincere gratitude for sending me the splendid mandala! I was extremely interested in your letter, and I agree with everything you wrote. It is just your view of Christ which seems to me in various aspects unclear. But it is impossible to write about it. This time we need to talk about it. Please, tell me when it would be opportune for you to come, so that I can arrange myself accordingly. I really admire your effort for discernment and value the importance you give to the subject.

With my best regards and gratitude for the dreams you sent

Yours faithfully

C.G. Jung[8]

It is unknown whether the meeting offered by Jung to Reichstein happened. However, in the same month, in October 1943, Jung sent Reichstein one copy of the Eranos-Jahrbuch 1940/1941 with the title 'On the Psychology of the Trinity'.[9]

Many of the concepts Reichstein discussed with Jung were presented in his paper 'Psychology and Religion', which was originally written in English in 1937 and was based on a series of lectures delivered at Yale University, published in German in 1940. In his introductory lecture at Yale, Jung explained that he would adopt an empirical point of view as he approached the themes and revisited the issues he intended to present as follows:

I restrict myself to the observation of the phenomena and I eschew any metaphysical or philosophical considerations. [. . .] My first lecture will be a sort of introduction to the problem of practical psychology and religion.

> The second is concerned with facts that demonstrate the existence of an authentic religious function in the unconscious. The third deals with the religious symbolism of unconscious process.[10]

Most of the themes in Reichstein's letters are related to Jung's text described earlier, indicating that the bound book she sent to him was possibly the German publication of the Yale lectures.

There is a gap in the available correspondence after Jung's last answer, because the next available letter is from 1947, when Reichstein wrote to Jung again. This time she asked for Jung's help with clarifications, because she was in discussion with one of his pupils. As we shall see in the subsequent letters, the pupil was most probably Riwkah Schärf-Kluger (1907–1987), who was a student and, like Reichstein, former patient of C.G. Jung. She attended the Psychological Club and was the first Swiss Jungian analyst to move to the USA. Schärf-Kluger was particularly interested in religious themes, and her work 'The Figure of Satan in the Old Testament' was included in Jung's publication *Symbolik des Geistes* in 1948. The available material from Reichstein is a draft of the original letter sent to Jung. It runs as follows:

> Dear Mr Doctor[11]
>
> During many months I had discussions with one of your pupils on certain basic points, about which we couldn't reach a consensus. [. . .] I would like to present briefly our discussion theme, and afterwards my opinions and my commentaries on them.
>
> In the opinion of your pupil there exists one always established hierarchy between consciousness, the subconscious and the unconscious. The elements in this hierarchy change *in themselves* and *against each other*, but never *into each other*. [. . .] Man is *outlying* from God (doesn't matter how one imagines this God), as one being separated from Him, an Ego-like being detached, created, with his own consciousness and functions. [. . .] The union of God and man consists of this becoming conscious. This is the highest state that man may ever achieve.
>
> In my opinion, this conscious Ego separated from God, this Ego who is only himself and not God any longer, is the final result of a divine differentiation process. [. . .] The *definitive* union of man and God as the goal of individuation process, which lies in an incalculable future, is the *elimination of the conflict*, once this God in His highest spiritual form comes into existence in the quaternity form of the conscious structure of man. They are opposites and therefore they are in one another mutually exclusive. There is an opposition between man and his God, despite their unity.
>
> What I wrote to you is essentially a repetition of what I wrote to you many years ago, only using other words, and for which I got your approval. But I was perplexed with the opposition of your pupil and therefore would like to have your endorsement again.[12]

In the sequence of the letter, Reichstein presents the passages of Jung which, in her opinion, validate her understanding of the issues mentioned. Jung answered the letter as follows:

> Küsnacht, 3 November 1947
>
> Dear Mrs Doctor!
>
> I would like to ask you to accept my apologies for making you wait so long for my answer. I was ill again for a while, with a gallbladder infection and I am late with all my activities because of it. I can only endorse your views. As far as our experience reaches, we cannot in principle differentiate between the symbol of the Self and the images of God. Accordingly, God would manifest in the Self and as the Self. This is the meaning of the Gospels, namely that God Himself has become human. Man seems to be a particle of God, with relative autonomy. Like one can become conscious of the personal unconscious, one can too at least partially become conscious of the col. unconscious, like an approximation of the Spirit of God, which means *Sapientia Dei*, and as it was always understood as such. The goal of the individuation process seems to be the union with the divine, in which the Self and God form a not-differentiable unity for us. This must be a strange 'pupil' of mine. He obviously totally misunderstood the essence of the process of transformation, which I often described. The embroidered robe is wonderful. I truly gazed at it and admired the technique and the meaning. It is waiting to be fetched.
>
> With best regards
>
> Yours faithfully
>
> C.G. Jung[13]

In the next letter, Reichstein wrote how she went to Küsnacht to fetch the robe, but Jung was not at home and she was disappointed that she did not see him. She further wrote that she received a positive feedback, including from her brother-in-law Ignaz Epper and other artists, about her embroidery work, which was shown in an exhibition with other artists of a shop in Zürich.[14] She also wrote that someone was interested in using her material in textile production. She was very happy with the compliments she got and at the end of this undated letter Reichstein wrote:

> I say all this to you because I believe that you will be content as well. I was your patient and I know that without you I would not develop these things and my relationship to you prepared the way that I went through. Even with the actual problems, which I quite frequently find demanding, it means life fulfilment as soon as I begin to work with it. Therefore, I will not stop being grateful to you.[15]

Jung's interest in Reichstein's discussion of religious motifs went on in a letter dated only with the year 1949. Reichstein mentioned a discussion in which no agreement was found, which was related to the question on the incarnation of Christ and the meaning of his sacrifice for mankind. Reichstein mentioned passages of Jung's book *Psychology and Alchemy*, published in German in 1944, and Jung's articles 'Transformation Symbolism in the Mass' and 'A Psychological Approach to the Dogma of the Trinity' from 1942, and invited Jung to comment on her arguments. Jung replied to this letter from Reichstein as follows:

> Bollingen April 1949
>
> Dear Mrs Reichstein
>
> Now, about your letter with the important question!
>
> It has to do with a difficult problem, to which the answer far surpasses my knowledge. I can offer only suppositions and a weakly constructed hypothesis. The myth of the incarnation of God and His Calvary that brings the salvation to man can only be understood by us psychologically. God is represented inside us as the Imago Dei, the image of God, which cannot be differentiated from the Self and therefore the equality God = Self. Before the incarnation the Self was absolutely unconscious, i.e., absolutely projected as God. In this condition man is totally dependent upon a God outside, who (as Job shows) is unpredictable and unjust. He (God) does not know Himself. But Job holds a mirror in front of Him. After that (historically) God decided to become human, i.e., in an absolutely unconscious condition the Self is daemonic, good and evil in his self-unconsciousness, therefore not confronted with himself and amoral. The incarnation means that he unites with the human judgment, which consummates the separation of the opposites for knowledge: The Self appears as double, namely as the benevolent Father and as the Devil, the opponent of God. It means that through the partial (act) of becoming conscious, the Self gets into an inner conflict, which corresponds to the suffering, the highest aspect of which is the crucifixion, i.e. the reconciling of the opposites in the *quaternio*. For instance:
>
> Spiritual
Good ┼ Evil
Physical
>
> The Self gets in such a way into the human that it dies, i.e., it loses its divinity and force and falls as victim to the human Ego-consciousness. It will be buried in the earth, i.e., in the body, i.e., in the dark physis, or in the unconscious per se. It is as a grain in the earth, and through it, by the presence of the sleeping Self, the body becomes Mana. It is the mother of a resurrected Self, (ascension, resurrection, etc.). From it comes the important mystical meaning of the body-sphere in the individuation process. This consists that God (the Self) will be reborn from the unconscious, i.e.,

as the sun appears in our sky and there deposes the Ego (the fall of Lucifer) as Jesus says: 'I saw Satan fall like lightning from heaven'. The body (= mother of God) found a new appreciation in consciousness (Assumption of Mary), which comes out of the reborn God and became, instead of the Ego, the centre of our psychic structure.

Mortal man is the vessel for this event. The Self, as a transcendental content of the unconscious, lives in a psychic relation to the time-space-continuum. From this perspective, it is relatively 'eternal'. Through consciousness, man has a link with the Self and through his body he has even the rebirth. It seems possible that the conscious Self in man or something crucial from him is taken with him into the immortality, and with that is guaranteed the eternal consciousness of God (otherwise the incarnation would make no-sense!). God, the creator, is unconscious and with that He would be responsible for the scandals of this world. But the world is obviously prepared for consciousness, i.e., God must become totally human to become conscious. It must, so to say, disappear in humanity (atheisms and materialisms!). Here is the dangerous moment of inflation (dictators, communism, etc.).

One must find the seed of God inside (redemption of Anima Mundi from matter! the rotundum, etc.) Now, one does not like to do it, for in this world that which contains God is despised and spat upon. It is the most scornful. One prefers to stay in the inflation, or, even more, one protects oneself from this process by hiding oneself behind clergy-men, those who guard themselves from God. God loves only those penitent sinners, who give Him the rebirth, more than the righteous, because the last ones for God's sake cannot bend themselves down to commit sins. Out of the black comes the white. It seems to me that there is no difference between archetype and atom, besides the different aspects. This is related to the thoughts on synchronicity. Unfortunately, it cannot be explained.

With best regards,

Yours faithfully.

C.G. Jung[16]

After the last letter, the ones which followed are mostly related to Jung asking for Reichstein's help in checking translations of his books in Dutch or mentioning other books in Dutch. Reichstein went on in her discussions about religious motifs and sent to Jung details of another discussion with Riwkah Schärf-Kluger about God, cosmogony, the incarnation of God and the integration of parts of the personality in 1957. Jung's answer runs as follows:

Dear Mrs Doctor

Thank you very much for the detailed letter, the contents of which interested me greatly. I am particularly impressed by the fact that in the conversation between you and Mrs Kluger there was constantly discussion about 'God', and about what He does or who He is. I miss here the clear recognition of the limits of the epistemology. [. . .]

Concerning the question of incarnation, the idea of the descent of God to human nature is a genuine mythologem. What lies at the basis of this image that we can empirically know is the process of individuation, in which becomes clear the notion of a greater human than our Ego. The unconscious itself marked this human with the same symbols of the deity, from which we can conclude that this figure corresponds to the Anthropos, most probably as the son of God, or the manifestation of God in the form of a human. [. . .]

Regarding the integration of the parts of the personality, one needs to stay aware of the fact that the Ego-personality as such does not contain the archetypes, but will only be affected by them; because the archetypes are universal and belong to the collective psyche, of which the I cannot dispose. Therefore, the Animus and Anima are images, which represent archetypal figures that mediate between consciousness and the unconscious. [. . .]

Naturally these are problems which cannot be discussed if we take seriously the perspective of epistemology. [. . .] I have the impression that considering the point of view of epistemology could significantly facilitate the theoretical discussion with Mrs Kluger.

With best regards

Yours faithfully

P.S. I allowed myself, under the condition of your agreement, to send a copy of the basic presentation in this letter to Mrs Kluger.[17]

To this letter, Reichstein answered to Jung criticising some of his considerations and arguments. She wrote as follows:

Dear Professor

Thank you very much for your letter. I am always grateful for your effort to answer my letter. However, your letter pushes me to a reply. The '*recognition of the limits of epistemology*' was for me such an evident condition that I did not consider it necessary to note. Naturally this recognition was always also present by Riwkah. It gave the common basis for our discussion. [. . .]

Regarding the incarnation of God in man, I certainly did not mean with the descent of God to the deepest level (until the extended Ego-personality of a man) that the greater man/self would become identical with the empirical man. In other words, that the Ego to some extent would be replaced by the self. [. . .]

Regarding the integration of parts of the personality, I am clearly aware of the fact, that, as you said, the Ego – personality, as such, does not contain the archetypes. But according to you the archetypes are the roots of consciousness after all. Does it not mean that the human consciousness and its associated functions grow out from the archetypes? [. . .] I am afraid that I begin to bore you. I would like to avoid that you misunderstand me, which in psychological areas happens so easily, and even more the deeper one tries to go into them.

With best regards – Yours M. Reichstein[18]

Reichstein's reply to Jung is undated, but in January 1958, Jung's secretary Aniela Jaffé wrote to Reichstein,[19] mentioning that Jung was in Bollingen to rest and he would not write letters for the time to come. Jung replied to Reichstein's letter a few months later. It runs as follows:

18th March 1958

Dear Mrs Doctor

Please accept my apologies that only today I respond to your letter. Too much work and the tiredness related to my old age prevented me from dealing with my correspondence. But I would like to tell you that I was glad to hear from you, and that you understood the problem of 'the limits of epistemology' correctly. The comprehension of the other questions depends upon it. I send to you enclosed the booklet of my wife, which was published by the Psychological Club of New York, as an expression of my gratitude for the many things you have done for me.

With my best greetings

Yours faithfully[20]

To Jung's last letter, Reichstein answered on the 25th of May 1958:

Dear Professor

Thank you so much for the booklet of your wife and your letter. I was very glad to receive both. I have been going regularly to the analysis with Miss Dr von Franz and I feel that I am in good hands. I hope with time and her impulses and help I will find satisfactory answers to some questions and the accentuation of immersed and still hidden (contents).

I wish you all the best for your health

With best regards

Yours M. Reichstein[21]

From the letters between Jung and Reichstein in the later years it is possible to observe that Jung, besides being grateful for her help with the Dutch translations, helped her to clarify her doubts and reflections on his ideas. Differently than in the case of Cabot, who also participated in Jung's circle in Zürich, but mainly in the social sphere, Reichstein's relation to Jung was based on the discussion of the themes and the exchange of ideas. Their exchange of letters shows an intense academic conversation on themes which were the focus of Jung's interest in his later writings. As we have seen, Jung maintained his correspondence with Reichstein until late in his life, and did so in a responsive and collegiate manner.

After Jung's death in 1961, Reichstein went on with her analysis with von Franz and continued with her studies in his psychology. Reichstein died on the 3rd of November 1975 at the age of 81 years.

Notes

1 Falzeder, 2015, p. 238.
2 I am grateful to Emmanuel Kennedy, who gave me this information in an interview.
3 See "Archaic man" in C.W. vol. 10.
4 PA – Document no. 13, Jung–Reichstein Letters.
5 Original in German: *Psychologie und Religion.*
6 Reichstein's letter is not dated, but in the envelope there is a note with the year 1943 (to and from Jung).
7 PA – Document no. 19, Jung–Reichstein Letters. Underlined by Reichstein.
8 PA – Document no. 20, Jung–Reichstein Letters.
9 Original in German: *Zur Psychologie der Trinitästidee.*
10 Jung, 1940, pars. 2–3, CW 11.
11 On the top of the letter there is a remark: Letter written to Jung in 1947.
12 PA – Document no. 22, Jung–Reichstein Letters. Underlined by Reichstein.
13 PA – Document no. 23, Jung–Reichstein Letters.
14 An article about the exhibition featured in the local journal. Conf.: Neue Zürcher Zeitung from 7 January 1947.
15 PA – Document no. 27, Jung–Reichstein Letters.
16 PA – Document no. 35, Jung–Reichstein Letters.
17 ETH – Letter from C.G. Jung to M. Reichstein from the 2nd of January 1957, Code Hs 1056:24928.
18 ETH – Letter from M. Reichstein to C.G. Jung (no date), Code Hs 1056:25722. Underlined by Reichstein.
19 ETH – Letter from A. Jaffé to Reichstein, Code Hs 1056:26486.
20 ETH – Letter from C.G. Jung to M. Reichstein from the 18th of March 1958, Code Hs 1056:26487.
21 ETH – Letter from M. Reichstein to C.G. Jung from the 25th of March 1958, Code Hs 1056:25271.

References

Falzeder, E., (2015) *Psychoanalytic Filiations: Mapping the Psychoanalytic Movement* (London: Karnac Books).

Jung, C.G. (1933b) "Archaic man" in *The Collected Works of C.G. Jung* (London: Routledge), 1991, vol. 10.

Jung, C.G. (1940) "Psychology and religion" in *The Collected Works of C.G. Jung* (London: Routledge), 1991, vol. 11.

19

CONCLUSION

The case of Mischa Epper sheds lights on the historical development of the technique of active imagination. Conversely, Reichstein's case gives us an example of how Jung used clinical material in his presentations. He focused on theoretical standpoints and symbolism, but mentioned little in relation to personal events, for he considered the latter less important. However, by highlighting archetypal symbolism to the detriment of the events in the lives of the patients, relevant elements for the understanding of their psychic condition were obliviated.

Comparing the available biographical information of Jung's patients, and the use of primary sources in the two new cases, allows us to draw a better picture of Jung's practice and his shaping of case material. This focus allows us a better understanding of how Jung used and framed clinical material in the context of his ideas, particularly in the way he presented his cases related to his postulations.

But I would like to return to the main questions that the material evoked once I received the correspondence between C.G. Jung and Maggy Reichstein from Mrs Lunin, namely: what impressed Jung with regard to their family story? And what did he mean by 'I learned a lot from you'?

Concerning the time when Jung encountered the sisters Mischa Epper and Maggy Reichstein: it happened during an important phase in the development of Jung's ideas, as he began to teach and apply the findings of his self-experimentation. In the cases of Mischa Epper and Maggy Reichstein, it may be inferred from the presented material that the events in their personal story impressed Jung. It gives us an idea about what he meant by the 'familial severities', namely: a) the difficulties of the family even before the birth of Mischa Epper and Maggy Reichstein, as their grandmother brought up her children alone after the early death of her husband; b) the repressive and dull ambiance in the aristocratic milieu which was negative for their development and a relevant cause for their rebellion; c) the birth of Reichstein in the East, which for her engendered conflicts with the European mentality as she grew up; d) the return to Holland after Reichstein had contracted malaria and the difficult emotional conditions caused by the health problems of their mother during the birth of Mischa Epper; e) the long suffering of the mother after the birth and her absence during their childhood; f) the early death of the mother; g) the nanny who was too severe and puritanical; h) the rigid education by the grandmother who had no interest in culture and art; i) the severe familial tensions among the grandmother, father and the children; j) the illness of Mischa Epper in her teenage years and the move to Zürich during the First World War in search for treatment; k) the suicide of the grandmother; and finally l) the anxiety symptoms of Reichstein, which led her to be treated by Jung.

The notes of Epper's diary showed the use of the technique of active imagination by Jung's collaborator Moltzer, and, in this respect, it sheds light upon a phase when Jung's technique was still in development. The reports in her diary also express criticism of Moltzer's treatment, which she experienced as focusing too much on the intuition and lacking contact with reality, compared to Jung's treatment, which was brief but constituted nevertheless an important help.

Therefore, the importance of the case of Mischa Epper can be summarised in three specific ways:

1 The time when Mischa Epper came to treatment sheds light upon an early phase of Jung's work on active imagination, and, concerning the development of the technique, the research fills the gap between the cases of Tina Keller-Jenny and Christiana Morgan. Summarising the development of this technique, there were differences that show how its focus developed: in the case of Keller-Jenny, which began in 1915, the focus of the technique was mostly on a careful observation of the material produced by the unconscious. In the case of Epper, who was treated in 1918, the main focus of the treatment given by Moltzer was on the expression and the interpretation of the fantasies and submission to the requests of the inner figures. And later, in 1926, in the case of Morgan, the focus was mainly on the experiencing of the relationship between the ego and the unconscious.
2 Her case provided Jung with the opportunity to work with a patient to whom visual arts were an important way to communicate in analysis, for she barely talked and expressed her fantasies in drawings. It was shortly after Jung himself began to draw his fantasies in the *Liber Novus*.
3 Finally, it gives us further information about the connection between Jung and Maria Moltzer, who was a close collaborator of his in the early days of analytical psychology.

Concerning Reichstein's analysis, Jung wrote that he learned from her and considered her material as exemplary, using it for different publications on different topics. One can conclude that her case can be situated among other important cases of his practice already known in the literature. Particularly relevant issues in her case are that a) he mentioned her as an example of the need for the analyst to re-evaluate his attitude towards the patient, as an important factor to be considered in the process of countertransference; b) he used it to indicate the problems of the lack of knowledge of the analyst, if he cannot understand the symbolism present in the material of the patient properly; c) he used her dreams to exemplify how dreams may indicate the patient's attitude to the doctor; d) he mentioned her case as an example of the stages of the individuation process relating it to Eastern symbolism; e) he presented her mandalas as examples of the appearance of symbols of the Self during analytical treatment; and, finally, f) he used her case as an example to show the problems of a one-sided development of the intellect and how it can be transformed by the occurrence of synchronistic events.

Outside of the analytical treatment and the discussion related to his publications, the correspondence with Reichstein showed that he considered her opinion, discussing different topics with her, particularly those containing religious motifs. Their letters show that Jung regarded her as one of the few people who could understand his ideas properly.

Considering the number of themes which Jung related to her, and the fact that he used her case as an example of his practice in different publications, the importance of Reichstein's case can be summarised in four specific ways:

1. Jung was caught in the transference with Reichstein, and his dream showing her in a high place led him to evaluate his attitude towards his patients. Therefore, it was a crucial element in his understanding of the process of transference and countertransference.
2. Jung understood the images in Reichstein's dreams, images and fantasies only after identifying the parallels between them and Eastern symbolism. Therefore, her case contributed to the development of Jung's theory in calling his attention to the relationship between Eastern and Western psychology.
3. The synchronistic events in Reichstein's case impressed Jung. He stated that before and after this event nothing comparable ever happened to him.
4. In his article 'Realities of Practical Psychotherapy' Jung used her case to demonstrate how the lack of knowledge of the doctor can impact on the psychological treatment and for the importance of that treatment not to be rigid in its methods, pointing out that fantasies and symptoms can be understood symbolically, as a process of higher development and not just as pathological events.

From the material presented, one may conclude that Jung was consistent in his use of the techniques he developed after his self-experiment. Furthermore, he improved and attuned his methods as he applied them to his patients. But in his writings, this research indicates that Jung's presentation of case material was biased to support his findings. The cases presented here show, however, that Jung did not falsify or invent any information about the case material in the story of Maggy Reichstein and Mischa Epper. If this were the case, this would call into question Jung's ethic in his publications. Particularly striking to this issue is the case of Reichstein, in which he was faithful to the events which happened to her. It is striking, because it refers to one of his most controversial postulations, namely, synchronicity. But it indicates that he considered the information in her case selectively, highlighting information to support his ideas and to substantiate his theories about the collective unconscious.

Therefore, prospective students of Jungian psychology should consider Jung's case presentation from a critical standpoint. These results also point to future researchers the need to verify when and where Jung was selecting information about his cases to highlight his postulations. This is valid particularly in his later writings, when there are indications that his memory was no longer accurate.

My conclusions, although consistent to the results of this research, cannot be considered as valid to all other cases of Jung. Essential information is still missing, such as Reichstein's notes of her treatment and her dreams diary. Such documents are known to have existed, but were not available or lost. Furthermore, Jung's documents about Reichstein's case are those found in the literature and in the documents presented here. Although this research was based on them and on primary sources, they give us only a partial picture of the whole. If new sources become available to future research studies, the conclusions presented here might change. Another limitation of this work is my own background as a Jungian analyst. It was a fascinating challenge to approach Jung from a historical perspective, but at the same time very demanding, because it required a critical view about a subject that I am involved with.

Independently of all these, for Maggy Reichstein and for Mischa Epper, the encounter with Jung was crucial. For Epper, he was a man greater than life, and for Reichstein, he gave her the sense of meaning in life. They were both grateful to him.

BIBLIOGRAPHY

Adler, A. (1907) *Studie über Minderwertigkeit von Organen* (Berlin und Wien: Urban and Schwarzenbach).

——— (1916) *The Neurotic Constitution: Outlines of a Comparative Individualistic Psychology and Psychotherapy* (New York: Moffat, Yard and Company).

——— (1920) *Praxis und Theorie der Individualpsychologie: Vorträge zur Einführung in die Psychotherapie für Ärzte, Psychologen und Lehrer* (München und Wiesbaden: Verlag von J.F. Bergmann).

Adler, G., ed. (1975) *C.G. Jung: Letters Vol. 2 1951–1961* (Princeton, NJ: Princeton University Press).

Baynes-Jansen, D. (2003) *Jung's Apprentice: A Biography of Helton Godwin Baynes* (Einsiedeln: Daimon Verlag).

Bernet, B. (2013) *Schizophrenie – Entstehung und Entwicklung eines psychiatrischen Krankheitsbild um 1900* (Zürich: Chronos Verlag).

Bernheim, H. (1887) *Suggestive Therapeutics: A Treatise on the Nature and Uses of Hypnotism* (New York: The Knickerbocker Press).

Bezzola, D. (1906/1907) "Zur Analyse psychotraumatischer Symptome" in *Journal für Psychologie und Neurologie* 8(3):S. 204–219.

Billinsky, J.M. (1969) "Freud and Jung (the end of a romance)" in *Andover Newton Quarterly* Nov;10(2).

Bleuler, E. (1911) *Dementia Praecox oder Gruppe der Schizophrenien* (Leipzig und Wien: Franz Deuticke).

Blom, P. (2008) *The Vertigo Years: Europe, 1900–1914* (New York: Basic Books).

Borch-Jacobsen, M. and Shamdasani, S. (2012) *The Freud Files: An Inquiry into the History of Psychoanalysis* (New York: Cambridge University Press).

Carotenuto, A. (1982) *A Secret Symmetry: Sabina Spielrein between Freud and Jung* (New York: Pantheon).

Dadó, A. (1978) *Mischa Epper: Quarles van Ufford 1901–1978* (Ascona: Museo Epper).

Darlington, B. (2015) "Kristine Mann: Jung's Miss X and a pionier in psychoanalysis" in *Spring: A Journal of Archetype and Culture* (New Orleans, LA: Spring Journal Books), vol. 92.

Dejerine, J. and Gauckler, E. (1913) *The Psychoneuroses and Their Treatment by Psychotherapy* (Philadelphia and London: J.B. Lippincott Company).
de Moura, V. (2014) "Learning from the patient: The East, synchronicity and transference in the history of an unknown case of C.G. Jung" in *Journal of Analytical Psychology* 59:391–409.
Douglas, C. (1993) *Translate This Darkness: The Life of Christiana Morgan* (New York: Simon & Schuster).
———, ed. (1997) *Jung, C.G. Visions: Notes of a Seminar Given in 1930–34* (Princeton, NJ: Princeton University Press), vol. 1 and 2.
Dubois, P. (1909) *The Psychic Treatment of Nervous Disorders: The Psychoneuroses and Their Moral Treatment* (New York and London: Funk and Wagnalls Company).
Ellenberger, H. (1970) *The Discovery of the Unconscious* (New York: Basic Books).
——— (1991) "The story of Helene Preiswerk: A critical study with new documents" in *History of Psychiatry* 2:41.
Falzeder, E. (1994) "My grand-patient, my chief tormentor: A hitherto unnoticed case of Freud's and the consequences" in *Psychoanalytic Quarterly* 63:297–331.
——— (2015) *Psychoanalytic Filiations: Mapping the Psychoanalytic Movement* (London: Karnac Books).
Fordham, M. (1967) "Active imagination: Deintegration or disintegration?" in *The Journal of Analytical Psychology* Jan;12:51–66.
Forel, A. (1907) *Hypnotism or Suggestion and Psychotherapie* (New York: Rebman Company).
Freud, S. (1904/1905) "On psychotherapy" *The Standard Edition of the Complete Psychological Works of Sigmund Freud, Volume VII* Psychoanalytic Electronic Publishing-PEP Online Version.
Fusar-Poli, P. (2012) "Sabina Spielrein" in *The American Journal of Psychiatry* 169(1): 21.
Gauld, A. (1992) *A History of Hypnotism* (Cambridge: Cambridge University Press).
Gurney, E., Myers, F.W.H. and Podmore, F. (1886) *Phantasms of the Living* (London: Trübner and Co.).
Haule, J.R. (1999) *Jung in Contexts: A Reader* (London and New York: Routledge).
Heuer, G. (2012) "A most dangerous- and revolutionary-method: Sabina Spielrein, Carl Gustav Jung, Sigmund Freud, Otto Gross, and the birth of intersubjectivity" in *Psychotherapy and Politics International* Oct;10(3):261–278.
Hofer, A. (2001) "Jung's analysis of Sabina Spielrein and his use of Freud's free association method" in *The Journal of Analytical Psychology* Jan;46(1):117–128.
Jaffé, A., ed. (1973) *C.G. Jung: Briefe* (Olten und Freiburg im Breisgau: Walter-Verlag), Band 1 und 2.
———, ed. (1989) *Memories, Dreams, Reflections, by C.G. Jung* (New York: Vintage Books).
Janet, P. (1976) *Psychological Healing: A Historical and Clinical Study* (New York: Arno Press), vol. 1 and 2.
Jung, C.G. (1902a) "On the so-called Occult Phenomena" in *The Collected Works of C.G. Jung* (London: Routledge), 1993, vol. 1.
——— (1902b) "A case of hysterical stupor in a prisoner in detention" in *The Collected Works of C.G. Jung* (London: Routledge), 1993, vol. 1.
——— (1905) "The psychological diagnosis of evidence" in *The Collected Works of C.G. Jung* (London: Routledge), 1992, vol. 2.
——— (1906) "Psychoanalysis and association experiment" in *The Collected Works of C.G. Jung* (London: Routledge), 1992, vol. 2.
——— (1907) "The psychology of Dementia Praecox" in *The Collected Works of C.G. Jung* (London: Routledge and Kegan Paul), 1981, vol. 3.

——— (1908a) "The content of the psychosis" in *The Collected Works of C.G. Jung* (London: Routledge and Kegan Paul), 1981, vol. 3.
——— (1908b) "The Freudian theory of hysteria" in *The Collected Works of C.G. Jung* (London: Routledge), 1993, vol. 4.
——— (1911) "Morton Prince, 'The mechanism and interpretation of dreams: A critical review'" in *The Collected Works of C.G. Jung* (London: Routledge), 1993, vol. 4.
——— (1912a) *Wandlungen und Symbole der Libido – Beiträge zur Entwicklungsgeschichte des Denkens* (Leipzig und Wien: Franz Deuticke).
——— (1912b/1952) "Symbols of transformation" in *The Collected Works of C.G. Jung* (London: Routledge and Kegan Paul), 1986, vol. 5.
——— (1913a) "General aspects of psychoanalysis" in *The Collected Works of C.G. Jung* (London: Routledge), 1993, vol. 4.
——— (1913b) "The theory of psychoanalysis" in *The Collected Works of C.G. Jung* (London: Routledge), 1993, vol. 4.
——— (1913c) "A comment on Tausk's criticism of Nelken" in *The Collected Works of C.G. Jung* (London: Routledge), 1993, vol. 18.
——— (1914) "Crucial points in psychoanalysis" in *The Collected Works of C.G. Jung* (London: Routledge), 1993, vol. 4.
——— (1916/1957) "The transcended function" in *The Collected Works of C.G. Jung* (London: Routledge), 1991, vol. 8.
——— (1917) *Der Psychologie der Unbewussten Prozess* (Zürich: Rascher und Cie.).
——— (1921) "Psychological types" in *The Collected Works of C.G. Jung* (London: Routledge), 1989, vol. 6.
——— (1929a) "The problems of modern psychotherapy" in *The Collected Works of C.G. Jung* (London: Routledge), 1993, vol. 16.
——— (1929b) "Commentary on *The secret of the golden flower*" in *The Collected Works of C.G. Jung* (London and Henley: Routledge and Kegan Paul), 1981, vol. 13.
——— (1930) "Richard Wilhelm: In memoriam" in *The Collected Works of C.G. Jung* (London: Routledge), 1990, vol. 15.
——— (1931) "The spiritual problem of modern man" in *The Collected Works of C.G. Jung* (London: Routledge), 1991, vol. 10.
——— (1933a) "The practical use of dream-analysis" in *The Collected Works of C.G. Jung* (London: Routledge), 1993, vol. 16.
——— (1933b) "Archaic man" in *The Collected Works of C.G. Jung* (London: Routledge), 1991, vol. 10.
——— (1935a) "Analytical psychology: Its theory and practice: The Tavistock Lectures" in *The Collected Works of C.G. Jung* (London: Routledge), 1993, vol. 18.
——— (1935b) "Principles of practical psychotherapy" in *The Collected Works of C.G. Jung* (London: Routledge), 1993, vol. 16.
——— (1936) "Yoga and the West" in *The Collected Works of C.G. Jung* (London: Routledge), 1991, vol. 11.
——— (1937) "The realities of practical psychotherapy" in *The Collected Works of C.G. Jung* (London: Routledge), 1993, vol. 16.
——— (1940) "Psychology and religion" in *The Collected Works of C.G. Jung* (London: Routledge), 1991, vol. 11.
——— (1950a) "A study in the process of individuation" in *The Collected Works of C.G. Jung* (London: Routledge), 1991, vol. 9i.
——— (1950b) "Concerning mandala symbolism" in *The Collected Works of C.G. Jung* (London: Routledge), 1991, vol. 9i.

——— (1952) "Synchronicity: An acausal connecting principle" in *The Collected Works of C.G. Jung* (London: Routledge), 1991, vol. 8.
——— (1953) "Psychology and alchemy" in *The Collected Works of C.G. Jung* (London: Routledge), 1992, vol. 12.
——— (1954a) "The philosophical tree" in *The Collected Works of C.G. Jung* (London and Henley: Routledge and Kegan Paul), 1981, vol. 13.
——— (1954b) Foreword to "Beelden uit het Onbewuste – een Geval van Jung" (1957) van Helsdingen, Dr. R.J., Van Loghum Slaterus-Arnhem, in *The Collected Works of C.G. Jung* (London: Routledge), 1993, vol. 18.
——— (1955) "Letter on synchronicity" in *The Collected Works of C.G. Jung* (London: Routledge), 1993, vol. 18, par. 1208.
——— (1955/56) "Mysterium coniunctionis" in *The Collected Works of C.G. Jung* (London: Routledge), 1992, vol. 14.
——— (1984) *Dream Analyses: Notes of the Seminar Given in 1928–1930 by C.G. Jung* (London, Melbourne and Henley: Routledge and Kegan Paul).
Kerr, J. (1993) *A Most Dangerous Method: The Story of Jung, Freud and Sabina Spielrein* (New York: Alfred A. Knop).
Kreis, G. (2014) *Insel der unsicherer Geborgenheit – Die Schweiz in den Kriegsjahren 1914–1918* (Zürich: Verlag Neue Zürcher Zeitung).
Leitner, M. (2001) *Ein gut gehütetes Geheimnis: die Geschichte der psychoanalytischen Behandlungstechnik von den Anfängen in Wien bis zur Gründung der Berliner Poliklinik im Jahr 1920* (Giessen: Psychosozial. Verlag).
Lindorff, D. (2004) *Pauli and Jung: The Meeting of Two Great Minds* (Wheaton, IL: Quest Books).
Lothane, Z. (1999) "Tender love and transference: Unpublished letters of C.G. Jung and Sabina Spielrein" in *International Journal of Psycho-Analysis* 80:1189–1204.
Main, R. (2004) *The Rupture of Time: Synchronicity and Jung's Critique of Modern Western Culture* (New York: Brunner and Routledge).
——— (2013) "Myth, synchronicity, and re-enchantment" in *Myth, Literature and the Unconscious* (London: Karnac Books).
Mauskopf, S.H. and Mc Vaugh, M.R. (1980) *The Elusive Science* (Baltimore and London: Johns Hopkins University Press).
McGuire, W., ed. (1974) *The Freud-Jung Letters* (Princeton, NJ: Princeton University Press).
——— (1990) *C.G. Jung: Analytical Psychology Notes of the Seminar Given in 1925* (London: Routledge).
Micale, M., ed. (1993) *Beyond the Unconscious: Essays of Henri F. Ellenberger in the History of Psychiatry* (Princeton, NJ: Princeton University Press).
Mitchell, S.W. (1884) *Fat and Blood: An Essay on the Treatment of Certain Forms of Neurasthenia and Hysteria* (Philadelphia: J.B. Lippincott & Co.).
Nunberg, H. and Federn, E., eds. (1906–1908/1976) *Protokolle der Wiener Psychoanalytischen Vereinigung* (Frankfurt a. M: Fischer), vol. 1.
Percheron, S. (1982) "Interview Jung to Suzanne Percheron" in *C.G. Jung, Emma Jung, Toni Wolff* (San Francisco: The Analytical Psychology Club of San Francisco, Inc).
Prince, M. (1910) "The psychological principles and field of Psychotherapie" in *Psychotherapeutics: A Symposium* (Boston and Toronto: The Gorham Press).
Reid, J.C. (2001) *Jung, My Mother and I: The Analytic Diaries of Catharine Rush Cabot* (Einsiedeln: Daimon Verlag).
Schröter, M., ed. (2012) *Sigmund Freud- Eugen Bleuler "Ich bin zuversichtlich, wir erobern bald die Psychiatrie" Briefwechsel 1904–1937* (Basel: Schwabe Verlag).

Shamdasani, S. (1990) "A woman called Frank" in *Spring: Journal of Archetype and Culture* 50:25–56.

——— (1992) "Two unknown early cases of Jung" in *Harvest: Journal for Jungian Studies* 38:38–43.

———, ed. (1996) *The Psychology of Kundalini Yoga: Notes of the Seminar Given in 1932 by C.G. Jung* (London: Routledge).

——— (1998) *Cult Fictions* (London: Routledge and New Fetter Lane).

——— (2001) "The magical method that works in the dark: C.G. Jung, hypnosis, and suggestion" in *The Journal of Jungian Theory and Practice* 3(1).

——— (2003) *Jung and the Making of Modern Psychology: The Dream of a Science* (Cambridge: Cambridge University Press).

——— (2005) *Jung Stripped Bare by His Biographers, Even* (London: Karnac Books).

———, ed. (2009) *The Red Book: Liber Novus/C.G. Jung* (New York: Norton & Company).

——— (2012a) "Psychotherapy, 1909: Notes on a Vintage" in *After Freud Left: A Century of Psychoanalysis in America*, J. Burnham (ed.) (Chicago: University of Chicago Press).

——— (2012b) "After Liber Novus" in *The Journal of Analytical Psychology* 57:366–367.

Silberer, H. (1909) "Bericht über eine Methode, gewisse symbolische Halluzinations-Erscheinungen hervorzurufen und zu beobachten" in *Jahrbuch für psychoanalytische und psychopathologische Forschung* 1:513–525.

——— (1917) *Problems of Mysticism and Its Symbolism* (New York: Moffat, Yard and Company).

Skea, B. (2006) "Sabina Spielrein: Out from the shadow of Jung and Freud" in *Journal of Analytical Psychology* Sep; 51(4):527–552.

Staudenmaier, L. (2003) *Die Magie als experimentelle Naturwissenschaft* (Langen: Verlag Wolfgang Roller).

Swan, W. (2008) "C.G. Jung's psychotherapeutic technique of active imagination in historical context" in *Psychoanalysis and History* 10(2).

———, ed. (2011) *The Memoir of Tina Keller-Jenny: A Lifelong Confrontation with the Psychology of C.G. Jung* (New Orleans, LA: Spring Journals Books).

Taylor, W.S. (1928) *Morton Prince and Abnormal Psychology* (New York and London: D. Appleton and Company).

Van den Berk, T. (2014) *In de ban van Jung – Nederlanders ontdekken de Analytische Psychologie* (Zoetermeer: Uitgeverij Meinema).

Van Helsdingen, R.J. (1957) *Beelden uit het Onbewuste* (Arnhem: Van Loghum Slaterus), Pages No. from Internal Translation for the C.G. Jung Institute – Zürich by Marianne Wysma.

Webb, J. (1976) *The Occult Establishment* (La Salle, IL: Open Court Publishing Company).

Wehr, G. (1996) *Gründergestallten der Psychoanalyse Profile-Ideen-Schicksale* (Zürich: Artemis und Winkler).

Wieser, A. (2001) *Zur frühen Psychoanalyse in Zürich: 1900–1914.* Dissertation zur Erlangung der Doktorwürde der Medizinischen Fakultät der Universität Zürich, Zürich.

Woodroffe, J. (2003) *The Serpent Power* (Madras: Ganesh and Company).

Zumstein-Preiswerk, S. (1975) *C.G. Jungs Medium: die Geschichte von Helly Preiswerk* (München: Kindler).

INDEX

PLATE 1 Mandala figure no. 9

PLATE 2 Bird in the fontanelle

PLATE 3 Embroidery of the scarab made by Reichstein

For Product Safety Concerns and Information please contact our EU representative GPSR@taylorandfrancis.com Taylor & Francis Verlag GmbH, Kaufingerstraße 24, 80331 München, Germany

Batch number: 10777124

Printed by Printforce, the Netherlands